FISCAL YEAR 2014

BUDGET

OF THE U.S. GOVERNMENT

OFFICE OF MANAGEMENT AND BUDGET

BUDGET.GOV

GENERAL NOTES

1. All years referenced for budget data are fiscal years unless otherwise noted. All years referenced for economic data are calendar years unless otherwise noted.

2. Detail in this document may not add to the totals due to rounding.

3. At the time the President's 2014 Budget request was developed, none of the full-year appropriations bills for 2013 was enacted; therefore, the programs and activities normally provided for in the full-year appropriations bills were operating under a continuing resolution (Public Law 112–175). For those programs and activities, full-year appropriations data included in the current year column (2013) in the budget *Appendix*, and in tables that show details on discretionary spending amounts in the *Analytical Perspectives* volume, reflect the annualized level provided by the continuing resolution. In the main *Budget* volume and the *Historical Tables* volume, current year totals by agency and for the total Government will match the President's 2013 Budget request.

Table of Contents

THE BUDGET MESSAGE OF THE PRESIDENT

To the Congress of the United States:

Thanks to the hard work and determination of the American people, we have made significant progress over the last 4 years. After a decade of war, our brave men and women in uniform are coming home. After years of recession, our businesses have created over six million new jobs. We buy more American cars than we have in 5 years, and less foreign oil than we have in 20 years. Our housing market is healing, our stock market is rebounding, and consumers, patients, and homeowners enjoy stronger protections than ever before.

But we know that there are millions of Americans whose hard work and dedication have not yet been rewarded. Our economy is adding jobs—but too many people still cannot find full-time employment. Corporate profits have skyrocketed to all-time highs—but for more than a decade, wages and incomes have barely budged.

It is our generation's task to reignite the true engine of America's economic growth—a rising, thriving middle class. It is our unfinished task to restore the basic bargain that built this country— the idea that if you work hard and meet your responsibilities, you can get ahead, no matter where you come from, no matter what you look like, or whom you love.

It is our unfinished task to make sure that this Government works on behalf of the many, and not just the few; that it encourages free enterprise, rewards individual initiative, and opens the doors of opportunity to every child across this great Nation.

A growing economy that creates good, middle class jobs—this must be the North Star that guides our efforts. Every day, we should ask ourselves three questions as a Nation: How do we attract more jobs to our shores? How do we equip our people with the skills they need to get those jobs? And how do we make sure that hard work leads to a decent living?

This Budget seeks to answer each of these questions.

Our first priority is making America a magnet for new jobs and manufacturing. After shedding jobs for more than 10 years, our manufacturers have added more than 500,000 jobs over the past 3 years. Companies large and small are increasingly deciding to bring jobs back to America.

To accelerate this trend, the Budget builds on the success of the manufacturing innovation institute we created in Youngstown, Ohio last year, and calls for the creation of a network of 15 of these hubs across the Nation. In these innovation hubs, businesses will partner with universities and Federal agencies to turn regions around our country into global centers of high-tech jobs.

The Budget also includes new initiatives to support manufacturing communities, including a new tax credit to strengthen their ability to attract investments and jobs. And it expands my

1

Administration's SelectUSA initiative to help draw businesses and investment from around the world to our shores.

If we want to make the best products, we also have to invest in the best ideas. That is why the Budget maintains a world-class commitment to science and research, targeting resources to those areas most likely to contribute directly to the creation of transformational technologies that can create the businesses and jobs of the future.

No area holds more promise than our investments in American energy. The Budget continues to advance my "all-of-the-above" strategy on energy, investing in clean energy research and development; promoting energy efficiency in our cars, homes, and businesses; encouraging responsible domestic energy production; and launching new efforts to combat the threat of climate change.

Modeled after my successful Race to the Top education reform effort, the Budget includes a new Race to the Top energy efficiency challenge for States, rewarding those that implement the most effective policies to cut energy waste. And it establishes a new Energy Security Trust funded by royalty revenue from oil and gas leases to support initiatives to shift our cars and trucks off oil, cutting our Nation's reliance on foreign oil.

Over the last 4 years, we have begun the hard work of rebuilding our Nation's infrastructure. We have built or improved over 350,000 miles of road and more than 6,000 miles of rail. And we have repaired or replaced over 20,000 bridges. But to compete in the 21st Century economy and become a magnet for jobs, we must do more. We need to repair our existing infrastructure, and invest in the infrastructure of tomorrow, including high-speed rail, high-tech schools, and self-healing power grids. These investments will both lay the foundation for long-term economic growth and put workers back on the job now.

My Budget includes $50 billion for up-front infrastructure investments, including a "Fix-it-First" program that makes an immediate investment to put people to work as soon as possible on our most urgent repairs, like the nearly 70,000 structurally-deficient bridges across the country. And to make sure taxpayers do not shoulder the whole burden, the Budget creates a Rebuild America Partnership to attract private capital to upgrade what our businesses need most: modern ports to move our goods; modern pipelines to withstand a storm; and modern schools worthy of our children.

The Budget also supports efforts I announced earlier this year to modernize and improve the efficiency of the Federal permitting process, cutting through the red tape that has been holding back even some of the most carefully planned infrastructure projects. These efforts will help us to achieve the new goal I set to cut timelines in half for infrastructure projects, while creating new incentives for better outcomes for communities and the environment.

All of these initiatives in manufacturing, energy, and infrastructure will help entrepreneurs and small business owners expand and create new jobs. But none of it will matter unless we also equip our citizens with the skills and training to fill those jobs.

And that has to start at the earliest possible age. But today, fewer than 3 in 10 4-year-olds are enrolled in a high-quality preschool program, and the high cost of private preschool puts too much of a financial burden on middle class families.

The Budget therefore includes a proposal that ensures 4-year-olds across the country have access to high-quality preschool education through a landmark new initiative in partnership with the States. And it increases the availability of early learning for our youngest children to help their growth and development during the formative early years of life.

Providing a year of free, public preschool education for 4-year-old children is an important investment in our future. It will give all our kids the best start in life, helping them perform better in elementary school and ultimately helping them, and the country, be better prepared for the demands of the global economy. Not only that, it could save hard-working families thousands of dollars each year in child care costs. This is an investment we need to make, and it is fully paid for in this Budget by imposing a new tax on every pack of cigarettes sold.

The Budget also builds on the historic reforms made during my first term to improve our elementary and secondary school system by rewarding excellence and promoting innovation. To help ensure that our high schools are putting our kids on a path to college and a good job, the Budget includes a new competitive fund that will help redesign America's high schools to prepare students with the real world skills they need to find a job right away or go to college. The fund rewards schools that develop new partnerships with colleges and employers, and create classes focusing on science, technology, engineering and mathematics (STEM)—the skills today's employers seek to fill the jobs available right now and in the future.

Even with better high schools, most young people will still need some higher education. Through tax credits, grants, and better loans, we have made college more affordable for millions of students and families over the last 4 years. But skyrocketing costs are still pricing too many young people out of a higher education, or saddling them with unsustainable debt. And taxpayers cannot continue to subsidize higher and higher costs for higher education.

To encourage colleges to do their part to keep costs down, the Budget includes reforms that will ensure affordability and value are considered in determining which colleges receive certain types of Federal aid. My Administration has also released a new "College Scorecard" that parents and students can use to compare schools.

To further ensure our educational system is preparing students for careers in the 21ˢᵗ Century economy, the Budget includes additional measures to promote STEM education, such as launching a new STEM Master Teacher Corps, to leverage the expertise of some of America's best and brightest teachers in science and mathematics, and to elevate the teaching of these subjects nationwide. It also includes a reorganization and consolidation of STEM education programs to improve the effectiveness of Federal investments in this area.

The Budget takes other critical steps to grow our economy, create jobs, and strengthen the middle class. It implements the Affordable Care Act, giving every American access to the high-quality, affordable health care coverage they deserve, and reducing the deficit by more than $1 trillion over the next two decades. It implements Wall Street reform, ending too-big-to-fail and protecting consumers against the abuses and reckless behavior that contributed to the financial collapse in 2008. And it includes measures to strengthen our housing market and ensure that every responsible homeowner has the opportunity to refinance at today's rates, saving $3,000 a year on average.

Our economy is stronger when we harness the talents and ingenuity of striving, hopeful immigrants. That is why I have proposed a plan to fix our broken immigration system that secures our borders, cracks down on employers who hire undocumented workers, attracts highly-skilled entrepreneurs and engineers to help create jobs and drive economic growth, and establishes a responsible pathway to earned citizenship—a path that includes passing a background check, paying taxes and a meaningful penalty, learning English, and going to the back of the line behind the folks trying to come here legally. The Budget makes investments that will make our immigration system more efficient and fair and lay a foundation for this permanent, common-sense reform.

The Budget also builds on the progress made over the last 4 years to expand opportunity for every American and every community willing to do the work to lift themselves up. It creates new ladders of opportunity to ensure that hard work leads to a decent living. It rewards hard work by increasing the minimum wage to $9 an hour so an honest day's work pays more. It partners with communities by identifying Promise Zones to help rebuild from the recession. It creates pathways to jobs for the long-term unemployed and youth who have been hardest hit by the downturn. And it strengthens families by removing financial deterrents to marriage and supporting the role of fathers.

We also know that economic growth can only be achieved and sustained if America is safe and secure, both at home and abroad. At home, the Budget supports my initiative to help protect our kids, reduce gun violence, and expand access to mental health services. We can protect our Second Amendment rights while coming together around reforms like eliminating background check loopholes to make it harder for criminals to get their hands on a gun—common-sense reforms that will help protect our kids from the scourge of gun violence that has plagued too many communities across the country.

To confront threats outside our borders, the Budget ensures our military remains the finest and best-equipped military force the world has ever known, even as we wind down more than a decade of war.

Already, we have brought home more than 30,000 of our brave servicemembers from Afghanistan. Our remaining forces are moving into a support role, with Afghan security forces taking the lead. And over the next year, another 34,000 American troops will come home. This drawdown will continue and, by the end of next year, our war in Afghanistan will be over. Beyond 2014, the Budget supports our continued commitment to a unified and sovereign Afghanistan.

To maintain our national security, the Budget supports our ongoing fight against terrorists, like al Qaeda. The organization that attacked us on 9/11 is a shadow of its former self. But different al Qaeda affiliates and extremist groups have emerged—from the Arabian Peninsula to Africa. We will confront these emerging security challenges through the full range of U.S. capabilities and tools, including diplomatic, security, intelligence, and economic development.

The Budget also provides the resources we need to act on our commitment to and interests in global development, by promoting food security that reduces dependence and increases prosperity; by investing in the increasingly successful drive toward an AIDS-free generation; and by maintaining our leadership as a global provider of humanitarian assistance that saves lives and reflects American values.

We must also confront new dangers, like cyber attacks, that threaten our Nation's infrastructure, businesses, and people. The Budget supports the expansion of Government-wide efforts to counter the full scope of cyber threats, and strengthens our ability to collaborate with State and local governments, our partners overseas, and the private sector to improve our overall cybersecurity.

The Budget also focuses resources on the Asia-Pacific region, reasserting American leadership and promoting security, stability, democracy, and economic growth.

Importantly, the Budget upholds our solemn obligation to take care of our servicemembers and veterans, and to protect our diplomats and civilians in the field. It keeps faith with our veterans, investing in world-class care, including mental health care for our wounded warriors, supporting our military families, and giving our veterans the benefits, education, and job opportunities that they have earned.

The Budget does all of these things as part of a comprehensive plan that reduces the deficit. All of these initiatives and ideas are fully paid for, to ensure they do not increase the deficit by a single dime.

By making investments in our people that we pay for responsibly, we will strengthen the middle class, make America a magnet for jobs and innovation, and grow our economy, which will in turn help us to reduce deficits. But economic growth alone will not solve our Nation's long-term fiscal challenges.

As we continue to grow our economy, we must take further action to cut our deficits. We do not have to choose between these two important priorities—we have to do both.

Over the last 4 years, both parties have worked together to reduce the deficit in a balanced way by more than $2.5 trillion. That is more than halfway toward the goal of $4 trillion in deficit reduction that economists say we need to stabilize our finances. As we wind down two wars, we have protected our military families and veterans while cutting defense spending on outdated military weapons systems. Domestic discretionary spending is approaching its lowest levels as a share of the economy since President Eisenhower was in office; and we have moved aggressively to cut waste, fraud, and abuse. And together, we have begun to ask the wealthy to do their fair share while keeping income taxes low for middle class families. Overall, we have cut the deficit in a balanced way that protects the investments in education, manufacturing, clean energy, and small businesses we need to grow the economy and strengthen the middle class. There is more work to do, and this Budget is designed to finish the job.

But we should not do it by making harsh and arbitrary cuts that jeopardize our military readiness, devastate priorities like education and energy, and cost jobs. That is not how to grow the economy. We should not ask middle class senior citizens and working families to pay down the rest of our deficit while the wealthiest are asked for nothing more. That does not grow our middle class.

The American people understand that we cannot just cut our way to prosperity. That is why I have repeatedly called for a balanced approach to deficit reduction. And that is why I have offered proposals on multiple occasions that cut wasteful spending, strengthen entitlements, and eliminate special tax breaks and loopholes so the wealthiest pay their fair share.

In my negotiations with House Speaker Boehner in December over the so-called "fiscal cliff," I again offered a compromise proposal that was balanced and comprehensive, and would achieve our $4 trillion deficit reduction goal. That proposal is still on the table. I am including it in this Budget to demonstrate my commitment to making the kind of tough and balanced choices that are needed to put our Nation's finances in order.

To be clear, the package I am offering includes some difficult cuts that I do not particularly like. But these measures will only become law if congressional Republicans agree to meet me in the middle by eliminating special tax breaks and loopholes so millionaires and billionaires do their fair share to cut the deficit. I will not agree to any deal that seeks to cut the deficit on the backs of middle class families. I am willing to make tough choices that may not be popular within my own party, because there can be no sacred cows for either party. And I look forward to working with any member of Congress who takes a similar, balanced approach. This plan is built on the kind of common ground that Democrats and Republicans should be able to reach.

In total, the Budget will cut the deficit by another $1.8 trillion over the next 10 years, bringing the deficit below 2 percent of GDP by 2023 and putting our debt on a declining path. This is not an end in and of itself—the best way to grow the economy and cut the deficit is by creating good middle class jobs. But this plan to reduce the deficit in a balanced way is a critical step toward ensuring that we have a solid foundation on which to build a strong economy and a thriving middle class for years to come.

Finally, this Budget continues my commitment to reforming and streamlining our Government for the 21st Century. It builds on my Campaign to Cut Waste by further targeting and eliminating wasteful spending wherever we find it. It reorganizes and consolidates agencies and programs to make them leaner and more efficient. It increases the use of evidence and evaluation to ensure we are making smart investments with our scarce taxpayer dollars. And it harnesses new technologies to allow us to do more with less.

No single Budget can solve every challenge and every problem facing the country. But this Budget shows how we can live within our means while growing our economy, strengthening the middle class, and securing our Nation's future. It is not a Democratic plan or a Republican plan. It is an American plan. And it is a plan that I hope can serve as an outline for us to write the next great chapter of the American story…together.

BARACK OBAMA

THE WHITE HOUSE,
        APRIL 10, 2013.

STRENGTHENING THE MIDDLE CLASS AND MAKING AMERICA A MAGNET FOR JOBS

When the President first took office in 2009, the economy was experiencing the worst downturn since the Great Depression, shedding over 800,000 private sector jobs a month, and shrinking at a rate not seen in more than 60 years. Businesses—small and large—were struggling. The housing market was in free fall, our auto industry was near collapse, and the Nation was engulfed in costly and draining wars in Iraq and Afghanistan.

Through the President's decisive actions to bolster economic growth and jumpstart economic activity, including signing into law the Recovery Act, we successfully broke the back of the recession and pulled the Nation back from the brink. The economy is now on the mend. We have seen positive economic growth for 14 consecutive quarters, and 36 months of private sector job growth, with 6.4 million jobs created. The housing market is recovering, America's auto industry is once again resurgent, and we have successfully ended the war in Iraq and begun the process of bringing our troops home from Afghanistan.

But our work is not done. The economy is adding jobs, but too many Americans are still unemployed. Businesses are hiring again, but too many are still struggling to compete and find workers with the right skills to meet their needs. Home prices are rising at the fastest pace in six years and construction is expanding, but too many families with solid credit are still finding it difficult to buy a home or refinance. Although corporate profits are at an all-time high, wages and incomes for America's middle class have continued to stagnate.

The President believes we must invest in the true engine of America's economic growth—a rising and thriving middle class. He is focused on addressing three fundamental questions: How do we attract more jobs to our shores? How do we equip our people with the skills needed to do the jobs of the 21ˢᵗ Century? How do we make sure hard work leads to a decent living?

The Budget presents the President's plan to address each of these questions. To make America once again a magnet for jobs, it invests in high-tech manufacturing and innovation, clean energy, and infrastructure, while cutting red tape to help businesses grow. To give workers the skills they need to compete in the global economy, it invests in education and job training, supporting learning from cradle to career. To ensure hard work is rewarded, it builds ladders of opportunity to help every American and every community.

To further strengthen the economy, we must also harness the talents and ingenuity of a striving and hopeful immigrant population. That is why the President has presented a plan for common-sense immigration reform that continues to strengthen our borders, cracks down on employers who exploit American and immigrant workers, streamlines the legal immigration system to attract highly-skilled entrepreneurs and engineers to help create jobs and drive economic growth and reunite Americans with their families, and establishes a responsible pathway to earned citizenship. The Budget makes investments that will improve our immigration system and lay a foundation for this permanent, common-sense reform.

The Budget is also built on the recognition that economic growth can only be achieved if America is safe and secure, both at home and abroad. It supports the President's initiative to address gun violence, promote school safety, and care for the mentally ill. It reasserts our leadership in the Asia-Pacific region. It upholds our commitment to a unified and sovereign Afghanistan, while continuing our fight against terrorists, like al Qaeda. It confronts new dangers like cyber attacks that threaten our Nation's businesses and people. And it upholds our solemn duty to care for our veterans, who have given so much in service to our Nation.

The Budget does all of these things without adding a single dime to the deficit. Every new initiative in the plan is fully paid for. And, as discussed in chapter 2, the Budget also incorporates the President's compromise offer to House Speaker Boehner to achieve another $1.8 trillion in deficit reduction in a balanced way. When combined with the deficit reduction already achieved, this will allow us to exceed the goal of $4 trillion in deficit reduction, while growing the economy and strengthening the middle class.

INVESTING IN AMERICAN INNOVATION

To compete in the 21st Century economy, we must continue to invest in American innovation, reviving our manufacturing base and keeping our Nation at the forefront of technological advancement. To ensure our energy security and combat global climate change, we must continue to focus on energy production, the development of clean energy alternatives, and the promotion of energy efficiency efforts in both the public and private sectors.

Make America a Magnet for Manufacturing Jobs. President Obama is committed to making America a magnet for jobs and manufacturing so that we can continue to build things the rest of the world buys. After shedding jobs for more than 10 years, our manufacturers have added more than 500,000 over the past three. Manufacturing production has grown since the end of the recession at its fastest pace in over a decade. The Budget builds on that momentum by investing in American manufacturing.

- *Transform Regions Into Global Epicenters of Advanced Manufacturing.* To support investment in U.S. manufacturers' competitiveness and accelerate innovation in manufacturing, the Budget includes a one-time, $1 billion investment to launch a network of up to 15 manufacturing innovation institutes across the United States. Leveraging

the strengths of a particular region, each institute will bring together companies, universities and community colleges, and Government to co-invest in the development of world-leading manufacturing technologies and capabilities that U.S.-based manufacturers can apply in production. In August 2012, the Administration launched a pilot institute in Youngstown, Ohio with a $45 million funding commitment from five Federal agencies led by the Department of Defense. While the President will continue to push the Congress to act on his broader proposal, he will also take executive action to launch three new manufacturing innovation institutes in 2013, with an initial focus on manufacturing technologies that address critical national security and energy needs.

- *Strengthen Manufacturing Communities.* The President is proposing incentives for communities facing concentrated job losses—particularly hard-hit manufacturing communities—to help attract new investment and jobs. The incentives will help prevent the downward spiral that can occur following mass layoff events. The President is also directing Federal agencies to provide coordinated assistance to manufacturing communities through a new partnership designed to strengthen communities' ability to attract and sustain business investment. To support the partnership, the Budget includes $113 million at the Department of Commerce to provide targeted financial assistance to competitively-designated manufacturing communities, which would be matched by non-Federal funds to co-invest in state-of-the-art infrastructure projects, industrial parks, and research facilities.

- *Expand Federal Efforts to Attract Investment to Our Shores*. In 2011, the President launched SelectUSA at the Department of Commerce, creating the first Federal effort to actively attract business investment in the United States. The Budget significantly expands SelectUSA to create the capabilities and services to help our governors and mayors compete with foreign countries. The Administration will also host a SelectUSA Investment Summit this year, bringing together businesses from around the world with local leaders to attract jobs and investment to our shores.

- *Strengthen Manufacturing Supply Chains*. The Department of Commerce's Manufacturing Extension Partnership provides a range of business services to small manufacturers and is enhancing the program to help companies focus on upgrading technology to benefit from supply chain opportunities. The Budget includes a $25 million increase to launch Manufacturing Technology Acceleration Centers, which will be industry-specific centers that can facilitate expansions of firms' abilities to participate in key supply chains.

Invest in Research and Development. For many decades, the United States has been a world leader in research and development (R&D). We need to maintain our world-class commitment to science and research. The Budget does that by providing $143 billion for R&D overall, while targeting resources to those areas most likely to directly contribute to the creation of transformational technologies that can create the businesses and jobs of the future. It increases non-defense

R&D by nine percent from the 2012 levels, even as overall budgets decline. As part of business tax reform it expands and simplifies the Research and Experimentation Tax Credit and makes it permanent—providing certainty to businesses and increasing the credit's effectiveness.

Basic research has been one of America's great strengths, creating whole new industries and jobs. The Budget maintains the President's commitment to increase funding for basic research at three key science agencies: the National Science Foundation; the Department of Energy's Office of Science; and the laboratories of the National Institute of Standards and Technology. Within these agencies, funds will be focused on basic research directed at priority areas, such as clean energy technologies, advanced manufacturing, biotechnology, and new materials.

The Budget supports biomedical research at the National Institutes of Health. Tomorrow's advances in health care depend on today's investments in basic research on the fundamental causes and mechanisms of disease, new technologies to accelerate discoveries, innovations in clinical research, and a robust pipeline of creative and skillful biomedical researchers.

The Budget funds the National Aeronautics and Space Administration to develop innovative aeronautics and space technologies that will keep the aerospace industry—one of the largest net export industries in the United States—at the cutting edge in the years to come. It also increases funding for Department of Agriculture competitive peer-reviewed research grants to support research in human nutrition and obesity reduction, food safety, bioenergy, and climate change.

Build a Clean Energy Economy, Improve Energy Security, and Enhance Preparedness and Resilience to Climate Change. Cleaner energy will play a crucial role in meeting the President's goals of reducing greenhouse gas emissions in the range of 17 percent below 2005 levels by 2020, and enhancing national security by reducing dependence on oil. The Administration supports a range of investments and initiatives to help make the United States the leader in this sector and bring about a clean energy economy with its new companies and jobs:

- *Adopt "All-of-the-Above" Strategy to Energy.* The President is committed to an "all-of-the-above" approach that develops all American energy sources in a safe and responsible way and builds a clean and secure energy future, including:

  — **Invest in Clean Energy Research and Development.** The Budget continues to place a priority on funding for the Department of Energy's Office of Energy Efficiency and Renewable Energy to accelerate R&D and further increase the cost-competitiveness and deployment of renewable power, electric vehicles, next-generation biofuels, advanced energy-efficient manufacturing, and energy efficiency in homes and commercial buildings. The Budget also proposes increasing support in 2014 for the Department of Energy's Advanced Research Projects Agency–Energy to support breakthrough research in clean energy technologies. It funds research and development of next-generation renewable energy and high-value bio-based products at the Department of Agriculture. It invests in cleaner energy from fossil fuels like clean coal, as well as funding to develop small modular nuclear reactors, and provides incentives for the development of the first, natural gas combined cycle power plant to integrate carbon capture and storage.

  — **Commit to Safer Production of and Cleaner Electricity from Natural Gas.** Our domestic natural gas resources are reducing energy costs across the economy—from manufacturers investing in new facilities to families seeing heating costs drop. The Budget invests in research to ensure safe and responsible natural gas production and promote the development of the first natural gas combined cycle

power plant to integrate carbon capture and storage.

  — **Implement Responsible Nuclear Waste Strategy.** Under the President's direction, the Department of Energy created a Blue Ribbon Commission on America's Nuclear Future to recommend how to manage the challenges associated with the back end of the nuclear fuel cycle. The Administration has issued a report in response to the recommendations and looks forward to working with the Congress on implementing policies that ensure that nuclear power can continue to be part of our energy mix.

- *Make Energy Go Farther Across the Economy.* Cutting the amount of energy we waste in our cars and trucks, in our homes and buildings, and in our factories, will make us a stronger, more resilient, and more competitive economy. The Budget takes a number of steps to support these improvements, including:

  — **Set a New Goal to Double American Energy Productivity by 2030.** The President has set a new goal to cut in half the energy wasted by America's homes and businesses, with action aimed at doubling the economic output per unit of energy consumed in the United States by 2030, relative to 2010 levels.

  — **Challenge States to Cut Energy Waste, Support Energy Efficiency, and Modernize the Electricity Grid.** The Budget includes $200 million in one-time funding for Race to the Top performance-based awards to support State governments that implement effective policies to cut energy waste and modernize the electricity grid.

  — **Cut Carbon Pollution by Building on the Success of Existing Public and Private Energy Efficiency Partnerships.** Over the next four years, the President is also committed to accelerating progress on energy productivity through the Better Buildings Challenge, continuing to lead through Federal energy efficiency, improving energy data access for consumers through the "Green Button" initiative, and making appliances even more efficient—saving consumers money, spurring innovation, and strengthening domestic manufacturing.

— **Sustain Investments in Technologies That Promote Maximum Productivity of Energy Use and Reduce Waste in Manufacturing.** The Budget expands applied research and development of innovative manufacturing processes and advanced industrial materials, and builds on the President's Executive Order to accelerate investment in industrial energy efficiency, including setting a new challenge to achieve 40 gigawatts of new combined heat and power by 2020.

• *Invest in Energy Security.* Over the President's first term, the United States cut oil imports by more than 3.6 million barrels per day, more than under any other President. To ensure that we continue on a path towards greater energy security, the Budget would:

— **Set a Goal to Cut Our Oil Net Imports in Half by the End of the Decade.** Increased production of domestic oil and biofuels, and improvements in the fuel economy of our cars and trucks, allowed the United States to cut imports of oil by almost one-third since 2008. To build on this progress, the President will propose new policies and investments to set us on a course to cut imports of foreign oil in half by the end of the decade, relative to 2008 levels.

— **Establish an Energy Security Trust and Enact Reforms to Promote Responsible Oil and Gas Development on Federal Lands.** While the United States will continue to rely on responsibly produced oil and natural gas, the President is committed to a long-term policy that allows us to transition to cleaner energy sources. The Budget establishes an Energy Security Trust to help fund efforts to shift our cars and trucks off oil. This $2 billion investment over 10 years will support research into a range of cost-effective technologies and will be funded by revenue generated from Federal oil and gas development.

— **Make Energy Project Permitting More Robust.** The Interior Department is continuing to take steps to open public lands to develop American energy. The Budget will increase funding for energy programs of the Department of the Interior's Bureau of Land Management by roughly 20 percent supporting better permitting processes for oil and gas, renewable energy, and infrastructure, including the transition to an electronic, streamlined system for oil and gas permits.

— **Ensure U.S. Leadership in Advanced Vehicle Manufacturing.** Building on the Recovery Act investments and the fuel efficiency standards proposed through 2025, the Administration has proposed a strategy for deploying advanced vehicles in the United States, including a comprehensive package of incentives for consumers and businesses to spur advanced vehicle manufacturing and adoption, and increased investments in advanced vehicle technologies through the Department of Energy's EV Everywhere initiative. The Administration is also committed to accelerating the growth of private sector investments in natural gas fueling infrastructure across the United States just as natural gas vehicle research begins to make the technology more economically and environmentally effective.

— **Reduce Defense Department Energy Consumption.** The Department of Defense (DOD) consumes almost three-fourths of all energy used by the Federal Government. Consuming that much energy—whether fuel for planes, ships, and tanks, or electricity for bases, commissaries, and schools—has budgetary and strategic impacts. To mitigate those impacts, DOD seeks to be more deliberate about how it uses energy, in line with the Administration's overall approach to energy efficiency, such as by improving the fuel efficiency of existing equipment, developing and fielding innovative energy technologies, expanding renewable and low carbon energy sources and improving the energy efficiency of buildings.

* *Enhance Preparedness and Resilience to Climate Change.* The President recognizes that climate change poses an economic, security, and environmental threat that demands a decisive response. Even as we work to reduce the severity of climate change by cutting carbon pollution, we must also improve our ability to manage the climate impacts that are already being felt at home and around the world. Preparing for increasingly extreme weather and other unavoidable consequences of climate change will save lives and help to secure long-term American prosperity. To that end, the President is committed to building stronger, more resilient infrastructure and communities. The Budget would support this ongoing work to:

— **Safeguard Federal Investments, Ensuring Delivery of Federal Services, and Protecting Critical Resources in the Face of Climate Change.** Federal agencies have developed their first-ever climate change adaptation plans, which will help agencies better protect taxpayer investments and safeguard the health and safety of communities, economies, and infrastructure in the face of extreme weather and other impacts of climate change. Agencies have also been working together, along with State and local partners, to develop joint strategies to build a coordinated and comprehensive response to the impacts of climate change in cross-cutting sectors, such as fresh water management. The Administration is also working to incorporate climate change considerations into the design and repair of critical infrastructure.

— **Support Local Efforts to Build Resilience.** The Administration has also sought to encourage and accelerate local efforts to improve climate preparedness and resilience in the face of climate change by supporting community resilience planning and by working across agencies to provide local decision-makers actionable information on observed and projected changes in extreme events and other impacts of climate change. The Budget includes $200 million of innovation-spurring transportation investments to fund communities that include enhanced resilience to extreme weather and other impacts of climate change in their planning efforts. Planning by these communities will be supported by a broader Administration commitment to help communities improve their resilience through direct technical assistance, provision of useful data and tools on projected impacts, and support for planning.

— **Improve Understanding of Climate Impacts and Making this Information Accessible.** The Budget funds new investments in actionable science on climate change impacts and the development of technical resources, data, and tools for communities. It supports efforts to make information about the Earth that is collected in several Federal agencies consistent and more usable. Building on supplemental funding provided to East Coast communities impacted by Hurricane Sandy, the National Oceanic and Atmospheric Administration will help communities prepare for and respond to coastal storms, sea level rise, drought, and other climate-related hazards by providing data, information, and services, as well as risk assessment tools.

— **Strengthen International Efforts to Reduce Carbon Pollution and Build Global Climate Resiliency.** The Administration has led efforts in the international climate negotiations that have yielded, among other things, the first set of national greenhouse gas reduction commitments by all of the major developed and developing countries alike, the most robust transparency system to date, and historic global efforts in support of climate resiliency. At the same time, we have worked to advance climate and clean energy efforts through a range of international initiatives, including launching the Major Economies Forum on Energy and Climate, the Clean Energy Ministerial, and the Climate and Clean Air Coalition to Reduce Short-Lived Climate Pollutants.

Open Data to Spark Innovation. For decades, entrepreneurs have used Government data from Global Positioning Systems, weather monitoring stations, and other sources to power their products and services. This synergy between freely available Federal data and entrepreneurial innovation has benefited both the American economy and American citizens. The Administration's Open Data Initiative has already liberated unprecedented volumes of Government data related to energy, education, international development, public safety, and other key areas. The goal of these efforts is to connect the next generation of entrepreneurs and service providers to freely available Government data, while rigorously protecting privacy.

To continue to expand the economic growth and job creation fueled by this policy, the Administration will accelerate efforts to make Government information resources more publicly accessible in "machine-readable" form, easily usable as fuel for innovation. The information is posted on the *Data.gov* website, giving free public access to data that taxpayers have paid for and that the Government is giving back to them.

Protect Intellectual Property in Support of the Nation's Innovation and Creative Economies. Protecting America's intellectual property rights is fundamental to the global economic competitiveness of the United States, the security and capabilities of our military, and the health and safety of the American public. The Budget supports improved intellectual property enforcement domestically and overseas as set out in the *Joint Strategic Plan on Intellectual Property Enforcement*, released by the U.S. Intellectual Property Enforcement Coordinator in June 2010, and the Administration's new *Strategy on Mitigating the Theft of U.S. Trade Secrets*, released in February 2013.

The Budget proposes to strengthen the U.S. Patent and Trademark Office's (USPTO's) efforts to improve the speed and quality of patent examinations through reforms authorized by the America Invents Act, including providing the USPTO with full access to its user fee collections. In addition, the Administration continues to advance law enforcement efforts through the National Intellectual Property Rights Coordination Center (IPR Center). The IPR Center brings together 21 Federal and international agencies in order to leverage their respective resources, expertise, and authorities to better combat intellectual property theft and dismantle the criminal organizations seeking to profit from the manufacture, importation, and sale of counterfeit and pirated goods that threaten our economic stability, restrict the competitiveness of U.S. industry in world markets, and place the health and safety of the American people at risk.

BUILDING A 21ST CENTURY INFRASTRUCTURE

Since the President took office four years ago, America has begun the hard work of rebuilding our infrastructure: we have built or improved over 350,000 miles of road and more than 6,000 miles of rail, and we have repaired or replaced over 20,000 bridges. But to compete in the 21st Century economy and become a magnet for jobs, we must do more. We need to repair our existing infrastructure, and invest in the infrastructure of tomorrow, including high-speed rail, high-tech schools, and power grids that are resilient to future extreme conditions. These investments will both lay the foundation for long-term economic growth and put workers back on the job now. The Budget ensures these investments do not add to the deficit by making trade-offs within discretionary spending limits and reinvesting savings from capping Overseas Contingency Operations funding.

We also know that America works best when we are catalyzing the resources and ingenuity of a vibrant private sector. That is why the President's infrastructure plan calls for making it easier for the private sector to invest in rebuilding our Nation and cutting red tape through permitting reform that dramatically reduces project timelines.

Provide $50 Billion in Upfront Infrastructure Investments. The national transportation system continues to face an immense backlog of state-of-good-repair projects, a reality underscored by the fact that there are nearly 70,000 "structurally deficient" bridges in the United States today. To address this problem, the Budget includes $40 billion for "Fix it First" projects, to invest immediately in our Nation's infrastructure with an emphasis on reducing the backlog of deferred maintenance on highways, bridges, transit systems, and airports nationwide. The Budget also includes $10 billion for competitive programs to encourage innovative reform and help get high-value infrastructure projects from the planning stage to execution.

Boost Private Investment Through "Rebuild America Partnership." The President's plan will bring together an array of new and existing policies all aimed at enhancing the role of private capital in U.S. infrastructure investment as a vital additive to the traditional roles of Federal, State, and local governments.

* *Create a National Infrastructure Bank.* The President continues to call for the creation of an independent national Infrastructure Bank. The Bank will have the ability to leverage private and public capital to support infrastructure projects of national and regional significance. In addition, the Bank will be able to invest through loans and loan guarantees in a broad range of infrastructure projects, including transportation, energy, and water, and will operate as an independent, wholly-owned Government entity outside of political influence.

* *Enact America Fast Forward Bonds and Other Tax Incentives for Infrastructure Investment.* Recovery Act funding for "Build America Bonds" (BABs) helped to support more than $181 billion for new public infrastructure. The program's innovative design ensured that taxpayers as a whole received the best bang-for-the-buck when the Federal Government helped States, localities, and their private sector partners invest in new infrastructure. The President's new America Fast Forward (AFF) Bonds program will build upon the successful example of the BABs program, broadening it to include similar programs like the qualified private activity bonds program, while also relaxing certain limitations in the way the combined program could be used. AFF Bonds will attract new sources of capital for infrastructure investment—including from public pension funds and foreign investors that do not receive a tax benefit from traditional tax-exempt debt. As part of the AFF Bonds program, the Budget proposes to reduce the cost

of financing for building and repairing public schools, State universities, and school buildings sponsored by non-profit educational entities by issuing AFF school construction bonds, with an additional interest subsidy in 2014 and 2015 to encourage immediate investment in school construction. In addition, the Budget proposes changes to the Foreign Investment in Real Property Tax Act (FIRPTA) aimed at enhancing the attractiveness of investment in U.S. infrastructure and real estate to a broader universe of private investors.

- *Implement Newly Expanded TIFIA Program.* The Transportation Infrastructure Finance and Innovation Act (TIFIA) loan program received an eight-fold increase in funding in the recent surface transportation reauthorization. The program, which is especially important to mayors and local leaders, highlights the important role that infrastructure financing can play in catalyzing private investment.

Dedicate Funding for High-Speed Rail Investment. The Budget provides $40 billion over five years to fund the development of high-speed rail and other passenger rail programs as part of an integrated national transportation strategy. This national system will provide 80 percent of Americans with convenient access to a passenger rail system featuring high-speed service within 25 years. The Administration's proposal also benefits freight rail and significantly restructures Federal support for Amtrak, to increase transparency, accountability, and performance.

Modernize Air Traffic Control System. The Budget provides nearly $1 billion in 2014 for the Next Generation Air Transportation System (NextGen). NextGen is the multi-year effort to improve the efficiency, safety, capacity, and environmental performance of the aviation system, which will improve the travel experience for the traveling public and allow businesses to better serve their customers. These funds would continue to support the transformation from a ground-based radar surveillance system to a more accurate satellite-based surveillance system; the development of 21st Century data communications capability between air traffic control and aircraft to improve efficiency; and the improvement of aviation weather information.

Expedite Infrastructure Projects Through Permitting Reform. Major infrastructure projects typically require multiple permits and reviews from multiple agencies across multiple governmental jurisdictions, which can lead to confusion, duplication, and delay. In addition, project developers, citizens, and stakeholders can find navigating these governmental roles frustrating, time-consuming, and costly.

In order to accelerate economic growth and improve the competitiveness of the American economy, the Administration is taking action to modernize and improve the efficiency of the Federal permitting process, cutting through the red tape and getting more timely decisions on Federal permits and reviews, while ensuring that projects that are approved are protective of our communities and the environment. The President has established a new goal of cutting timelines in half for infrastructure projects in areas such as highways, bridges, railways, ports, waterways, pipelines, and renewable energy.

Expand Access to Wireless Broadband. The Administration and the Federal Communications Commission are continuing their work in 2014 to expand availability of spectrum for wireless broadband use through incentive auctions and by identifying spectrum used by Federal agencies that could be repurposed for commercial use. In addition, through the First Responder Network Authority, created by the Middle Class Tax Relief and Job Creation Act of 2012, the Administration is also working to develop a highly reliable, nationwide interoperable wireless broadband network for first responders.

OPENING GLOBAL MARKETS

The emergence of a global marketplace beyond our borders that includes 95 percent of the world's customers, as well as the globe's fastest-growing markets, creates an opportunity for America to export our goods and services to new customers and spur economic growth and job creation in the United States. To support international trade and the jobs that accompany it, the Administration is seeking to open global markets through a series of initiatives that would:

Encourage Growth Through National Export Initiative. A critical component of building a stronger American economy is ensuring that U.S. businesses, farmers, and ranchers can actively participate in international markets by increasing their exports of goods and services. The Administration launched the National Export Initiative (NEI) in January 2010 with the goal of doubling U.S. exports over five years while supporting two million new jobs. The Administration is currently making historic progress toward this target—in 2012, exports of goods and services reached record levels of over $2.2 trillion, 39 percent above 2009 levels. In addition, the number of jobs supported by exports climbed to 9.8 million in 2012—an increase of 1.3 million jobs since 2009, which is 60 percent of the way to the President's goal of two million additional export-supported jobs by the end of 2014. The Budget provides targeted increases for agencies involved in trade promotion and financing, development finance, and trade enforcement in support of the NEI. This funding will help strengthen efforts to promote exports from small businesses; increase export promotion activities in underserved markets around the world; help enforce domestic and international trade rules; fight to eliminate barriers on sales of U.S. goods and services; and improve the competitiveness of U.S. firms.

Complete Negotiations on Trans-Pacific Partnership. As the United States rebalances toward the Asia-Pacific region, a top priority is strengthening the regional economic architecture. By the end of 2013, the United States will work with Trans-Pacific Partnership (TPP) partners to bring TPP negotiations toward an ambitious conclusion—the goal put forward by President Obama and fellow TPP leaders in November 2012. TPP is a high-standard regional trade agreement that will link the United States to dynamic economies throughout the rapidly growing Asia-Pacific region and has the potential to provide a more robust and responsive trade model for the next generation—a model that addresses new challenges that have arisen in recent years. All TPP partners share a core mission of tackling these new challenges not only to help businesses and workers today, but to enhance regional trade for the next generation of producers, workers, and consumers in every Asia-Pacific economy.

Launch Negotiations on Transatlantic Trade and Investment Partnership with European Union (EU). President Obama announced his intention to launch negotiations with the EU on a comprehensive Transatlantic Trade and Investment Partnership (TTIP) in his 2013 State of the Union Address to the Congress. Such a partnership would include ambitious reciprocal market opening in goods, services, and investment, and would offer additional opportunities for modernizing trade rules and identifying new means of reducing the non-tariff barriers that now constitute the most significant obstacle to increased transatlantic trade. A successful agreement of this kind could generate new business and employment by expanding trade and investment opportunities in both economies, pioneer rules and disciplines that address challenges to global trade and investment that have grown in importance in recent years, and further strengthen the extraordinarily close strategic partnership between the United States and Europe.

Enhance Trade Enforcement. The Budget enhances trade enforcement with additional funding for Customs and Border Protection (CBP) officers who are responsible for conducting inspections on the goods entering the United States. More CBP officers will improve our trade enforcement capabilities, resulting in more seizures of counterfeit and fraudulent items, which will help protect U.S. businesses. The Budget continues to support CBP's Centers of Excellence and Expertise that are designed around key industry sectors in order to facilitate legitimate trade, enhance enforcement, and increase industry-based knowledge within CBP. It also supports the Interagency Trade Enforcement Center, an interagency effort created by the President in February 2012 to address unfair trade practices and barriers via a "whole-of-government" approach, helping ensure that America's trading partners abide by their obligations, including maintaining open markets on a non-discriminatory basis and following rules-based procedures in a transparent way.

Promote Trade, Travel, and Tourism, While Enhancing Security. The travel and tourism industry is a major contributor to U.S. economic growth, exports, and employment. That is why the President issued an Executive Order in January 2012 directing Federal agencies to aggressively expand the Nation's ability to attract and welcome visitors, while maintaining the highest standards of security. As a result of that direction, an interagency taskforce developed the

National Travel and Tourism Strategy to promote domestic and international travel opportunities throughout the United States and increase our market share of worldwide travel, with the goal of attracting 100 million international visitors to the United States annually by 2021, which is expected to generate $250 billion in spending.

To enhance security, the Budget adds 1,600 new CBP officers at our air, land, and sea ports of entry in 2014. These additional CBP officers will speed the entry of people and cargo into the United States, while increasing seizures of illegal items such as drugs, guns, currency, and counterfeit goods. In addition, the Budget includes new funding for hand-held mobile equipment and kiosks that will make inspections and processing more efficient and further reduce wait times and cut cargo processing.

The Administration's travel and tourism promotion efforts have already begun to bear fruit, with international tourists spending a record $168.1 billion in 2012 and supporting 7.7 million jobs in the third quarter of 2012.

PROVIDING MIDDLE CLASS TAX CUTS AND REBALANCING THE TAX CODE THROUGH TAX REFORM

The President believes that targeted tax relief can strengthen the economy and provide important support to middle class families.

Provide Permanent Tax Relief for Working Families and Students. The Budget starts from a baseline that makes permanent the American Opportunity Tax Credit (AOTC) and the improvements to the Earned Income Tax Credit (EITC) and Child Tax Credit enacted in 2009 and extended in 2010 and 2012. The AOTC provides a partially refundable tax credit of up to $2,500 per year to help finance up to four years of college. The credit is expected to help nearly 13 million families with students pay for higher education in 2013. The 2009 improvements to the EITC and Child Tax Credit reduce EITC "marriage penalties," that reduce the incentive to marry, provide additional assistance to families with three or

more children, and allow working families with moderate incomes to receive more of the benefits of the Child Tax Credit. The American Taxpayer Relief Act of 2012 (ATRA) made other middle class tax relief permanent, and extended these measures to assist working families and students through 2017.

The Budget proposes further targeted tax relief paid for by eliminating tax loopholes and making the system more fair, that will:

Incentivize Small Business Hiring and Wage Increases with a Payroll Tax Credit. Although the economy is recovering and private-sector employment is increasing, a tax credit designed to stimulate job creation and wage increases can help put more Americans back to work, provide targeted tax relief to America's small businesses, and strengthen the foundation of the economic recovery. The Budget proposes a one-time, temporary 10 percent tax credit for increases in companies' wage payments over wages paid in 2012, whether driven by new hires, increased wages or salaries, or both. The credit would be available to small businesses—those with less than $20 million of total wages paid in 2012—for up to $5 million of increased wages.

Encourage Retirement Savings with Automatic Individual Retirement Accounts and Support for Small Employers Who Offer Retirement Plans. About half of American workers have no workplace retirement plan. Yet fewer than 1 out of 10 workers who are eligible to make tax-favored contributions to an Individual Retirement Account (IRA) actually do so, while nearly 9 out of 10 workers automatically enrolled in a 401(k) plan continue to make contributions. The Budget would automatically enroll workers without employer-based retirement plans in IRAs through payroll deposit contributions at their workplace. The contributions would be voluntary—employees would be free to opt out—and matched by the Saver's Tax Credit for eligible families. Small employers would be eligible for tax credits to defray the administrative costs of setting up these savings plans. The Budget would also double the existing tax credit for small employers that start up new qualifying employer plans.

Expand Child and Dependent Care Tax Credit. Child care costs can be a major burden for working families and a barrier to employment for some individuals. To help defray these costs, the Budget increases the Child and Dependent Care Tax Credit available to working families with incomes between $15,000 and $103,000.

Rebalance the Tax Code. To raise revenue and pay for the tax cuts noted above, the Budget includes the following key offsets:

- *Tax Carried (Profits) Interests as Ordinary Income*. Currently, many hedge fund managers, private equity partners, and other managers in partnerships are able to pay a 20 percent capital gains tax rate on their labor income—income known as "carried interest." This tax loophole allows these financial managers to pay a lower tax rate on their income than other workers. The Budget eliminates the loophole for managers in investment services partnerships, and taxes carried interest at ordinary income tax rates, raising $16 billion over 10 years.

- *Prohibit Individuals from Accumulating Over $3 Million in Tax-Preferred Retirement Accounts*. Individual Retirement Accounts and other tax-preferred savings vehicles are intended to help middle class families save for retirement. But under current rules, some wealthy individuals are able to accumulate many millions of dollars in these accounts, substantially more than is needed to fund reasonable levels of retirement saving. The Budget would limit an individual's total balance across tax-preferred accounts to an amount sufficient to finance an annuity of not more than $205,000 per year in retirement, or about $3 million for someone retiring in 2013. This proposal would raise $9 billion over 10 years.

- *Return Estate Tax to 2009 Parameters and Close Estate Tax Loopholes*. The Budget returns the estate tax exemption and rates to 2009 levels beginning in 2018. Under 2009 law, only the wealthiest 3 in 1,000 people who die would owe any estate tax. As part of the end-of-year "fiscal cliff" agreement, congressional Republicans insisted on permanently cutting the estate tax below those levels, providing tax cuts averaging $1 million per estate to the very wealthiest Americans. It would also eliminate a number of loopholes that currently allow wealthy individuals to use sophisticated tax planning to reduce their estate tax liability. These proposals would raise $79 billion over 10 years.

- *Establish Financial Crisis Responsibility Fee*. The Administration is again calling for a Financial Crisis Responsibility Fee on the largest financial institutions to fully compensate taxpayers for the support they provided to the financial sector during the 2008–2009 economic crisis and to discourage excessive risk-taking going forward. The fee,

which would be restricted to financial firms with assets over $50 billion, would raise approximately $59 billion over 10 years.

IMPLEMENTING CORPORATE TAX REFORM TO CREATE JOBS HERE AT HOME AND FOSTER INNOVATION AND COMPETITIVENESS

Over the nearly three decades since the last comprehensive reform effort, the business tax system has been loaded up with special deductions, credits, and other tax expenditures that help well-connected special interests, but do little for economic growth. Now more than ever, we cannot afford a tax code burdened with costly special-interest tax breaks. In an increasingly competitive global economy, we need to ensure that our tax code contributes to making the United States an attractive location for entrepreneurship and business growth.

For this reason, the President is calling on the Congress to immediately begin work on corporate tax reform that will close loopholes, lower the corporate tax rate, encourage investment here at home, and not add a dime to the deficit. In February 2012, the President provided a framework for how business tax reform could achieve these goals. As a starting point for comprehensive reform, the Budget proposes a number of specific measures to keep America competitive, to make sure our tax system encourages jobs to be created here rather than abroad, and to begin eliminating special interest loopholes in the tax code.

Because the President favors adopting these measures as part of revenue-neutral business tax reform that would also cut the corporate rate and comprehensively reform tax subsidies, the Budget does not count the net savings from the business tax proposals described below toward its deficit reduction targets. However, the President's proposal for revenue neutral reform would prevent hundreds of billions of dollars from being added to the deficit if the Congress continues to extend temporary business tax incentives without paying for them.

The specific measures proposed in the Budget include:

Expand, Simplify, and Make Permanent the Research and Experimentation Tax Credit. The Research and Experimentation (R&E) Tax Credit is an important Federal incentive for research. But the R&E Tax Credit is less effective than it could be in spurring additional research because it is complicated and temporary. Currently, businesses must choose between using a complex, outdated formula that provides a 20 percent credit rate and a much simpler one that provides a 14 percent credit rate. The Budget would increase the rate of the simpler credit to 17 percent, which would make it more attractive and simplify tax filing for businesses. In addition, the Budget makes the basic and the simplified R&E credit permanent to provide certainty and increase effectiveness. These reforms would provide an additional $99 billion in incentives for research over the next 10 years.

Provide a Permanent Tax Incentive for Renewable Energy Production and Energy Efficiency. In order to provide a strong, consistent incentive to encourage investments in renewable energy technologies like wind and solar, the Budget would make permanent the tax credit for the production of renewable electricity. As with the R&E credit, the United States has to date provided only a temporary production tax credit for renewable electricity generation. This approach has created an uncertain investment climate, undermined the effectiveness of the tax incentive, and slowed the development of a clean energy sector in the United States. In addition, the structure of the current Production Tax Credit makes it difficult for new, growing firms to benefit, because they may not yet have tax liability.

The Budget would address this issue by making the Production Tax Credit refundable. The Budget would also reform and make permanent the deduction for energy efficient commercial property. Together, these measures would provide an additional $23 billion of incentives for renewable energy production and energy efficiency over the next 10 years.

Reform the International Tax System. The international provisions of the corporate tax code create opportunities for U.S. companies to reduce their taxes by locating their operations and profits abroad instead of in the United States. The tax system is also subject to gaming, as corporations manipulate complex tax rules to minimize their taxes and, in some cases, shift profits earned in the United States to low-tax jurisdictions. At the same time, the tax system should properly balance the need to reduce tax incentives to locate overseas with the need for U.S. companies to be able to compete overseas; some overseas investments and operations are necessary to serve and expand into foreign markets in ways that benefit U.S. jobs and economic growth. The Budget proposes specific reforms to combat abuses as potential elements of broader business tax reform, which the President has proposed should also include a minimum tax on foreign earnings. The specific proposals in the Budget would crack down on opportunities to shift profits on intellectual property to low-tax countries and restrict the ability of companies to claim interest deductions while deferring U.S. tax on the associated income. The Budget also proposes to disallow deductions for moving production overseas, while providing a new tax credit for bringing production back to the United States. Together, these reforms would save $157 billion over 10 years.

Eliminate Fossil Fuel Tax Preferences. The tax code currently subsidizes fossil fuel—oil, gas, and coal products—through loopholes and tax expenditures that benefit these industries over others. In accordance with the President's agreement at the G-20 Summit in Pittsburgh, Pennsylvania in December 2009 to phase out subsidies for fossil fuels so that we can transition to a 21st Century energy economy, the Budget repeals a number of these tax preferences. Eliminating these tax subsidies would save $44 billion over 10 years.

Reform the Tax Treatment of Derivatives. Derivatives contracts and other complex financial products are currently subject to varying tax rules. In addition to creating needless complexity and distorting choices among financial instruments, these rules allow major financial firms to defer taxes on profits indefinitely, selectively realize profits and losses for tax purposes, and pay the lower long-term capital gains rate on a portion of short-term gains. The Budget would require that all derivatives contracts be "marked to market" with resulting gains and losses taxed each year and treated as ordinary income. This reform would save $19 billion over 10 years.

Eliminate Special Depreciation Rules for Corporate Purchases of Aircraft. Under current law, airplanes used in commercial and contract carrying of passengers and freight can be depreciated over seven years. However, airplanes not used in commercial or contract carrying of passengers or freight, such as corporate jets, are depreciated over five years. The Budget would change the depreciation schedule to seven years for corporate planes that carry passengers, to be consistent with the treatment of commercial aircraft. This change would save $3 billion over 10 years.

REDUCING BURDENSOME REGULATION

The Administration is firmly committed to a regulatory strategy that protects the safety and health of all Americans, while promoting continued economic growth and job creation. Smart, cost-effective regulations, crafted with input from stakeholders inside and outside of Government, can save lives and prevent harm, while promoting growth and innovation.

As the economy continues to recover and create new jobs, it is critical for the Nation's regulatory strategy to enable American businesses to grow and innovate. That is why the Administration carefully weighs the costs and benefits of rules—not by reducing difficult questions to problems of arithmetic, but by carefully weighing economic effects and also by taking into account qualitative factors, including fairness and human dignity. The Administration uses objective data to assess the impact of rules and to assess alternatives. Moreover, the Administration looks for areas where it can promote transparency and disclosure as a low-cost, high-impact regulatory tool.

From automobile safety to energy efficiency to credit cards, this approach has been fruitful. In fact, the net benefits of regulations issued through the third fiscal year of the first term have exceeded $91 billion. This amount, including not only monetary savings, but also lives saved and injuries prevented, is over 25 times the net benefits through the third fiscal year of the previous Administration. At the same time, the number of final rules reviewed by the Office of Information and Regulatory Affairs and issued by Executive agencies was actually lower during the first term of the Administration than it was during the first term of the previous Administration.

To improve the regulatory process, the President issued an Executive Order calling for attention to the best available evidence, careful consideration of costs and benefits, greater coordination among agencies, and selection of flexible and least burdensome alternatives, and has called on independent Federal regulators to follow suit in their rulemakings. The Executive Order also called for a historic Government-wide review, or "look back," of existing rules. The review produced over 500 reform proposals across all Executive agencies. As a result, the Administration is on track to save more than $10 billion in the near term, with more savings to come. The President has also moved to institutionalize the Government-wide review of rules and called on independent agencies to follow the same cost-saving and burden-reducing principles that Executive agencies must follow.

In the coming year, agencies will continue to pursue the regulatory reforms identified in the review process, producing more in savings by simplifying rules, eliminating redundancies, and identifying more cost-effective ways of completing their mission and serving the American people.

EDUCATING A COMPETITIVE WORKFORCE

To compete in the 21st Century economy, America's workers must be prepared with the skills and knowledge to meet the demands of high-growth industries that fuel America's economy and innovation. That is why the President is calling for major investments and reforms in education and training to ensure our youth and adults have the opportunity to learn the skills they need. In addition to a major new commitment to early childhood education, the Budget sustains investments in elementary and secondary schools while ramping up innovation, redoubles our focus on science, technology, engineering, and mathematics (STEM) education to prepare our students for the jobs of tomorrow, and includes new initiatives to make college more affordable.

Increase Access to High-Quality Early Childhood Education. Today, far too many children are already behind academically and developmentally by the time they start school, and never truly catch up—compromising our ability to compete in a global economy and sidelining huge pools of untapped talent. The early years of a child's life are the most critical for building the foundation needed for success in life. Research has conclusively shown that supporting children at this stage leads to significant benefits in school and beyond. This is particularly true for low-income children who often start kindergarten academically behind their peers by many months. Providing high-quality early childhood education to all children will enable them to start school ready to learn and realize their full potential. Research has shown that taxpayers receive a high average return on investments in high-quality early childhood education, with savings in areas like improved educational outcomes, increased labor productivity, and a reduction in crime.

The Budget therefore includes a "Preschool for All" initiative, in partnership with the States, to provide all low- and moderate-income four-year-old children with high-quality preschool, while also incentivizing States to expand these programs to reach additional children from middle class families and establish full-day kindergarten policies. To support this effort, the Budget includes $750 million in discretionary Preschool Development Grants in 2014, to ensure that States willing to commit to expanding preschool access are able to make the critical investments necessary to serve their four-year-old children in high-quality programs. The preschool initiative is coupled with a companion investment at the Department of Health and Human Services in expanding voluntary home visiting programs, maintaining child care subsidies, and increasing the availability of high-quality care for infants and toddlers through new Early Head Start-Child Care Partnerships.

The investments in early childhood education and development on the mandatory side of the Budget are fully financed by raising the Federal tax on cigarettes from $1.01 to $1.95 per pack. In addition to financing important investments in early learning, the proposed tobacco tax increase would have substantial public health benefits, particularly for young Americans. Researchers have found that raising taxes on cigarettes significantly reduces consumption, with especially large effects on youth smoking.

Redesign High School. During the President's first term, the Department of Education initiated historic reforms in our elementary and secondary schools by rewarding excellence and promoting innovation. Early indications show impressive progress in raising academic standards, placing an effective teacher in every classroom, and turning around struggling schools. The

Budget continues to build on this progress with sustained investment and new reforms. New initiatives include a new, competitive fund to redesign high schools nationwide, in order to keep America's youth engaged, successful, and focused on the future. This initiative will strengthen college- and career-readiness by redesigning high school to focus on providing challenging, relevant experiences, and rewarding schools that develop new partnerships with colleges and employers to improve instruction and prepare students to continue on to postsecondary education or transition into skilled jobs. In addition, the Budget proposes to strengthen and reform career and technical education to better align programs with the needs of employers and higher education.

Prepare Students for STEM Careers in the 21st Century Economy. Our future competitiveness demands that we move American students from the middle or bottom to the top of the pack in science and mathematics, preparing our young people to learn deeply and think critically in these subjects. The Budget proposes a comprehensive reorganization of Federal STEM education programs to enable more strategic investment in STEM and more critical evaluation of outcomes, reflecting an Administration priority on using Government resources more effectively to meet national goals. This reorganization is designed to increase the impact of Federal investments in four areas: K-12 instruction; undergraduate education; graduate fellowships; and education activities that typically take place outside the classroom, all with a focus on increasing participation and opportunities for individuals from groups historically underrepresented in these fields. The Department of Education will also invest in recruiting and preparing 100,000 effective STEM teachers within a decade, and in creating a new STEM Master Teachers Corps, to help improve instruction in their schools and districts, and to serve as a national resource for improving STEM instruction across America.

Improve College Affordability and Value. Early in his first term, the President set a national goal for the United States to lead the world again with the highest share of college graduates by 2020. Higher education remains an important step toward the middle class, and earning a degree or certificate is no longer just a privilege for some, but rather a prerequisite for all.

Over the past four years, the Administration has taken important steps to help students afford college, including expanding grant aid and college tax credits for American families. The President also recognizes that affordability and value in higher education are responsibilities shared with State governments, colleges, and universities. All must do their part to rein in costs, provide good value for American families, and prepare students with the education and training they need for jobs in the global economy.

The Budget includes several measures designed to improve college affordability and value. These include: a $1 billion Race to the Top fund, which would support competitive grants to States that commit to driving reform in their higher education policies and practices, while doing more to contain tuition and make it easier for students to earn a degree; a $260 million First in the World fund to spur the establishment, validation, and scaling-up of cutting-edge innovations that can decrease college costs and boost attainment rates; and reforms to Federal campus-based aid to reward colleges that set responsible tuition policy, deliver good value and quality to students, and serve low-income and Pell-eligible students well. These efforts build on actions the Administration has already taken to provide students and families with clear information about college costs and quality, through the College Scorecard and Financial Aid Shopping Sheet. The Budget also continues the Administration's strong commitment to the Pell Grant program, offsetting the cost with reforms to existing loan programs, and proposes a cost-neutral student loan reform that will keep rates low this year, set interest rates to more closely follow market rates, and provide greater affordability for students in repayment.

TRAINING AND SUPPORTING WORKERS IN A CHANGING ECONOMY

As the economy changes, training and employment programs must innovate and adapt to help American workers gain the skills they need to find new jobs and careers. At the same time, we must maintain critical protections to ensure our workers are treated fairly and safely in the jobs they hold. The Budget includes several initiatives to ensure these goals are achieved, including:

Modernize, Streamline, and Strengthen the Delivery of Training and Employment Services. Today more than 40 programs at 11 Federal agencies deliver job training and employment services. The Administration believes we should be doing everything we can to make it easier for people who need help to find a job or build their skills for a better one, and for employers who need to find well-qualified workers. The Administration is exploring opportunities to revisit how the Federal Government funds job training and employment services, including the possibility of reorganizing some of the existing training programs. For example, the Budget proposes a universal displaced worker program that will reach up to a million workers a year with a set of core services, combining the best elements of two more narrowly-targeted programs. Any reform must ensure that the needs of particularly vulnerable job-seekers and workers continue to be met and ensure greater accountability and transparency about the performance of federally-supported job training providers and programs. The Administration looks forward to working with the Congress and other stakeholders on job training reform in the coming year.

Drive Innovation in Training and Employment Services. To spur innovation, the Budget provides $150 million for the Workforce Innovation Fund. The Fund tests new ideas that States and regions bring forward to implement systemic reforms and replicate evidence-based strategies for training and helping workers find jobs. The Department of Labor (DOL) will continue to administer the Fund, working closely with agencies that support educational, employment, and related services. Within the Fund, $10 million is dedicated to building knowledge of which interventions are most effective for disconnected youth. The Budget also provides $80 million to increase the set-aside for governors in the Workforce Investment Act formula grants from 5 percent to 7.5 percent, in order to boost States' capacity to engage in program improvements and reform. In addition, the Budget provides $25 million to support new, evidence-informed efforts to improve employment outcomes for older Americans.

Reform Community Colleges to Meet Employer Needs. A large share of the Nation's skills training is delivered by community colleges. The Budget funds an $8 billion Community College to Career Fund jointly administered by DOL and the Department of Education to support State and community college partnerships with businesses and other stakeholders to build the skills of American workers; this is a successor initiative to the Trade Adjustment Assistance Community College and Career Training Grants, for which 2014 provides the final year of funding.

Maintain Strong Support for Worker Protection. The Budget includes nearly $1.8 billion for DOL's worker protection agencies, putting them on sound footing to meet their responsibilities to protect the health, safety, wages, working conditions, and retirement security of American workers. The Budget preserves recent investments in rebuilding DOL's enforcement capacity and makes strategic choices to ensure funding is used for the highest priority activities.

HELPING SMALL BUSINESSES GROW AND CREATE JOBS

The President recognizes that small businesses are a crucial engine of economic growth and a ladder for many to the middle class. The Budget continues the Administration's strong focus on providing tools to nurture entrepreneurs and grow small businesses through beneficial tax changes, such as eliminating capital gains and extending expensing for small business investments, and doubling deductions for start-up expenses, as well as financing and technical assistance. The Budget supports key initiatives through the Small Business Administration (SBA) to boost access to capital, increase small business contracting opportunities, and improve counseling resources.

To increase financing available to small businesses, the Budget supports development of SBA ONE, a streamlined one-stop lending platform aimed at simplifying the loan process for lenders and borrowers, from application to closure. To increase the share of Federal contracts going to small businesses, the Budget provides for additional SBA Procurement Center Representatives, who will be strategically embedded across the Federal Government to assist agencies in structuring Federal procurement awards to be accessible for small businesses. The Budget also proposes to create a new program at SBA to help existing small business owners take their business to the next level through an intensive, several months-long small business leadership program. This program will include immersion in core business concepts such as accounting and finance, peer-to-peer review among fellow business owners, tailored mentorship from experienced entrepreneurs, introductions to capital access and revenue opportunities, and culminate in the creation of a targeted growth plan for each business owner. The program will be modeled as a public-private partnership that is built on the best practices of other working private sector and non-profit models.

To make all of these resources more accessible to the public, the Budget continues to support the leading role that SBA and the Department of Commerce have played in the Administration's BusinessUSA initiative, a one-stop shop for businesses looking to do business with the Federal Government or obtain information about Federal business assistance resources.

REJUVENATING THE HOUSING MARKET

As the financial crisis and recession was deepening in 2009, the Administration took immediate steps to help millions of responsible homeowners who were facing foreclosure or were at risk of losing their homes. This began with the Administration's effort to establish a broad set of programs designed to stabilize the housing market and keep millions of Americans in their homes. The initiative included: Treasury's mortgage-backed securities purchase program, which along with mortgage-backed securities purchases by the Federal Reserve, has helped maintain liquidity to lenders to keep mortgage interest rates at historic lows; the first-time homebuyer tax credit, which helped millions of Americans to purchase homes, bolstering economic recovery; the low-income housing tax credit and housing finance agency programs to support affordable housing; and the Home Affordable Modification Program through the Troubled Asset Relief Program, which provides eligible homeowners the opportunity to significantly reduce their monthly mortgage payments, remain in their homes, and avoid foreclosures.

Finish the Task on Universal Refinancing for Responsible Homeowners. The housing market is showing signs of healing and growth. Home prices are increasing, inventories are down, and sales and construction are increasing. However, too many Americans are still paying mortgage interest rates far above today's historic low market rates because the reduction in their home value over the past five years made them worth less than their mortgage and ineligible for refinancing. Last year, the Administration worked with housing regulators and the Government Sponsored Enterprises (GSEs) Fannie Mae and Freddie Mac to double the number of underwater homeowners assisted with refinancing through the Home Affordable Refinance Program (HARP). Around 1.1 million borrowers refinanced through HARP in 2012, bringing the total number of borrowers who have refinanced through HARP since its inception to 2.1 million.

While this is an important step, the Administration believes that more aggressive action is needed and is calling on the Congress to take additional steps so virtually every family that has a standard mortgage and has been making its payments on time will have the opportunity to refinance their mortgage at today's historically low rates. Specifically, legislation is needed to fully streamline HARP to increase access and lower costs for borrowers and provide those responsible Americans who happen not to have a loan guaranteed by the GSEs with access to a comparable streamlined refinance program. Helping families refinance will help homeowners get into more sustainable loans, save each family on average $3,000 annually, enable many more to stay in their homes, and boost local economies.

Rebuild Communities Most Devastated by the Housing Crisis. Rising home prices in the last year have lifted an estimated 1.4 million homeowners from being underwater to having positive equity in their homes. But some areas are still experiencing high levels of negative equity. For example, just five States account for 34 percent of the total negative equity in the United States. In these communities hit hardest by the foreclosure crisis, the weight of foreclosed and vacant properties will continue to hold back growth and increase poverty and crime. To address this problem, the President implemented the Neighborhood Stabilization Program (NSP), which has played a critical role rebuilding communities that have been hit hardest by foreclosure and abandonment. To date, NSP has made over 600 grants that are helping to rehabilitate or demolish more than 100,000 damaged or vacant properties.

The President is proposing two programs to extend the success of NSP while creating construction jobs to rehabilitate properties. The Budget provides funding for neighborhood stabilization activities to continue mitigating the impacts of the foreclosure crisis. This funding will provide essential new resources to help communities while creating jobs through rehabilitating, repurposing, and demolishing vacant and blighted properties. In addition, the Budget includes funding for Project Rebuild, to help launch or support public-private land banks, provide grants to the hardest hit areas where there are high-levels of vacancies or severe blight, and offer loan subsidies to stimulate private investment.

IMPLEMENTING HEALTH INSURANCE REFORM

A key component of the Administration's drive to strengthen the middle class and provide a foundation for a strong economy is the implementation of the Affordable Care Act (ACA), the landmark comprehensive health insurance reform law passed in 2010. Although not yet fully implemented, the ACA is already holding insurance companies more accountable, lowering health insurance costs, and increasing choices and quality of health care for all Americans. Importantly, the law is projected to reduce the deficit by more than $1 trillion over the next two decades, according to the Congressional Budget Office's latest analysis.

The reforms effective in 2014 will implement some of the most important pieces of the legislation, providing every American access to affordable, comprehensive coverage through Health Insurance Marketplaces, also known as Affordable Insurance Exchanges. Most insurers will no longer be able to discriminate against individuals with pre-existing conditions, and individuals without access to affordable coverage from their employer or other programs will be eligible to purchase coverage with new tax credits to lower the cost of coverage. While Medicaid already provides critical health care coverage to low-income children, seniors, and individuals with disabilities, the ACA also provides unprecedented Federal assistance to States that expand Medicaid to cover low-income adults. When fully phased in, these provisions will provide insurance to millions of Americans who are uninsured today.

Because of the ACA, most insurers already are required to offer coverage to children with a pre-existing condition and cannot rescind an individual's coverage due to a technical error on an application, lifetime dollar limits on health benefits are banned, and most insurers must cover preventive care without charging a deductible or co-payment. Beginning in 2014, most insurers will be prohibited from denying coverage or charging more to any person due to a pre-existing condition or their gender. Limits on annual benefits will also be prohibited.

Since its enactment, the ACA has benefited millions of middle class Americans. Over three million previously uninsured young adults have obtained health insurance largely due to the ACA's requirement that young adults under age 26 can be covered by their parent's insurance. Over 6.1 million seniors benefited from the health care law's assistance to help cover prescriptions drugs in the Part D donut hole, saving them almost $6 billion on prescription drugs. More than 100,000 Americans with pre-existing conditions have gained coverage through the Pre-existing Condition Insurance Plan Program. Hundreds of thousands of small businesses have received tax credits to offer health insurance coverage to their employees, benefiting millions of workers.

More reforms also are taking effect. To ensure that dollars are going to patient care, the ACA requires insurance companies to spend at least 80 or 85 percent, depending on their market, of premium dollars on medical care and quality improvements, instead of administrative costs and profits. If they fail to meet these standards, insurance companies are required to provide a rebate to their customers. The first rebates went out in the summer of 2012, and the Department of Health and Human Services (HHS) estimates that these rebates totaled $1.1 billion in 2012.

Additionally, the ACA brings an unprecedented level of scrutiny and transparency to health insurance rate increases. Large premium increases proposed by health insurance companies in the individual and small group markets will now be evaluated by experts to make sure they are based on reasonable cost assumptions and solid evidence, and insurance companies have to publicly justify unreasonable rate increases. HHS estimates that rate review reduced premiums by about $1 billion in 2012.

The Administration has been working diligently with States to prepare for the ACA's health insurance expansion in 2014. Health Insurance Marketplaces will help ensure that every American can access high-quality, affordable health insurance coverage beginning in 2014. These competitive marketplaces will provide millions of Americans and small businesses with "one-stop shopping" for affordable coverage in every State. HHS has provided nearly $3.4 billion in grant funding to 37 States and the District of Columbia to establish Marketplaces.

In addition, numerous ACA reforms aimed at improving quality, efficiency, and coordination of care have already taken effect. Hospital Value-Based Purchasing and the Hospital Readmissions Reduction Program tie Medicare payments to hospitals to achievement of indicators of high-quality care. The Medicare Shared Savings Program launched nationwide, and has created new opportunities for patient-centered, integrated care for Medicare beneficiaries. Further, the Administration launched several initiatives to improve care for individuals eligible for both Medicare and Medicaid, including developing and testing new models designed to incentivize States and providers to create efficiencies through integration of care and improved care coordination. In addition, the ACA provided significant new tools and resources to crack down on waste and fraud in health care.

IMPLEMENTING WALL STREET REFORM

In addition to health care reform, the Administration is committed to implementing the Dodd-Frank Wall Street Reform and Consumer Protection Act of 2010 (Wall Street reform), the most far-reaching reform to the U.S. system of financial regulation since the Great Depression, and another critical element of the Administration's effort to secure the middle class and lay a foundation for long-term growth and prosperity for all Americans. Through the law's authorities, the Administration is taking necessary steps to create a more stable and responsible financial system. Financial regulators have made significant progress implementing reforms designed to fill gaps in market oversight, rein in predatory and abusive lending, and bring principles of fairness and accountability to all corners of our Nation's financial markets. And thanks in part to this important reform effort, our financial system has become smaller as a share of the economy and significantly less leveraged, helping reduce our vulnerability to future crises.

Our economy is benefitting from the many reforms now in place. Our financial system is safer now that banks will pay for their own bad bets.

Banks' balance sheets have grown stronger, with capital requirements for the largest firms effectively doubled, and capital levels in U.S. banks overall up 75 percent from three years ago. In addition, we have a new orderly liquidation framework in place for protecting the financial system, the economy, and taxpayers from the consequences of the failure of a large financial company. Eleven of the largest bank holding companies have already submitted their "living wills" to the Federal Reserve and the Federal Deposit Insurance Corporation, providing a roadmap to regulators should they ever fail, with the remaining plans due by the end of this year. This new liquidation framework will help ensure that the costs of resolving a failed financial company will never again be borne by taxpayers, but, instead, by the company's stockholders, creditors, and culpable management.

Another critical safeguard established under Wall Street Reform was the creation of the Financial Stability Oversight Council (FSOC). This new council of financial regulators headed by the Secretary of Treasury has become a central figure in monitoring and addressing risks to the financial system. Although FSOC members are required by law to meet only quarterly, the FSOC has been far more active than that—meeting 12 times in 2012 alone. This forum has enabled regulators to quickly coordinate their responses to events such as the failure of MF Global and the disruptions caused by Hurricane Sandy. In addition, in July 2012 the FSOC designated eight financial market utilities as systemically important institutions, subjecting them to more stringent risk-management standards and coordinated oversight by the financial regulators.

With the Consumer Financial Protection Bureau (CFPB) now able to exercise the full scope of its authorities, a new cop is on the beat, setting high and uniform standards across the financial services marketplace, improving financial literacy for all Americans, and helping to end profits based on misleading financial product sales pitches and hidden traps. Unlike years past, today banks and other financial companies must compete vigorously for consumers only on the basis of price and quality. In 2012, the CFPB began supervising payday lenders, credit reporting agencies, and debt collectors—three types of businesses that amazingly had never before been regulated. The CFPB has also been hard at work cracking down on abusive practices in the mortgage industry, making financial contracts simpler, and ending many hidden fees so that families are in a better position to understand their financial obligations when they buy a home. In total, these reforms put in place the strongest consumer financial protections in history.

Wall Street Reform also expanded enforcement authorities and whistleblower rules at the Securities and Exchange Commission and the Commodity Futures Trading Commission (CFTC), providing investors with increased protections. In addition, the agencies' vigorous enforcement efforts should serve as a greater deterrent to those who consider breaking the rules to get ahead. In addition, thousands of publicly-traded companies have exercised their right to vote on executive compensation packages as a result of new say-on-pay provisions.

Leading up to the financial crisis, many banks got into trouble because they were exposed to hidden risks from several exotic financial products. Regulators have begun implementing new Wall Street Reform rules in the over-the-counter derivatives market, significantly reducing the risks associated with these products by bringing much-needed transparency for both market participants and regulators. As a result of new reporting requirements, the price and volume of certain swap transactions are now available to regulators and the public, at no charge; reporting for additional asset classes will begin later in 2013. In addition, swap dealers now have to register with the CFTC and adhere to new standards for business conduct and recordkeeping.

To ensure that agencies and departments have the resources they need to implement Wall Street Reform, the Administration has called for adequate funding levels for them for 2013, and continues this commitment in the 2014 Budget.

REFORMING OUR IMMIGRATION SYSTEM

For generations, the United States has been enriched by a steady stream of hardworking and talented people who have helped make America an engine of the global economy and a beacon of hope around the world. The President is committed to building a fair, effective immigration system that lives up to our heritage as a nation of laws and a nation of immigrants. That system should demand responsibility from everyone—both the 11 million workers here in the shadows

and those who hire them—and reward the hard work of legal immigrants whose entrepreneurship and skills help build our economy.

The President has laid out a plan for common-sense immigration reform that would continue investments in border security, crack down on companies that hire undocumented workers, improve the legal immigration system for employment-sponsored and family-sponsored immigrants, and establish a responsible pathway to earned citizenship. The plan would require anyone who is undocumented to pay their taxes and a penalty, move to the back of the line, learn English, and undergo background checks.

There is a growing consensus in support of common-sense immigration reform across America. The vast majority of Americans support reform, as do stakeholders in the business, law enforcement, civil rights, labor, agriculture, and faith communities. The American people expect their elected officials in Washington to get the job done once and for all. The President is committed to working with the Congress to pass legislation that will permanently fix our broken immigration system.

The Budget supports the foundation for common-sense reform by continuing investments in strengthening our border, making our immigration enforcement effort smarter by focusing on individuals who are a threat to public safety, streamlining legal immigration by reducing barriers for immigrant entrepreneurs and innovators and families, and by expanding support for the integration of individuals on the path to citizenship. Moreover, the President will ensure that common-sense immigration reform legislation includes the resources required to responsibly and efficiently build the 21st Century immigration system America deserves.

BUILDING LADDERS OF OPPORTUNITY

There's a basic bargain in America. It says that no matter who you are or where you're from, if you're willing to work hard and play by the rules, you should be able to find a good job, feel secure in your community, and support a family. The Budget builds on the progress made over the last four years to expand opportunity for every American and every community willing to do the work to lift themselves up. It creates new ladders of opportunity to ensure that hard work leads to a decent living. It expands early childhood learning to give children a foundation for lifelong learning, as noted earlier in this chapter. It partners with communities to help them thrive and rebuild from the recession. It creates pathways to jobs for the long-term unemployed and youth who have been hardest hit by the downturn. It rewards hard work and reduces inequality and poverty by supporting an increase in the minimum wage. It also strengthens families by removing financial deterrents to marriage and supporting the role of fathers.

Partner With Communities to Help Them Rebuild. A child's zip code should never determine her destiny. But today, the neighborhood a child grows up in can diminish her odds of graduating high school, health outcomes, and lifetime economic opportunities. To address this problem, the Administration is building on the success of its Promise Neighborhoods and Choice Neighborhoods programs and partnering with some of the highest-poverty communities across the Nation. The Administration will designate Promise Zones through a transparent, competitive process that can draw on a number of resources in the Budget, including: using Department of Justice funding for local law enforcement and community leaders to reduce violent crime; leveraging Department of Housing and Urban Development grants to attract private investment to tear down distressed public housing and build new mixed income homes, while ensuring that low-income residents do not get displaced; and using Department of Education funding to improve educational opportunities and provide students and their families with a continuum of educational supports from cradle to college or career. The Budget also includes Promise Zone tax incentives to stimulate growth and investments in targeted communities, such as tax credits for hiring workers and incentives for capital investment within the Zone. In addition, the Budget supports direct Federal partnership with local leaders, helping them to navigate Federal programs, cut red tape, and use Federal resources more effectively.

Create Pathway to Work for Every American. The Budget includes a Pathways Back to Work Fund that offers incentives to hire the long-term unemployed and low-income adults, helps low-income youth find summer and year-round jobs, and provides the real-world skills Americans need to find a job. These steps are critical to ensuring that our economic recovery reaches the broadest possible swath of Americans.

Raise Minimum Wage to $9.00. No one who works full time should have to raise his or her family in poverty. Raising the minimum wage would directly boost wages for 15 million workers and would help our growing economy. That is why the President is calling on the Congress to raise the Federal minimum wage from $7.25 to $9.00 per hour by the end of 2015, and index it to inflation thereafter.

Strengthen Families. The Budget supports the President's commitment to promoting healthy marriages for all families and supporting the critical role that fathers play in enhancing the intellectual, emotional, and financial well-being of their sons and daughters. The Budget proposes to allow existing Federal programs, like the child support program, to implement models that get more men working and engaging with their children. It also supports States in testing strategies to overcome financial deterrents to forming safe and stable marriages.

MAKING COMMUNITIES SAFER BY REDUCING GUN VIOLENCE

The Budget supports the President's comprehensive approach to improving gun safety and reducing gun violence, including expanded background checks for firearm sales, improved tracing and ballistics analysis, and enhanced efforts to keep guns out of the hands of dangerous criminals and other prohibited persons.

To maximize success, the Budget combines these efforts with programs to improve school safety, enhance police officer protection, and implement new mechanisms to prevent the use of firearms by unauthorized users. It provides $112 million in new funds to help schools develop and implement emergency preparedness plans, create safer and more nurturing school climates through evidence-based behavioral practices, provide support and services to children exposed to pervasive violence, collect data on school safety and climate, and highlight best practices regarding school discipline policies, including the equitable implementation of these policies. This investment will complement Departments of Justice, Health and Human Services, and Homeland Security programs designed to support comprehensive school safety strategies.

The Budget expands mental health services for youth and families with a $130 million initiative to help teachers recognize signs of mental illness in students, improves mental health services for young people ages 16-25, and trains 5,000 more mental health professionals with a focus on serving students and young adults. The Budget also includes $30 million to support a nationwide violent deaths surveillance system and additional research on the causes and prevention of gun violence. Together, these initiatives can help identify mental illness early and create a clear pathway to treatment for those in need, increase gun safety, and keep communities safe from the immeasurable tragedies resulting from gun violence.

KEEPING AMERICA SAFE FROM THREATS OUTSIDE OUR BORDERS

Economic growth can only be achieved if America is safe and secure, both at home and abroad. Looking outside our borders, the Budget supports American leadership in the critical Asia-Pacific region; it upholds our commitment to a unified and sovereign Afghanistan, while continuing our fight against terrorists, like al Qaeda; and it confronts new dangers like cyber attacks that threaten our Nation's businesses and people. The Budget also upholds our solemn duty to care for our veterans, who have given so much in service to our Nation.

Invest in Long-Term Partnerships in Iraq, Afghanistan, and Pakistan. The Budget continues support for U.S security, diplomatic, and development goals in Afghanistan, Pakistan, and Iraq, while scaling down funding for operations and assistance. It includes resources for the State Department and the U.S Agency for International Development (USAID) to support strong, long-term partnerships with these countries. In addition, Overseas Contingency Operations (OCO) funding is provided for near-term development assistance related to stabilization and counterinsurgency programs, extraordinary costs of operating in a high-threat environment, protection of civilian personnel, and oversight activities of the Special Inspector General for Afghanistan Reconstruction.

Support Counterterrorism Efforts. Protecting the United States from terrorism remains a critical priority. The Budget continues to support counterterrorism efforts by a variety of Federal agencies consistent with the National Strategy for Counterterrorism. It will also support the gradual drawdown of U.S. forces and the transition to full Afghan responsibility for their country's security by the end of 2014. Because final policy decisions about the pace of this drawdown are pending, the Budget includes a placeholder for Department of Defense (DOD) OCO costs. The Administration will submit a Budget amendment to the Congress describing the OCO request as soon as possible.

Continue Investments in Nonproliferation and Counterterrorism Programs. The Budget continues to support the President's vision of a world without nuclear weapons by providing key investments in nonproliferation programs. This funding includes resources for flagship counterterrorism programs that develop partner capabilities to prevent terrorist attacks on the United States and other countries and to prevent the development, acquisition, trafficking, and use of weapons of mass destruction by terrorists.

Rebalance American Engagement with the Asia-Pacific Region. The United States and its interests are inextricably linked with Asia's economies and security, and it welcomes economic prosperity across the Asia-Pacific region. The Budget makes strategic, coordinated and Government-wide investments in a wide range of tools across the Asia-Pacific region, which will help create American jobs, empower American businesses, and maintain the security and stability necessary for economic growth.

Address Cyber Threats. Cyber attacks targeting the financial industry, other critical infrastructure, and Government demonstrate that no sector, network, or system is immune to infiltration by those seeking financial gain, perpetrating malicious and disruptive activity, or stealing commercial or Government secrets and property. Cyber threats are constantly evolving and require a comprehensive response.

To address cyber threats, the Administration is working across Government, with our State and local and international partners, and in conjunction with the private sector. Top priorities include securing Federal networks, protecting critical infrastructure, improving incident response, and engaging internationally. The President is also directing the Administration to help shape the future by prioritizing research, development, and technology transition, and harnessing private sector innovation while ensuring our activities continue to respect the privacy, civil liberties, and rights of everyone.

The Budget includes funding to support the expansion of information sharing programs and the Administration's cross-agency priority goal for cybersecurity, which are designed to enhance situational awareness of emerging cyber threats, identify and mitigate network and system vulnerabilities, and enhance the Nation's ability to rapidly respond to cyber attacks. The Budget will also support implementation of Executive

Order 13636, which is designed to improve the cybersecurity of U.S. critical infrastructure.

Re-Prioritize Investments in Weapons Systems. One of the Administration's priorities is to provide servicemembers with the modern equipment they need to implement the new defense strategy. To achieve this goal, the Budget, for example, continues funding the Joint Strike Fighter program, which is designed to counter the threats posed by a sophisticated adversary, and the VIRGINIA class submarine, which improves the Navy's ability to operate in coastal waters. DOD is also working to upgrade the command and control equipment on the Army's Stryker combat vehicles, and the suspension and drive train of Paladin self-propelled howitzers to improve troop protection, survivability, and mobility.

While the Administration is committed to continuing its investment in new weapons systems needed to ensure that America's military remains the finest in the world, it is also focused on maintaining and improving existing systems. For example, DOD will continue to use the highly-capable C-130 airlift aircraft rather than procure a new airlifter such as the C-27. In addition, although DOD will continue to use new Global Hawk Block 30 Unmanned Aerial Vehicles that have already been procured, together with the proven U-2 reconnaissance aircraft, for the critical task of providing intelligence to our troops, it will terminate further procurement of Block 30 Global Hawks. DOD will also retain and upgrade proven systems such as the F-15 and F-16 fighter aircraft and the B-2 bomber.

Assist Countries in Transition and Promote Reforms in Middle East and North Africa. Building on the Administration's ongoing response to the transformative events in the Middle East and North Africa region, the Budget continues Department of State and USAID funding to support the economic and security sectors in the region. It continues or expands our bilateral economic support in countries such as Egypt, Tunisia, and Yemen. In addition, the Budget funds the Middle East and North Africa Incentive Fund, which will support countries in transition

and provide incentives for long-term economic and political reforms. This fund builds upon several Arab Spring initiatives, including Enterprise Funds, fiscal stabilization support through cash transfers and loan guarantees, and various initiatives through the G8's Deauville Partnership, including technical assistance, trade, and asset recovery initiatives. In addition, base funding for diplomatic operations in the region is increased by $39 million, supporting both increased engagement and measures to protect diplomatic personnel.

Support Global Health by Investing in High-Impact Interventions. Administration investments will accelerate progress toward the goals of achieving an AIDS-free generation and an end to preventable child and maternal deaths. The Budget supports the achievement of aggressive HIV/AIDS prevention and treatment targets the President laid out on World AIDS Day in 2011, and continuing progress toward eliminating pediatric AIDS. Consistent with the Child Survival Call to Action, it increases USAID investments aimed at addressing malaria, malnutrition, pneumonia, and complications in childbirth. In recognition of the Global Fund to Fight AIDS, Tuberculosis, and Malaria's key role as a multilateral partner and its progress in instituting reforms, the Budget provides $1.65 billion to leverage pledges from other donors and accelerates progress against these three diseases. In addition, the Budget funds the balance of the Administration's pledge to the Global Alliance for Vaccines and Immunization.

Fight Hunger by Improving Food Security in Poor Countries. As part of a multi-year plan to combat hunger, the Budget increases USAID funding for agriculture development and nutrition programs. Administration programs are intended to reduce extreme poverty, increase food security, and reduce malnutrition for millions of families by 2015. The Budget provides bilateral assistance for Feed the Future, including the New Alliance for Food Security and Nutrition, and funding for the multi-donor Global Agriculture and Food Security Program. The Budget also maintains strong support for food aid and other humanitarian assistance, including over $4.1 billion to help internally-displaced persons, refugees, and victims of armed conflict and natural disasters.

SUPPORTING OUR NATION'S SERVICEMEMBERS, VETERANS, AND THEIR FAMILIES

Our Nation has a solemn obligation to take care of our servicemembers and veterans. To deliver on this commitment, the Budget provides significant resources to support veterans' medical care, help military families, assist soldiers transitioning to civilian life, reduce veterans' homelessness, and improve the claims system at the Department of Veterans Affairs.

Care for Wounded, Ill, and Injured Servicemembers. The Budget provides $49.4 billion for the DOD Unified Medical Budget that supports the DOD Military Health System and delivers quality health care for the Nation's 9.6 million eligible beneficiaries. Caring for wounded, ill, and injured servicemembers is a priority for the Administration, and the Budget sustains strong programs that support these servicemembers and their families. DOD is also improving its support for servicemembers' mental and emotional health by increasing collaboration among suicide prevention programs and working to eliminate the stigma associated with accessing mental health services.

Support Military Families. The Budget provides for a broad spectrum of programs and services for servicemembers and their families including: mental health and counseling services; deployment assistance; child care and youth programs; morale, welfare, and recreation programs; commissaries; DOD-run schools for military dependents; and military spouse employment programs. DOD is working to improve its support to the All-Volunteer Force by discontinuing redundant or less effective military family programs, while increasing support for programs that are proven to serve military families well.

Improve Career Transitions for Newly-Separated Veterans. To help lower the veterans' unemployment rate, the Administration is proposing the first major redesign of veterans' transition assistance in over 20 years. This new program, Transition GPS (Goals, Plans, and Success), will help servicemembers more effectively capitalizes on the skills they have developed through their service. DOL is also providing increased access to intensive reemployment services for post-9/11 veterans, helping employers take advantage of tax credits for hiring veterans, and continuing its work to connect veterans with disabilities or other barriers to employment. DOD is also working to help servicemembers and veterans better communicate to civilian employers the skills they learned.

The Administration also continues its support of tax credits that will help employ veterans. The Returning Heroes Tax Credit, which provides up to $5,600 to employers, and the Wounded Warrior Tax Credit, which provides up to $9,600 to hire long-term unemployed veterans with service-connected disabilities, were recently extended for one more year in the American Taxpayer Relief Act of 2012. These credits are a part of the Work Opportunity Tax Credit (WOTC), which contains other categories targeted to hiring veterans. The Budget proposes to permanently extend the WOTC.

Through their Joining Forces initiative, the First Lady and Dr. Jill Biden have led an effort to challenge the private sector to hire or train 100,000 veterans and their spouses by the end of 2013. Joining Forces has already exceeded that goal, partnering with more than 2,100 companies to hire or train 155,000 veterans and spouses. The Administration has set a new goal for companies to hire more than 250,000 veterans and spouses by the end of 2014.

The Budget also supports the President's proposed Veterans Job Corps initiative. This initiative will put up to 20,000 veterans back to work over the next five years rebuilding and protecting America. By leveraging our returning service-members' skills and talents as police officers, firefighters, and in conservation jobs, the Veterans Job Corps will result in an America as strong as those who have defended her.

Reduce Veteran Homelessness. The Budget's proposed services for homeless and at-risk veterans will help combat veterans' homelessness through collaborative partnerships with local governments, non-profit organizations, and the Departments of Housing and Urban Development, Justice, and Labor.

Address VA Benefit Claims Backlog. The Budget includes $136 million for a Veterans Claims Intake Program that will allow VA to directly receive and convert paper evidence, such as medical records, into a digital format for increased efficiency in claims processing. It also supports continued development of a digital, near-paperless environment that allows for greater exchange of information and increased transparency for veterans. Specifically, the Budget enables the Veterans Benefit Management System to reduce the processing time and the claims backlog, facilitate quality improvements through rules-based calculators, and automate claims tracking.

PAYING FOR NEW INVESTMENTS

The Budget shows that it is possible to achieve the deficit reduction needed to put the Nation on a sustainable fiscal path while still investing in initiatives that will help our economy grow and support the middle class. All of the new investments proposed in the Budget are fully paid for. The Budget's new discretionary spending is financed within the current discretionary caps of the Budget Control Act, as adjusted by the American Taxpayer Relief Act—which grow at less than the rate of inflation between 2013 and 2014. The Budget pays for new infrastructure proposals and short-term measures to support the ongoing economic recovery with savings from reducing operations in Iraq and Afghanistan and from capping Overseas Contingency Operations funding, which will prevent future efforts to evade agreed-upon discipline in defense spending. The Budget pays for new early childhood investments by increasing the tobacco tax, which will also save thousands of lives. In addition, the Budget pays

for new tax cuts by closing tax loopholes and rebalancing the tax code so it does not unfairly benefit the wealthiest Americans.

The Budget also fully pays for a range of mandatory investments designed to support the middle class and promote economic growth, such as sustaining the current maximum Pell award for all eligible students, providing assistance for displaced workers, and establishing an Energy Security Trust Fund to support shifting cars and trucks off of oil. All of these initiatives are fully offset with savings from smart reforms to mandatory programs, including the Unemployment Insurance program and higher education.

As a result of these tough but responsible decisions, the Budget is able to make essential investments in the Nation's future while also reducing the deficit.

REDUCING THE DEFICIT IN A SMART AND BALANCED WAY

By making investments in our people and infrastructure, we will strengthen the middle class, make America a magnet for jobs and innovation, and grow our economy, which will in turn help us to reduce deficits. But economic growth alone will not solve our Nation's long-term fiscal challenges.

Over the past few years, Democrats and Republicans have cut the deficit by more than $2.5 trillion through a mix of spending cuts and tax reform, including more than $1.4 trillion in spending cuts to discretionary programs in the Budget Control Act (BCA) and appropriations bills since 2011, and over $600 billion in new revenue in the American Taxpayer Relief Act (ATRA) from raising income tax rates on the highest income Americans. When interest savings are included, this amounts to over $2.5 trillion of deficit reduction, more than halfway toward the goal of $4 trillion in deficit reduction. That amount is what economists find is needed to bring deficits below three percent of Gross Domestic Product (GDP), put our debt on a downward trajectory, and put us on a fiscally sustainable path.

On multiple occasions, the President has presented comprehensive plans that would achieve this $4 trillion deficit reduction goal—in his April 2011 Framework for Shared Prosperity and Shared Fiscal Responsibility, in his July 2011 offer to Congressional Republicans during negotiations over extending the debt ceiling, in his September 2011 submission to the Joint Select Committee on Deficit Reduction, in his 2013 Budget, and in his latest offer to Congressional Republicans during negotiations that led to the passage of the ATRA at the start of this year.

The President stands by the compromise offer he made to Speaker Boehner in December 2012. This Budget includes all of the proposals in that offer. These proposals would achieve nearly $1.8 trillion in additional deficit reduction over the next 10 years, bringing total deficit reduction to $4.3 trillion. This represents more than enough deficit reduction to replace the damaging cuts required by the Joint Committee sequestration. The key elements of the offer include:

- About $580 billion in additional revenue relative to ATRA, from tax reform that closes tax loopholes and reduces tax benefits for those who need them least;

- About $400 billion in health savings that build on the health reform law and strengthens Medicare;

- About $200 billion in savings from other mandatory programs, such as reductions to farm subsidies and reforms to Federal retirement contributions;

- About $200 billion in additional discretionary savings, with near equal amounts from defense and non-defense programs;

- $230 billion in savings from using a more accurate measure of inflation for cost-of-living adjustments throughout the Budget, with protections for the most vulnerable;

- Almost $200 billion in savings from reduced interest payments on the debt, discretionary effects of program integrity cap adjustments, and other effects; and

- $50 billion for immediate infrastructure investments, as described in chapter 1, to repair our roads and transit systems, create jobs, and build a foundation for economic growth.

Because all of the President's proposed investments are fully paid for with additional savings not counted toward the totals above, the Budget locks in the nearly $1.8 trillion in deficit reduction from the President's offer to Speaker Boehner.

As a result, deficits under the Budget fall to below three percent of GDP in 2016, and the Federal debt begins to decline as a share of the economy. Over the next 10 years, deficits fall to about two percent of GDP, and debt continues to decline, reaching 73 percent of GDP in 2023, the last year of the budget window. Putting our Budget on a sustainable fiscal path is a critical step toward ensuring that we have a solid foundation on which to build a strong economy and a thriving middle class for years to come.

REFORMING THE INDIVIDUAL INCOME TAX CODE—ASKING EVERYONE TO PAY THEIR FAIR SHARE

While the ATRA raised revenue from higher tax rates, the next stage of deficit reduction will require additional revenue from reforming the tax code. To reach the goal of $4 trillion in total deficit reduction, the President is proposing more than $1 trillion in savings from spending cuts, entitlement reforms, and interest savings. But he is also proposing to do what leaders of both parties have suggested: save hundreds of billions of dollars through tax reform that reduces tax benefits for high-income households. Tax reform holds the potential to improve economic growth by reducing complexity for individuals and small businesses, improving efficiency, and lowering the deficit. Without it, reducing the deficit through spending cuts alone will undermine growth by slashing investments in education, energy, and medical research, and endangering Medicare and Social Security. The Administration believes in a balanced approach that cuts spending and reforms entitlements responsibly, but also raises revenue from tax reform that closes special interest loopholes and addresses deductions and exclusions that let some of the wealthiest members of society pay a smaller fraction of their income in taxes than many middle class families.

As a first step toward balanced deficit reduction and tax reform, the President proposes that the Congress immediately enact two measures that would raise $583 billion in revenue by broadening the tax base and reducing tax benefits for those who need them the least:

Reduce the Value of Itemized Deductions and Other Tax Preferences to 28 Percent for Families with Incomes in the Highest Tax Brackets. Currently, a millionaire who contributes to charity or deducts a dollar of mortgage interest enjoys a deduction that is more than twice as generous as that for a middle class family. The Budget would limit the tax rate at which high-income taxpayers can reduce their tax liability to a maximum of 28 percent, a limitation that would affect only the top three percent of families in 2014. This limit would apply to: all itemized deductions; foreign excluded income; tax-exempt interest; employer sponsored health insurance; retirement contributions; and selected above-the-line deductions. The proposed limitation would return the deduction rate to the level it was at the end of the Reagan Administration.

Observe the Buffett Rule. The Budget also puts forward a specific proposal to comply with the Buffett Rule, requiring that wealthy millionaires pay no less than 30 percent of income—after charitable contributions—in taxes. This proposal will prevent high-income households from using tax preferences, including low tax rates on capital gains and dividends, to reduce their total tax bills to less than what many middle class families pay.

Beyond these measures, the President is committed to working with the Congress to further reform the tax code to make it more fair, promote economic growth and job creation, and improve competitiveness.

BUILDING ON SAVINGS IN THE HEALTH CARE LAW

Health care comprises one-quarter of non-interest Federal spending, and the health care costs of an aging population are a major driver of future deficit growth. To help reduce health care costs, the President signed into law the Affordable Care Act (ACA). This law has already contributed to significant reductions in the growth of private and public health care spending. In addition, according to the Congressional Budget Office's latest analysis, the health care law will reduce the deficit by more than $1 trillion over the next two decades. Realizing this deficit reduction and efficiencies in the health care system will reduce cost and improve quality requires effective implementation of the ACA. The President is committed to ensuring ACA implementation is effective, efficient, and swift. Repealing or failing to implement the health care law would return the Nation to a path of rapidly increasing health care costs and add trillions of dollars to deficits over the long-run.

To continue our commitment to make health care affordable and strengthen Medicare, Medicaid, and other health programs, the Budget includes $401 billion in health savings over 10 years that build on the ACA by eliminating excess payments and fraud and supporting reforms that boost the quality of care. It accomplishes this without shifting significant risks onto individuals, slashing benefits, or undermining the fundamental compact these programs represent to our Nation's seniors, people with disabilities, and low-income families. These reforms will extend Medicare's solvency by approximately four years.

Encourage Adoption of New Physician Payment Models. The Administration is committed to working with the Congress to reform Medicare physician payments to provide predictable payments that incentivize quality and efficiency in a fiscally responsible way. The Administration supports a period of payment stability lasting several years to allow time for the continued development of scalable accountable payment models. Such models would encourage care coordination, reward practitioners who provide high-quality efficient care, and hold practitioners accountable, through the application of financial risk, for consistently providing low-quality care at excessive costs. Following the period of stability, practitioners will be encouraged to partner with Medicare by participating in an accountable payment model, and over time, the payment update for physician's services would be linked to such participation.

Reduce Medicare Coverage of Bad Debts. This proposal will align Medicare policy more closely with private sector standards by reducing bad debt payments from 65 percent generally to 25 percent for all eligible providers over three years starting in 2014. This proposal will save approximately $25 billion over 10 years.

Better Align Graduate Medical Education Payments with Patient Care Costs. Medicare compensates teaching hospitals for the indirect costs created from residents "learning by doing." The Medicare Payment Advisory Commission (MedPAC) has determined that these Indirect Medical Education (IME) add-on payments are significantly greater than the additional patient care costs that teaching hospitals experience. This proposal will modify these payments and save approximately $11 billion over 10 years.

Better Align Payments to Rural Providers with the Cost of Care. Medicare makes a number of special payments to account for the unique challenges of delivering medical care to beneficiaries in rural areas. These payments continue to be important; however, in specific cases, the adjustments may be greater than necessary to ensure continued access to care. The Budget proposes to improve the consistency of payments across rural hospital types, provide incentives for efficient delivery of care, and eliminate higher than necessary reimbursement, saving approximately $2 billion over 10 years.

Encourage Efficient Post-Acute Care. Medicare covers services in skilled nursing facilities (SNFs), long-term care hospitals (LTCHs), inpatient rehabilitation facilities (IRFs) and home health agencies. Over the years, MedPAC has noted that expenditures for post-acute care have increased dramatically, and payments are in excess of the costs of providing high-quality and efficient care, placing a drain on Medicare. Recognizing the importance of these services, the Administration supports policies that will encourage efficient utilization of services and improve the quality of care. The Budget's proposals include adjusting payment updates for certain post-acute care providers and equalizing payments for certain conditions commonly treated in IRFs and SNFs, which will save about $81 billion over 10 years. The Budget encourages appropriate use of inpatient rehabilitation hospitals and adjusts SNF payments to reduce unnecessary hospital readmissions, saving almost $5 billion over 10 years. Also, the Budget proposes to restructure payments for post-acute care services using a bundled payment approach, saving about $8 billion over 10 years.

Improve Payment Accuracy for Medicare Advantage. Medicare Advantage plans receive a minimum statutory adjustment to their payment to account for differences in coding of medical conditions between Medicare Advantage and fee-for-service providers. The Government Accountability Office (GAO) has identified this minimum adjustment as inadequate to account for overpayments resulting from this difference. Therefore, the Budget proposes to increase the minimum coding intensity adjustment beginning in 2015. This proposal will save approximately $15 billion over 10 years. In addition, MedPAC has identified potential changes to the way employer group waiver plans are paid. The Budget proposes to align employer group waiver plan payments with the average individual Medicare Advantage plan bid in each Medicare Advantage payment area beginning in 2015. This proposal is estimated to save $4 billion over 10 years.

Align Medicare Drug Payment Policies with Medicaid Policies for Low-Income Beneficiaries. The Department of Health and Human Services Office of Inspector General has found substantial differences in rebate amounts and net prices paid for brand name drugs under Medicare and Medicaid, with Medicare receiving significantly lower rebates and paying higher prices than Medicaid—even for Medicaid beneficiaries also enrolled in Medicare. Moreover, Medicare per capita spending in Part D is expected to grow significantly faster over the next 10 years than spending in Parts A or B under current law. This proposal would allow Medicare to benefit from the same rebates that Medicaid receives for brand name and generic drugs provided to beneficiaries who receive the Part D Low-Income Subsidy beginning in 2014. This option is estimated to save $123 billion over 10 years.

Accelerate Manufacturer Drug Rebates to Provide Relief to Medicare Beneficiaries in the Coverage Gap. The Affordable Care Act closes the coverage gap in Part D by 2020 through a combination of manufacturer discounts and Federal subsidies. Since the law's enactment, over six million Medicare beneficiaries have saved on their prescription drug costs. The Budget proposes to increase manufacturer discounts for brand name drugs from 50 to 75 percent in 2015, effectively closing the coverage gap for brand name drugs in 2015, five years sooner than under current law. This proposal is estimated to save approximately $11 billion over 10 years.

Increase Income-Related Premiums Under Medicare Parts B and D. Under Medicare Parts B and D, higher income beneficiaries pay higher premiums. Beginning in 2017, the Budget proposes to restructure income-related premiums under Parts B and D by increasing the lowest income-related premium five percentage points, from 35 percent to 40 percent and also increasing other income brackets until capping the highest tier at 90 percent. The proposal maintains the income thresholds associated with income-related premiums until 25 percent of beneficiaries under Parts B and D are subject to these premiums. This will help improve the financial stability of the Medicare program by reducing the Federal subsidy of Medicare costs for those beneficiaries who can most afford them. This proposal will save approximately $50 billion over 10 years.

Promote Targeted, Shared Responsibility for New Beneficiaries. The Budget proposes three targeted policies to promote appropriate use of health care for new enrollees in Medicare starting in 2017. First, to strengthen program financing and encourage beneficiaries to seek high-value health care services, the Budget proposes to apply a $25 increase in the Part B deductible in 2017, 2019, and 2021 for new beneficiaries. Second, Medicare beneficiaries currently do not make co-payments for Medicare home health services. This proposal would create a home health copayment of $100 per home health episode for new beneficiaries, applicable for episodes with five or more visits not preceded by a hospital or other inpatient post-acute care stay. This proposal is consistent with a MedPAC recommendation to establish a per episode copayment. Third, to encourage more efficient health care choices, the Budget proposes a Part B premium surcharge equivalent to about 15 percent of the average Medigap premium for beneficiaries that purchase Medigap policies with particularly low cost-sharing requirements.

Medigap policies sold by private insurance companies cover most, or all, of the cost-sharing Medicare requires. This protection, however, gives individuals less incentive to consider the costs of health care services and thus raises Medicare costs and Part B premiums. Together these proposals will save approximately $7 billion over 10 years.

Strengthen the Independent Payment Advisory Board (IPAB) to Reduce Long-Term Drivers of Medicare Cost Growth. IPAB has been highlighted by economists and health policy experts as a key contributor to Medicare's long term solvency, and this proposal would lower the target rate from the GDP per capita growth rate plus one percentage point to plus 0.5 percentage point.

Encourage the Use of Generic Drugs By Low Income Beneficiaries. Medicare provides Part D cost-sharing subsidies for beneficiaries with incomes below 150 percent of the Federal poverty level. Evidence has shown that low income subsidy (LIS) individuals have higher rates of brand name drug utilization than other beneficiaries. To increase generic utilization by LIS beneficiaries, the Budget proposes in most instances to increase specified copayments for brand drugs from their current law level, while lowering specified copayments for generic drugs by more than 15 percent. Beneficiaries would continue to be charged the current law amounts for brand drugs if a generic substitute is not appropriate or available. This proposal will save approximately $7 billion over 10 years.

Cut Waste, Fraud, and Abuse in Medicare and Medicaid. In this fiscal environment, we cannot tolerate waste, fraud, and abuse in Medicare, Medicaid, and the Children's Health Insurance Program (CHIP), or any Government program. That is why the Administration has made targeting waste, fraud, and abuse a priority. The Administration is aggressively implementing new tools for fraud prevention included in the Affordable Care Act, as well as the fraud prevention system, a predictive analytic model similar to those used by private sector experts. In addition, the Budget proposes a series of policies to build on these efforts that will save nearly $4.1 billion over the next 10 years. Specifically, the Budget proposes new initiatives to reduce improper payments in Medicare; require prior authorization for advanced imaging; direct States to track high prescribers and utilizers of prescription drugs in Medicaid to identify aberrant billing and prescribing patterns; expand authorities to investigate and prosecute allegations of abuse or neglect of Medicaid beneficiaries in additional health care settings; and affirm Medicaid's position as a payer of last resort by removing exceptions to the requirement that State Medicaid agencies reject medical claims when another entity is legally liable to pay the claim. In addition, the Budget would alleviate State program integrity reporting requirements by consolidating redundant error rate measurement programs to create a streamlined audit program with meaningful outcomes, while maintaining the Federal and State Government's ability to identify and address improper Medicaid payments.

Limit Medicaid Reimbursement of Durable Medical Equipment (DME) Based on Medicare Rates. Under current law, States have experienced challenges in preventing overpayments for DME. This proposal, starting in 2014, would limit Federal reimbursement for a State's Medicaid spending on certain DME services to what Medicare would have paid in the same State for the same services. This proposal is projected to save $4.5 billion over 10 years.

Better Align Medicaid Disproportionate Share Hospital (DSH) Payments with Expected Levels of Uncompensated Care. Supplemental DSH payments are intended to help support hospitals that provide care to disproportionate numbers of low-income and uninsured individuals. The ACA reduced State DSH allotments from 2014 through 2020 to reflect the reduced need as a result of the increased coverage provided in the Act, and these reductions have since been extended in legislation through 2022. To better align DSH payments with expected levels of uncompensated care, the Budget proposes to begin the reductions in 2015, instead of 2014, and to determine future State DSH allotments based on States' actual DSH allotments as reduced by the Affordable Care Act. This proposal is projected to save $3.6 billion over 10 years.

Lower Drug Costs. The Budget includes a number of policies to lower drug costs to taxpayers and consumers. It proposes targeted adjustments in Medicaid prescription drug financing by clarifying the definition of brand drugs, excluding authorized generic drugs from average manufacturer price calculations for determining manufacturer rebate obligations for brand drugs, making a technical correction to the ACA alternative rebate for new drug formulations, and calculating Medicaid Federal upper limits based only on generic drug prices. These proposals are projected to save $8.8 billion over 10 years. In addition, beginning in 2014, the Budget proposes to increase the availability of generic drugs and biologics by authorizing the Federal Trade Commission to stop companies from entering into anti-competitive deals, known also as "pay for delay" agreements, intended to block consumer access to safe and effective generics. Such deals can cost consumers billions of dollars because generic drugs are typically priced significantly less than their branded counterparts. The Administration's proposal will generate $11 billion over 10 years in savings to Federal health programs including Medicare and Medicaid. The Budget also proposes to accelerate access to affordable generic biologics by modifying the length of exclusivity on brand name biologics. Beginning in 2014, this proposal would award brand biologic manufacturers seven years of exclusivity, rather than 12 years under current law, and prohibit additional periods of exclusivity for brand biologics due to minor changes in product formulations, a practice often referred to as "evergreening." The proposal will result in $3 billion in savings over 10 years to Federal health programs including Medicare and Medicaid.

Modernize the Federal Employee Health Benefits Program (FEHBP). The health insurance marketplace has changed significantly since the FEHBP was enacted in 1959, and the current governing statute leaves little flexibility for the program to evolve with the changing market. The Budget proposes to modernize FEHBP by taking several steps beginning in 2015: employees would be given the option to enroll in a "self plus one" coverage option rather than being limited to just self or family options; domestic partners of Federal employees and new retirees would be eligible for health benefits; the Office of Personnel Management (OPM) would be authorized to contract with modern types of health plans rather than being limited to the current four statutorily-defined plans reflective of the 1950s insurance market; OPM would be authorized to contract separately for pharmacy benefit management services; and OPM would be given authority to make adjustments to premiums based on an enrollee's tobacco use and/or participation in a wellness program. These proposals are estimated to save $8.4 billion over 10 years.

Encourage Additional Provider Efficiencies. The Budget contains several proposals encouraging more appropriate compensation for the efficient provision of services under the Medicare program. MedPAC cautions that physician self-referral of ancillary services leads to a higher volume when combined with fee-for-service payments, a finding consistent with GAO analysis. The Budget encourages more appropriate use of ancillary services by only allowing providers who meet certain accountability standards to self-refer radiation therapy, therapy services, and advanced imaging services. In addition, the Budget would modernize Medicare payments for clinical laboratory services by more closely aligning payment levels with the private sector and granting the Secretary authority to make other appropriate payment adjustments, as well as supporting policies to encourage electronic reporting of laboratory results. The Budget would also expand the availability of Medicare data released to physicians and other providers for performance improvement, fraud prevention, value-added analysis, and other purposes. In addition, the Budget would reduce payment of physician administered Part B drugs from 106 percent of average sales price to 103 percent of average sales price. These proposals would save approximately $20 billion over 10 years.

MAKING FURTHER TOUGH CHOICES TO REDUCE THE DEFICIT

As part of a balanced deficit reduction plan, the Budget includes other tough choices to cut spending and find further savings in other mandatory programs across the Government. These additional savings proposals include:

Maintain Farm Safety Net While Making Common-Sense Reforms. The President is committed to building a strong rural economy by ensuring targeted investments in renewable energy, infrastructure, conservation, and agricultural, food, and environmental research. The farm sector continues to be one of the strongest sectors of our economy, with net farm income expected to reach $128 billion in 2013, a nominal record and the highest level in real terms since 1973. With the continuing high value of both crop and livestock production, income support payments based upon historical levels of production can no longer be justified. The Budget proposes to reform agricultural programs while reducing spending by $38 billion over 10 years.

A key reform and cost savings is the elimination of "direct payments," while providing mandatory disaster assistance to livestock and orchard producers to protect them from significant losses, such as those experienced in the recent drought. The Budget also proposes to reduce subsidies for crop insurance companies by establishing a reasonable rate of return to participating crop insurance companies and reducing the reimbursement rate of administrative and operating costs. In addition, the Budget proposes to reduce producers' premium subsidy by three basis points for policies with subsidies greater than 50 percent and reducing the subsidy for the harvest price option by two basis points. Conservation programs are strengthened by the creation of a new agricultural conservation easement program, which would combine programs designed to preserve wetlands, agriculture land, and grasslands under one streamlined program. To offset the cost of the new program, the Budget proposes to reduce the Conservation Reserve Program to 25 million acres from 32 million acres and cuts the Conservation Stewardship Program from 12.7 million to 10.3 million acres. At the same time, the Budget targets funding for priorities such as bioenergy, specialty crops, organic foods, and beginning farmer assistance.

Restrain Increases in Federal Civilian Worker Pay. Putting the Nation back on a sustainable fiscal path will take some tough choices and sacrifices. Federal civilian employees are central to the Federal Government's success in serving the American people. They assure the safety of the country's food and airways, defend the homeland, provide health care to the Nation's veterans, search for cures to devastating diseases, and provide vital support to our troops at home and abroad. The men and women who serve their fellow Americans as civilian Federal workers are patriots who work for the Nation often at great personal sacrifice; they deserve our respect and gratitude. But just as families and businesses across the country are tightening their belts, so too must the Federal Government. On his first day in office, the President froze salaries for all senior political appointees at the White House. Starting in 2011, the President proposed and the Congress enacted a two year pay freeze for all civilian Federal workers, which is expected to save more than $60 billion over the next 10 years. And in 2013 and again in 2014, the President is proposing to freeze the pay for senior political officials. However, a permanent pay freeze for the remaining civilian employees is neither sustainable nor desirable. In light of the fiscal constraints we are under, the Budget proposes a one-percent increase in civilian pay for 2014. Compared to the baseline, this slight increase in civilian pay would free up $1 billion in 2014 and $18 billion over 10 years to fund programs and services and is one of the measures the Administration proposes to help meet the discretionary caps.

Reform Federal Civilian Worker Retirement. The President's 2011 Plan for Economic Growth and Deficit Reduction proposed to increase the Federal employees' contributions toward their accruing retirement costs, from 0.8 percent to 2.0 percent of pay, over three years, beginning in 2013. In response, the Congress created the Revised Annuity Employee retirement plan for Federal employees hired after 2012, through which those employees contribute 3.1 percent of their pay toward their pensions. In order to make reasonable adjustments to contributions made by those who joined the workforce prior to 2013, the Budget again proposes to increase contributions of those employees by 1.2 percent of pay, over three years, beginning in 2014. While Federal agency contributions for currently accruing costs of employee pensions would decline, these Federal employers would pay an additional amount toward unfunded liabilities of the retirement system that would leave total agency contributions unchanged.

Under the proposed plan, the amount of the employee pension would remain unchanged. This proposal is estimated to save $20 billion over 10 years. In addition, the Budget again proposes to eliminate the FERS Annuity Supplement for new employees. These changes are expected to neither negatively impact on the Administration's ability to manage its human resources, nor inhibit the Government's ability to serve the American people.

Adjust TRICARE Fees to Better Reflect Costs. Over the past decade, U.S. health care costs have grown substantially and the Military Health System (MHS) costs have been no exception. Although the Congress recently permitted small increases in the TRICARE Prime enrollment fees for working age retirees and some adjustments to Pharmacy copays, the savings from these changes are not enough to control the large increases in health care costs. For example, in 1996 a working age retiree's family of three who used TRICARE civilian care contributed on average roughly 27 percent of the total cost of their health care through fees and copays. Today that percentage has dropped to less than 11 percent, which is substantially less than the average 40 percent contribution paid by Federal employees. The Department of Defense continues to seek efficiencies within the MHS, but also requires additional savings. The Budget includes small TRICARE benefit adjustments to address health care cost increases and make the health benefit more sustainable. TRICARE fee adjustments include increased Prime enrollment fees, annual Standard/Extra enrollment fees with adjusted deductibles and catastrophic caps. In addition, the Budget makes targeted increases to TRICARE pharmacy benefit copayments and establishes annual TRICARE-For-Life Enrollment fees. Survivors of members who died while on active duty and disability retirees and their family members will be exempt from the fee and copay adjustments.

Reform Aviation Passenger Security Fee to Reflect Costs More Accurately. Reflecting its commitment to keeping air travel and commerce safe, the Administration has invested heavily in personnel, technology, and infrastructure to mitigate the constantly evolving risks to aviation security. As risk changes, so too must the way in which we fund our aviation security efforts. Since its establishment in 2001, the Aviation Passenger Security Fee has been statutorily limited to $2.50 per enplanement, with a maximum fee of $5.00 per one-way trip. This recovers less than 30 percent of the Transportation Security Administration's aviation security costs, including overhead and the Federal Air Marshal Service, which have risen over the years while the fee has remained the same. The Budget proposes to replace the current "per enplanement" fee structure so that passengers pay the fee only one time per one-way trip; remove the current statutory fee limit and replace it with a statutory fee minimum of $5.00, with annual incremental increases of 50 cents from 2015 to 2019, resulting in a fee of $7.50 in 2019 and thereafter; and allow the Secretary of Homeland Security to adjust the fee through regulation when necessary. The proposed fee would collect an estimated $9 billion in additional fee revenue over five years, and $25.9 billion over 10 years. Of this amount, $18 billion will go towards debt reduction.

Share Payments More Equitably for Air Traffic Services. All flights that use controlled air space require a similar level of air traffic services. However, commercial and general aviation can pay very different aviation fees for those same air traffic services. To reduce the deficit and more equitably share the cost of air traffic services across the aviation user community, the Budget proposes to create a $100 per flight fee, payable to the Federal Aviation Administration, by aviation operators who fly in controlled airspace. All piston aircraft, military aircraft, public aircraft, air ambulances, aircraft operating outside of controlled airspace, and Canada-to-Canada flights would be exempted. This fee would generate an estimated $7.3 billion over 10 years. Assuming the enactment of the fee, total charges collected from aviation users would finance roughly three-fourths of airport investments and air traffic control system costs. To ensure appropriate input from stakeholders on the design of the fee, the proposal would also establish an expert Commission that could recommend to the President a replacement charge, or charges, that would raise no less in revenue than the enacted fee.

Provide Postal Service Financial Relief and Undertake Reform. The Budget includes a comprehensive and balanced legislative proposal to provide short-term financial relief and longer term reforms to the financially strapped Postal Service. It includes flexibilities that will allow the Postal Service to realign its business plan to better compete in the changing marketplace of increasingly digital communication, including provisions that enable the agency to reduce its costs and increase its revenues. These reforms will result in savings of more than $20 billion over 10 years, and build on the Postal Service's ongoing initiatives to implement operating efficiencies and business solutions to return it to sustainability.

Strengthen Pension Benefit Guaranty Corporation to Protect Worker Pensions. The Budget gives the Board of Directors of the Pension Benefit Guaranty Corporation (PBGC) discretion to increase premium rates to generate up to an additional $25 billion beginning in 2015. This reform is necessary to ensure the continued financial soundness of PBGC, which currently has a deficit of $35 billion. PBGC premiums are currently much lower than what a private financial institution would charge for insuring the same risk, and unlike private insurers (or even other similar agencies, such as the FDIC), the PBGC is currently unable to adjust the premiums it assesses from plan sponsors to cover potential liabilities.

Strengthen UI Safety Net and Improve Program Integrity. The combination of chronically underfunded reserves and the economic downturn has placed a considerable financial strain on States' Unemployment Insurance (UI) operations. Currently, 23 States owe more than $28 billion to the Federal UI trust fund, and employers in those States are now facing automatic Federal tax increases.

The Budget would put the UI system back on the path to solvency by providing immediate tax relief to employers to encourage job creation now and reestablishing State fiscal responsibility going forward. Under this proposal, employers in

States that are indebted to the Federal UI trust fund would receive tax relief for two years. To encourage State solvency, the Budget would also raise the minimum level of wages subject to unemployment taxes in 2016 to $15,000, a level slightly less in real, inflation-adjusted terms than it was in 1983, after President Reagan signed into law the last wage base increase. The higher wage base would be offset by lower tax rates to avoid a Federal tax increase.

To enhance UI program integrity, the Budget also includes a discretionary cap adjustment for UI improper payment reviews and reemployment and eligibility assessments. Reducing UI improper payments is a top management challenge identified by GAO and the Department of Labor's Inspector General. The Budget expands an initiative begun in 2005 to finance in-person interviews to assess UI beneficiaries' need for employment services and their continued eligibility for benefits. The resulting savings in UI benefit payments would total $1.24 billion.

The Budget further enhances program integrity by requiring States to use the Treasury Offset Program to recover UI debts stemming from overpayments due to fraud or failure to report earnings, and the State Information Data Exchange System, or a successor system, to obtain information from employers necessary to determine a claimant's eligibility.

Step Up Efforts to Reduce Social Security Payment Errors and Boost Program Integrity. The Budget provides a dedicated source of mandatory funding for the Social Security Administration (SSA) to conduct Continuing Disability Reviews (CDRs) in the Social Security Disability Insurance (SSDI) and Supplemental Security Income (SSI) programs, as well as redeterminations of eligibility for SSI. This dedicated funding will enable SSA to work down a backlog of CDRs and ensure that only those eligible for benefits continue to receive them. The resulting savings come from reduced spending on benefits in SSDI, SSI, Medicare (since SSDI beneficiaries generally qualify for Medicare), and Medicaid (since SSI beneficiaries automatically qualify for Medicaid).

CDRs and redeterminations generate significant deficit reduction, with a return on investment for CDRs of approximately $9 in lifetime program savings for every $1 spent on these activities, and a return on investment for redeterminations of approximately $5 to $1.

Dispose of Excess or Under-Utilized Federal Property. With over 1.1 million buildings, structures, and land parcels, the Federal Government is the largest property owner in the United States. Over time, agencies have accumulated more properties than the Government needs to effectively meet its mission. That is why, from his first days in office, the President has made it a priority to eliminate wasteful spending on Federal real estate. We have already made significant progress. In June 2010, the President directed agencies to accelerate efforts to shed unneeded property, reduce operating costs, and adopt more efficient real estate management practices to achieve $8 billion in savings by the end of 2012. The President's directive included two parts: $5 billion in savings through the Base Realignment and Closure Commission (BRAC) process, as well as $3 billion in non-BRAC savings. As of the end of 2012, agencies achieved $5.1 billion in BRAC savings and $3.5 billion in non-BRAC savings, exceeding the President's goals.

Building on the lessons learned from this real estate savings initiative, the Administration's new real property goal will track the square footage baseline from its recent "Freeze the Footprint" guidance, which will limit the growth of the Federal real property inventory even further. In addition, individual agency co-location, consolidation, and disposal projects will be tracked on *Performance.gov*.

The Administration will also continue to pursue enactment of the Civilian Property Realignment Act (CPRA), which it first proposed in the 2012 Budget. Building on the best practices of BRAC, CPRA would create an independent board of experts to identify opportunities to consolidate, reduce, and realign the Federal footprint, as well as expedite the disposal of properties. The proposal utilizes bundled recommendations, a fast-track congressional procedure, streamlined disposal and consolidation authorities, and a revolving fund to provide logistical and financial support to agencies.

The Administration's continuing efforts to dispose of unneeded Federal property will generate at least $2 billion in net deficit reduction over the next 10 years.

Reform Federal Oil, Gas, and Coal Management. The U.S. Treasury receives billions of dollars annually from oil and gas development on Federal lands and waters, but recent studies from GAO and others have found that taxpayers could earn a better return through policy changes and more rigorous oversight. The Budget proposes a package of legislative and administrative reforms to improve the management of the Department of the Interior's (DOI) onshore and offshore oil and gas programs, with a key focus on increasing the return to taxpayers from the sale of these Federal resources and on enhancing transparency and oversight. Proposed changes include royalty reforms and incentives to diligently develop leases, such as shorter primary lease terms, stricter enforcement of lease terms, and monetary incentives to get leases into production through a new per-acre fee on nonproducing leases. Revenue collection improvements include simplification of the royalty valuation process, elimination of interest accruals on company overpayments of royalties, and permanent repeal of DOI's authority to accept in-kind royalty payments. States will also be asked to help pay for the costs of administering energy and mineral receipts from which they receive benefits, but they will also benefit from higher Federal revenue sharing payments as a result of the other reforms. Some States that have already completed reclamation of priority abandoned coal mines would no longer receive unrestricted payments from the abandoned coal mine land fund. Collectively, these reforms will generate over $3 billion in net revenue to the Treasury over 10 years.

LOWERING CAPS ON DISCRETIONARY SPENDING

In August 2011, the President signed into law the BCA, which put in place a down payment toward deficit reduction. The BCA included a cap on discretionary spending that would achieve approximately $1.2 trillion in deficit reduction over ten years, including savings on interest payments. ATRA, signed into law in January 2013, reduced those caps even further, achieving an additional $12 billion in savings. Because of those caps, by the beginning of the next decade, domestic discretionary spending will drop to its lowest level as a share of the economy since at least the 1950's, when Dwight D. Eisenhower sat in the Oval Office.

Importantly, although discretionary spending represents only one-third of Federal spending, it supports critical investments in education, infrastructure, energy, and scientific research, all of which are engines of job creation and economic growth. Cutting discretionary spending in these areas hinders our ability to innovate and compete in the 21st Century economy and jeopardizes the Nation's long-term economic strength, as well as its national security.

However, in the interest of reaching bipartisan agreement on a balanced deficit reduction package, the Budget proposes to lower the discretionary caps even further, reducing discretionary spending by an additional $202 billion over the next decade. The proposed cuts are almost evenly distributed between defense and non-defense spending, and are timed to take effect beginning in 2017, after the economy is projected to have fully recovered. While the President would not support lowering the discretionary caps on their own, because doing so will make it more difficult for the country to make needed investments to grow the economy, he is willing to accept this level of cuts as part of a balanced compromise that will put the country on a sustainable long-term fiscal path.

USING A MORE ACCURATE MEASURE OF INFLATION

In the interest of achieving a bipartisan deficit reduction agreement, beginning in 2015 the Budget would change the measure of inflation used by the Federal Government for most programs and for the Internal Revenue Code from the standard Consumer Price Index (CPI) to the alternative, more accurate chained CPI, which grows slightly more slowly. Unlike the standard CPI, the chained CPI fully accounts for a consumer's ability to substitute between goods in response to changes in relative prices and also adjusts for small sample bias. Most economists agree that the chained CPI provides a more accurate measure of the average change in the cost of living than the standard CPI.

Switching to the chained CPI, which will reduce deficits and improve Social Security solvency, has been proposed in almost every major bipartisan deficit reduction plan put forward over the past several years, including the Bowles-Simpson Fiscal Commission plan, the Bipartisan "Gang of Six" plan, and the Domenici-Rivlin Bipartisan Policy Center plan.

The President has made clear that any such change in approach should protect the most vulnerable. For that reason, the Budget includes protections for the very elderly and others who rely on Social Security for long periods of time, and only applies the change to non-means tested benefit programs. The switch to chained CPI will reduce deficits by at least $230 billion over the next 10 years.

CREATING A 21ST CENTURY GOVERNMENT

In order for our country to continue leading in the 21st Century economy, we need a 21st Century Government. We need a Government that is lean, efficient, and continuously striving to do more with less, ensuring that every taxpayer dollar is used wisely and to the maximum effect. We need a Government that is responsive to the needs of its citizens and businesses, and is willing to embrace the rapid pace of technological innovation underway, ensuring that we remain globally competitive.

That is why, under the President's direction, the Administration will continue its efforts to streamline Government operations, improve performance, adopt new technologies, and provide greater value to the American taxpayer. The Budget builds on the President's Campaign to Cut Waste by taking further steps across the Government to cut unnecessary and wasteful spending. It includes new proposals to consolidate and reorganize Federal agencies and programs to eliminate duplication, overlap, and inefficiency. It includes new incentives to promote the use of evidence, evaluation, and technology to get better results, including the adoption of best practices from the private sector. It also continues to drive performance improvement with ambitious goals and frequent measurement.

CUTTING WASTE WHEREVER WE FIND IT

Whether the Budget is in surplus or deficit, wasting taxpayer dollars on programs that are outdated, ineffective, or duplicative is wrong. Given the current fiscal environment, it is critical that we redouble our efforts to scour the Budget for waste and make tough decisions about reducing funding or ending programs that are laudable, but not essential. This exercise is difficult but necessary, and it builds on efforts the Administration has undertaken since the President first took office.

We have already made significant progress in cutting waste in areas across the Government. We are terminating unneeded or underperforming military weapons systems. We are closing or consolidating underutilized field offices. We are eliminating duplicative or overlapping programs. We are cutting unnecessary travel and conference spending. We are selling off excess Federal real estate. We are leveraging the buying power of the Federal Government to save money on the purchase of commodities such as office supplies and shipping services.

The Budget builds on these efforts by including a total of 215 cuts, consolidations, and savings proposals. For example, one of largest savings measures in the Budget is the Administration's proposal to align Medicare drug payment policies with Medicaid rebate policies for low-income beneficiaries, allowing Medicare to benefit from lower drug prices. This change alone will save $123 billion over the next 10 years. The Budget takes other critical steps to save money, such as closing the loophole in current law that allows people to collect both full disability benefits and unemployment benefits that cover the same period of time. Shutting this loophole will save $1 billion over 10 years. As detailed later in this chapter, the single biggest consolidation proposed this year is in the area of science, technology, engineering, and mathematics (STEM) education, where the Administration is proposing a bold restructuring of STEM education programs—consolidating 90 programs and realigning ongoing STEM education activities to improve the delivery, impact, and visibility of STEM efforts.

In total, these proposals are projected to save more than $25 billion in 2014, and $539 billion through 2023, including savings from program integrity proposals, totaling $98 billion through 2023. Program integrity proposals are detailed in the Budget Process chapter of the Analytical Perspectives volume. The Cuts, Consolidations, and Savings section of this Budget includes tables detailing discretionary and mandatory proposals, as well savings activities agencies are undertaking that require no further action by the Congress, many of which were suggested through the President's SAVE Award.

Some of the broader Administration efforts to address unnecessary and wasteful spending include:

Cut Improper Payments. Every year, the Federal Government wastes billions of dollars on improper payments to individuals, organizations, and contractors. These are payments made in the wrong amount, to the wrong person, or for the wrong reason. When the President took office in 2009, the rate of wasteful Government-wide improper payments was on the rise. Since then, the Administration has taken forceful steps to cut down on improper payments, such as putting in place new measures to increase transparency and accountability, directing agencies to intensify and expand efforts to recover improper payments, establishing a "Do Not Pay" list for agencies to check before making payments, and implementing the landmark Improper Payments Elimination and Recovery Act of 2010 and the Improper Payments Elimination and Recovery Improvement Act of 2012. The Administration has also moved quickly to deploy cutting-edge forensic technologies to crack down on waste, fraud, and abuse.

As a result of these efforts, the Government-wide error rate decreased to 4.35 percent in 2012, having steadily declined from its high-water mark of 5.42 percent in 2009. In total, over the last three years the Government has avoided over $47 billion in improper payments and has recaptured a record $4.4 billion in overpayments to contractors.

Reduce Administrative Overhead. As part of the Administration's focus on reducing spending and finding efficiencies, in November 2011 the President issued an Executive Order to promote efficient spending that called for agencies to make a 20 percent reduction in their 2013 spending on administrative areas such as travel, advisory contracts, printing, employee Information Technology (IT) devices, extraneous promotional items, and transportation. To identify further savings, in May 2012 the Administration outlined a series of actions for reining in spending and increasing both transparency and oversight of Federal conference and travel activity. As a result, agencies have reduced travel and conference spending by more than $2 billion thus far. Overall, agencies have saved nearly $11 billion on administrative activities, which agencies are redirecting to higher priority programs.

Consolidate Data Centers. Under the President's Federal Data Center Consolidation Initiative, the Administration has been working to consolidate unnecessary Federal data centers across the Nation. Since agencies began executing their data center consolidation plans in 2011, nearly 400 data centers have been closed, leading to a net reduction in data centers for the first time in over a decade. Shutting these facilities down increases agency IT efficiencies, strengthens our cybersecurity posture, and decreases the Government's energy and real estate footprint.

Save Billions of Dollars in Contracting. The Administration has consistently challenged Federal agencies to strengthen their acquisition and contracting practices by eliminating inefficiencies, reducing risk, and buying smarter. In response, agencies reduced contract spending by over $20 billion in 2012 compared to 2011, marking the largest single-year decrease on record. This continues a three-year trend that has brought a $35 billion decline in spending from 2009 through 2012—a dramatic reversal of the unsustainable 12 percent annual contract spending growth rate experienced from 2000 through 2008.

Savings are being achieved by buying less and buying smarter. For example, in 2012 agencies spent $7 billion, or 15 percent, less than they did in 2010 for management support services. Agencies have also been making more concerted efforts to coordinate the Government's buying power through strategic sourcing. Government-wide strategic sourcing of items such as office supplies and domestic shipping services has already saved nearly $200 million since 2010, and agency-level strategic sourcing of goods like IT and medical equipment have saved hundreds of millions more.

In 2014, to accelerate the pace of savings, agencies with the largest procurement spending will begin pursuing multiple new Government-wide strategic sourcing solutions under the coordination of the Strategic Sourcing Leadership Council headed by the Office of Management and Budget. The Small Business Administration will work alongside participating agencies to help maximize the participation of small businesses in these critical cost-savings efforts. A portal will also be established to begin capturing the prices agencies pay for commonly used goods and services so that contracting officials can identify the best prices.

Under current law, contractors that are paid based on their incurred costs may demand reimbursement for executive and employee salaries up to the level of the Nation's top private sector CEOs and other senior executives. These salaries and benefits have increased by more than 300 percent since the law was enacted in the mid-1990s. In 2011, when the cap reached $763,000, the President called on the Congress to establish a new, sensible limit that is on par with what the Government pays its own executives and employees. The Administration was encouraged by the proposal in the 2013 Senate's National Defense Authorization bill to cap reimbursement for defense contractors at the level of the Vice President's salary, which is currently $230,700. The Budget urges the Congress to expand the Senate's proposal to cover all contractor employees—both defense and civilian—and pass a law that allows agencies to pay above this cap on an exception basis only, when it is necessary to ensure the agency has continued access to the skills and capabilities of specialists to achieve mission outcomes.

Reform Military Acquisition. The Department of Defense (DOD) has a respnsibility to procure weapon systems and critical goods and services needed by the Armed Forces to successfully execute our national security mission. The military departments (the Air Force, Army, and Navy) and defense agencies have a portfolio of 84 ongoing major weapon system acquisition programs, and DOD contracts account for approximately 70 percent of all Federal procurement.

Through its "Better Buying Power" (BBP) reform, DOD is charting a path to greater productivity in the military acquisition system. New BBP initiatives address current fiscal realities, including enforcing affordability caps, measuring cost performance, and aligning contractor profitability with acquisition goals. DOD has also instituted best practices, including applying lessons learned, expanding strategic sourcing, establishing acquisition professional reviews, and instituting peer reviews to ensure effective competition.

REORGANIZING, CONSOLIDATING, AND STREAMLINING GOVERNMENT

Over the years, the Federal Government has become increasingly complex, as agencies have been assigned new missions and duties in their service to the American people. At times, this has resulted in agencies with duplicative and overlapping responsibilities that have wasted taxpayer resources and made it harder for the public to navigate their Government. The Administration has been working to address this problem over the last four years. In its last report on duplication within the Federal Government, the Government Accountability Office concluded that more than three-quarters of its recommendations for Executive Branch action had been addressed in some way.

However, the Administration is committed to doing more to consolidate and streamline Government operations. That is why the President is again asking the Congress to revive an authority that Presidents had for almost the entire period from 1932 through 1984—the ability to submit proposals to reorganize the Executive Branch via a fast-track procedure. In effect, the President is asking to have the same authority that any business owner has to reorganize or streamline operations to meet changing circumstances and customer demand.

Building on the progress already made, the Budget includes a series of proposals to consolidate and reorganize Executive Branch departments, including to:

Consolidate Business and Trade Promotion Into a Single Department. As the President indicated in 2012, if he is given Presidential reorganization authority, his first proposal would be to consolidate a number of agencies and programs into a new Department with a focused mission to foster economic growth and spur job creation. The proposal would consolidate six primary business and trade agencies, as well as other related programs, integrating the Government's core trade and competitiveness functions into one new Department. Specifically, the new Department would include the Department of Commerce's core business and trade functions, the Small Business Administration, the Office of the U.S. Trade Representative, the Export-Import Bank, the Overseas Private Investment Corporation, and the U.S. Trade and Development Agency. It would also incorporate related programs from a number of other departments, including the Department of Agriculture's business development programs, the Department of the Treasury's Community Development Financial Institutions Fund program, the National Science Foundation's (NSF) statistical agency and industry partnership programs, and the Bureau of Labor Statistics from the Department of Labor. Creating a department solely focused on economic growth would also require moving the National Oceanic and Atmospheric Administration from the Department of Commerce to the Department of the Interior.

By bringing together the core tools to expand trade and investment, grow small businesses, and support innovation, the new Department would coordinate these resources to maximize the benefits for businesses and the economy. With more effectively aligned and deployed trade promotion resources, strengthened trade enforcement capacity, streamlined export finance programs, and enhanced focus on investment in the United States, the Government could more effectively implement a strong, pro-growth trade policy. This reorganization would also help American businesses compete in the global economy, expand exports, and create more jobs at home. These changes could generate approximately $3 billion in savings over the next 10 years, with roughly half of the savings coming from reducing overhead and consolidating offices and support functions. Additional comparable savings would be generated through programmatic cuts once the synergies from consolidation are realized.

Consolidate 90 STEM Education Programs. Currently, Federal initiatives to promote STEM education are spread across the

Government in more than 200 programs within 13 different agencies. The Budget is proposing a bold reorganization of STEM education programs into four key areas: K-12 instruction; undergraduate education; graduate fellowships; and education activities that typically take place outside the classroom, all with a focus on increasing participation and opportunities for individuals from groups historically underrepresented in these fields. This reorganization involves a consolidation of 90 of these programs and realignment of ongoing STEM education activities to improve the delivery, impact, and visibility of STEM efforts. Nearly $180 million would be redirected from programs across the Government to the Department of Education, NSF, and the Smithsonian Institution. The Department of Education's role will include developing STEM innovation networks to reform STEM instruction and supporting Master Teachers who can serve as a national resource for improving STEM teaching and learning. NSF will focus on efforts to improve STEM undergraduate education and to reform graduate fellowships so they reach more students and align with national needs. The Smithsonian Institution will improve the reach of informal education activities by ensuring they are aligned with State standards and are relevant to the classroom.

Modernize, Streamline, and Strengthen the Delivery of Training and Employment Services. As the economy changes, Federal training and employment programs must continually innovate and adapt to help American workers gain the skills they need to find new jobs and careers. Today more than 40 programs at 11 Federal agencies deliver job training and employment services. We should be doing everything we can to make it easier for Americans to find a job or build their skills for a better one, and for employers who need to find well-qualified workers. The Administration is therefore exploring opportunities to revisit how the Federal Government funds job training and employment services, including the possibility of reorganizing some of the existing training programs that serve overlapping populations. For example, the Budget proposes a universal displaced worker program that will reach up to a million workers a year with a set of core services, combining the best elements of two more narrowly-targeted programs. Any reform must ensure that the needs of particularly vulnerable job-seekers and workers continue to be met and ensure greater accountability and transparency about the performance of federally supported job training providers and programs. The Administration looks forward to working with the Congress and other stakeholders on job training reform in the coming year.

Reform TVA. Since its creation in the 1930s during the Great Depression, the federally owned and operated Tennessee Valley Authority (TVA) has been producing low-cost electricity and managing natural resources for a large portion of the Southeastern United States. TVA's power service territory includes most of Tennessee and parts of Alabama, Georgia, Kentucky, Mississippi, North Carolina, and Virginia, covering 80,000 square miles and serving more than nine million people. TVA is a self-financing Government corporation, funding operations through electricity sales and bond financing. In order to meet its future capacity needs, fulfill its environmental responsibilities, and modernize its aging generation system, TVA's current capital investment plan includes more than $25 billion of expenditures over the next 10 years. However, TVA's anticipated capital needs are likely to quickly exceed the agency's $30 billion statutory cap on indebtedness. Reducing or eliminating the Federal Government's role in programs such as TVA, which have achieved their original objectives and no longer require Federal participation, can help put the Nation on a sustainable fiscal path. Given TVA's debt constraints and the impact to the Federal deficit of its increasing capital expenditures, the Administration intends to undertake a strategic review of options for addressing TVA's financial situation, including the possible divestiture of TVA, in part or as a whole.

Realign and Streamline GSA Operations. The General Services Administration (GSA) provides real estate, acquisition, and technology services to the Federal Government. A more efficient and effective GSA translates into cost savings for Federal agencies and taxpayers. Based on a comprehensive review of GSA's operations, the Budget is proposing realignment and streamlining of key GSA functions that will result in estimated cost savings exceeding $200 million over 10 years. Consolidating reporting structures within GSA will increase accountability in decision-making in areas such as finance, human resources, and IT, and generate cost savings by eliminating redundancies. Further reforms to GSA's Public Buildings Service and Federal Acquisition Service are designed to deliver consistency across organizational units, particularly in service delivery and policy application, ensuring GSA serves Federal agencies as a single national solutions provider.

Reform Food Aid. The existing P.L. 480 Title II food aid program, which is administered by the U.S. Agency for International Development and funded through the U.S. Department of Agriculture, includes numerous requirements that raise the cost of providing food aid and reduce its timeliness and effectiveness in responding to humanitarian crises and fighting hunger abroad. The proposed reform replaces P.L. 480 Title II funding with an equivalent amount of flexible discretionary funding that will provide aid to over two million more people annually. At the same time, the less rigid funding stream will give the United States far greater ability to provide aid when, where, and in the form that it can be most effective. The program will use a majority

of emergency food aid funding to purchase and ship food from the United States, will supplement the existing level of support for certain militarily useful ships, and will facilitate the retention of U.S. mariners. In addition to helping more people in crisis, the reform will reduce mandatory spending—and the deficit—by an estimated $500 million over a decade.

Prioritize Immigration Detention Resources. The Administration has focused its immigration enforcement efforts on identifying and removing individuals who pose a danger to national security or a risk to public safety, including aliens convicted of crimes, with particular emphasis on violent criminals, felons, and repeat offenders. To ensure the most cost-effective use of Federal dollars, the Budget focuses detention capabilities on priority and mandatory detainees, while allowing low-risk, non-mandatory detainees to enroll in lower cost, parole-like alternatives to detention programs, such as electronic monitoring and intensive supervision. As the Administration continues to focus on priority removal cases, it will work to reduce the time removable aliens spend in immigration detention custody. To achieve this goal, U.S. Immigration and Customs Enforcement is improving its ability to expedite removal of convicted criminal aliens, so they do not require lengthy stays in U.S. immigration detention custody prior to deportation.

USING EVIDENCE TO GET BETTER RESULTS

In its first term, the Administration developed innovative grant programs that drive resources to evidence-based practices and require strong evaluations to build knowledge of what works. In partnership with policy officials, researchers, and program managers, the Administration will expand the use of these models in other priority program areas in 2014.

Pay for Success. To ensure taxpayers get the best possible return on their investment in social programs, the Administration is expanding the Pay for Success program model started in 2012.

Pay for Success leverages philanthropic and private dollars to fund preventive services up front, with the Government paying providers only after they generate results that save taxpayer money. In 2012, the Department of Justice awarded grants to two States for Pay for Success projects to prevent recidivism, and in 2013 the Department of Labor expects to support training programs using this model. In 2014, the Administration will broaden its support for Pay for Success, reserving up to $195 million in the areas of job training, education, criminal justice, housing, and disability services.

The President's Budget is also proposing a new $300 million incentive fund at the Department of the Treasury to help State and local governments implement Pay for Success programs with philanthropies. The fund will provide credit enhancements for philanthropic investments and outcome payments for money-saving services. This approach borrows from the Outcomes Finance Fund, a similar fund established in the United Kingdom. The Administration will also make available up to five percent of proceeds from the sale of excess Federal property under the proposed Civilian Property Realignment Act for innovative homeless programs, including Pay for Success projects that save taxpayer money by reducing homelessness.

Invest in Innovation Using a Tiered Evidence Model. Federal grant programs should build evidence of what works and create incentives for grantees to adopt proven practices. Even in a period of constrained resources, the Budget increases funding by 44 percent over the 2012 enacted level for innovation funds that use a tiered model to provide more resources for programs that demonstrate evidence of success. For example, the Budget includes $215 million for the Department of Education's Investing in Innovation (i3) program. The program uses development, validation, and scale-up grants to grow the base of evidence on effective teachers and leaders, improving low-performing schools, and parent engagement strategies that increase student learning at the K-12 level. The Budget also provides $260 million to launch a companion First in the World fund at the Department of Education to spur the establishment, validation, and scaling-up of cutting-edge innovations that can decrease college costs and boost postsecondary attainment rates.

The Budget also includes $150 million for the Department of Labor's Workforce Innovation Fund, to engage States and localities in developing more effective training and placement services for the unemployed, and invests $25 million in new, evidence-informed efforts to improve employment outcomes for older Americans.

Evidence will also be a focus of the new initiatives that the Department of Education, NSF, and the Smithsonian implement under the STEM reorganization discussed earlier in this chapter. Rigorous evaluations will be a core strategy in this effort to help distinguish truly effective approaches from well-intended ones with little impact.

Generate Stronger Results in Formula Grant Programs with Competitive Grants. The Budget also takes important steps to improve the effectiveness of formula grant programs by using competitive grants to encourage adoption of evidence-based approaches such as:

- In the Department of Justice, the Budget couples the Byrne Justice Assistance Grant and Juvenile Accountability Block Grant programs with competitive incentive funds that provide "bonuses" to States and localities for evidence-based use of formula funds.

- In the Department of Health and Human Services (HHS), the Budget proposes to require that States use five percent of their mental health block grant allocation for grants that use the most effective evidence-based prevention and treatment approaches.

- The Department of Education proposes to reform the Career and Technical Education formula grant to require that States award the funds competitively at the local level and to create an innovation fund that will drive the use and development of evidence-based practices to make sure young people gain the skills needed to succeed in today's economy.

All of these reforms capitalize on research conducted over several decades to learn what works for different communities and populations. The proposals do not mandate that State and local governments adopt federally prescribed solutions, but require that a portion of funding is spent on approaches backed by strong evidence.

Create Performance Partnerships That Provide Flexibility While Demanding Results. Inconsistent and overlapping Federal program requirements sometimes prevent States and localities from effectively coordinating services or using funding to support strategies that are likely to achieve the best outcomes. For 2014, the Budget proposes establishing a limited number of Performance Partnership pilots designed to improve outcomes for disconnected youth, including young adults who have dropped out of school and are not employed. Approved performance partnerships designed at the State or local level could blend discretionary funds for youth-serving programs at the Departments of Education, HHS, Labor, Justice, Housing and Urban Development (HUD), and other agencies, in exchange for greater accountability for results. Performance indicators, such as education and employment outcomes, would be used to gauge progress, and evaluations would study what locally designed strategies work best. The Administration will learn from community leaders about the potential for similar performance partnerships, exchanging greater flexibility over funds for greater accountability for results, to revitalize distressed communities and reduce youth violence.

Inject Performance Focus Into More Programs. The Budget takes other steps to inject an emphasis on outcomes into programs that have lacked that focus for too long. For example, the Budget consolidates and establishes new performance requirements in programs ranging from rural and cooperative grant programs at the Department of Agriculture to the Federal Emergency Management Agency first responder grants. The Budget also continues the implementation of the historic requirement for low-performing Head Start grantees to compete for funding, establishes performance standards in the Community Services Block Grant program and requires competition for programs below those standards, and allocates Senior Corps funding on a competitive basis.

Support Initiatives That Can Produce Cost-Effective Results. The Budget makes additional investments in programs where the evidence suggests long-term savings outweigh short-term costs. For example, the President's historic investment in early childhood education reflects the deep body of research showing that high-quality early interventions can yield lasting savings to the Government and society through improvements in children's educational, employment, health, and other outcomes. New criminal justice investments, including State partnerships through the Justice Reinvestment Act, and grants through the Second Chance Act, may not only reduce crime and imprisonment, but also generate savings over the long run. This is also true of the Hawaii Opportunity Probation and Enforcement program's "swift and certain" approach to sanctions for probationers, which the Budget proposes to continue expanding and evaluating. To support and evaluate these efforts, the Budget strongly encourages cost-benefit analyses in States, as well as Federal agencies.

STRENGTHENING EVALUATION AND SHARING WHAT WORKS

Rigorous evaluations identify what works, under what conditions, and at what cost. They can also show what doesn't work and should stop. Innovative companies constantly use data and experimentation this way—to drive learning and improvement. Building on their lessons, the Administration is intensifying its use of evaluation and experimentation to build a culture of learning and continuous improvement to ensure Americans receive maximum value for their tax dollars.

Learn and Share What Works. The Budget supports new evaluations across the Government to analyze program impacts such as investigations into how to: structure student aid in order to increase college access for low-income students; strengthen the impact of Federal technical assistance to small businesses; strengthen performance benchmarking and create new efficiencies across Federal health care programs operated by the Departments of Veterans Affairs (VA), Defense, and HHS; use evidence-based home visiting programs to improve birth outcomes, reduce low-birth weight, and improve infant health, and; use increased local flexibility in housing assistance to achieve positive outcomes for families, including increased employment and self-sufficiency. The Administration will also help policymakers, program managers, and practitioners access strong evidence by continuing to expand "what works" clearinghouses for proven practices, such as the Department of Justice's *CrimeSolutions.gov*, the Department of Education's What Works Clearinghouse, the Substance Abuse and Mental Health Services Administration's National Registry of Evidenced-based Programs and Practices, and the Department of Labor's new Clearinghouse of Labor Evaluation and Research.

Share Data Across Agencies. Federal agencies are also beginning to reduce the costs of high-quality evaluations by using existing sources of data within the Government rather than conducting costly new surveys. The Budget provides funds to link data across programs in order to support high-quality, low-cost research. HHS and HUD, for instance, are sharing data to analyze how housing interventions affect the health care use and costs of residents. VA and HUD are also collaborating to streamline reporting by homelessness programs and to create a more comprehensive picture of homelessness trends and interventions. The Census Bureau is also working in partnership with agencies to expand capacity for researchers to securely access and analyze data to evaluate programs in ways that safeguard privacy and confidentiality.

Strengthen Agency Capacity for Data Analytics and Evaluation. The Administration is building a more robust evaluation and data analytics infrastructure within agencies to support rigorous research focused on important policy priorities. Building on an approach that has been successful at the Department of Labor, the Budget includes funding for a Chief Evaluation Officer at the Department of Agriculture to work closely with program offices to develop and implement evaluation agendas set by policy officials. As an example of cross-agency collaboration, evaluation officials from the Departments of Education, Labor, HHS, and NSF are developing common evidence standards for research studies, which can be a resource for improving the quality of studies throughout the Federal Government.

Interagency learning networks comprised of program, performance management, and evaluation officials are now forming to develop shared evaluation agendas and tools in areas as diverse as reviewing outcomes for business technical assistance programs, improving enforcement programs that oversee compliance with health, safety and environmental laws, operating financial literacy programs, and strengthening and evaluating STEM programs.

MANAGING FOR RESULTS

To improve the effectiveness and efficiency of Federal agencies, the Administration is implementing goal-focused, data-driven approaches to set priorities, benchmark progress, and ensure staff and resources across the Government are coordinating their efforts for maximum impact.

Use Goals and Frequent Data-Driven Reviews. To emphasize and enhance performance improvement practices across the Federal Government, in 2009 the Administration directed agency leaders to set high-priority performance goals (Priority Goals). Agencies set Priority Goals every two years, with the current set established for 2012-2013. The Deputy Secretary or Chief Operating Officer of each agency runs quarterly progress reviews and designates a senior accountable official responsible for driving progress on each Priority Goal. Goal Leaders are expected to select strategies based on evidence, set milestones, and assess progress at least once a quarter. They are also expected to use appropriately rigorous evaluations and other studies to refine understanding of problems and opportunities and to improve results.

The Administration also identified 14 Federal Cross-Agency Priority (CAP) Goals to help deliver on the President's commitment to strengthen future economic growth and job creation. CAP Goals have been set for: exports; entrepreneurship and small businesses; STEM education; broadband infrastructure; energy efficiency; job training; and transitioning returning veterans to civilian jobs. CAP Goals have also been set to improve sustainability, cybersecurity, and other aspects of Federal Government operations.

Communicate Performance. To support transparency, accountability, learning, and inter-agency coordination, the Administration established *Performance.gov*. This website makes it easier for the public to see what the Federal Government is trying to accomplish, why, how, and how well. It also serves as a tool to keep agency executives and Priority Goal leaders focused on finding better ways to accomplish their objectives. It supports collaboration on shared goals, facilitates learning across agencies and delivery partners, and invites public suggestions for performance improvement.

HARNESSING INFORMATION TECHNOLOGY TO DO MORE WITH LESS

The American people expect the Government to use information technology (IT) to provide the same level of service they experience in their everyday lives. As part of the President's Campaign to Cut Waste the Administration is transforming how the Government uses IT to improve productivity, lower the cost of operations, and streamline service delivery, all while bolstering cybersecurity.

The Administration has also focused on a cut and reinvest strategy for IT that acknowledges the need to cut waste and keep costs down, while at the same time encouraging investment in innovative and higher value technologies that can help us build a more efficient and citizen-friendly Government. By requiring Federal agencies to identify specific IT programs they would eliminate or pare back before proposing new ones, the Administration is accelerating the adoption of newer, more effective technologies, while forcing tough decisions on the ones that have outlived their usefulness.

Launch New Digital Government Strategy. New expectations require the Federal Government to be ready to deliver and receive digital information and services anytime, anywhere, and on any device. It must do so safely, securely, and with fewer resources. To build for the future, the Administration has launched a comprehensive Digital Government Strategy that embraces the opportunity to innovate more with fewer resources, and enables entrepreneurs to better leverage Government data to improve the quality of services. These imperatives are not new, but modern tools and technologies enable us to seize the opportunity to fundamentally change how the Federal Government serves both its internal and external customers—by building a 21st Century platform to better serve the public.

Use PortfolioStat to Target Duplicative and Low-Value IT Spending. Building on the success of the Administration's TechStat sessions, which focus on identifying and solving problems in specific IT projects, in 2012 the Administration launched PortfolioStat, a new tool for agencies to assess the current maturity of their entire IT portfolio, enabling them to identify and eliminate duplicative or low value technology investments, and adopt intra- and inter-agency IT shared services, where applicable. Through the first year of the PortfolioStat initiative, agency Chief Operating Officers have set targets to reduce commodity IT spending through 98 consolidation opportunities, targeting over $1 billion in spending reductions in 2014.

Expand BusinessUSA. In October 2011, the President issued a challenge to Government agencies to think beyond their organizational boundaries in the best interest of serving America's business community, and to start thinking and acting more like the businesses they serve.

He directed the creation of *BusinessUSA.gov*, a centralized, one-stop platform to make it easier for businesses to access services to help them grow and hire. BusinessUSA implements a "no wrong door" approach for small businesses and exporters by using technology to quickly connect businesses to the services and information relevant to them, regardless of where the information is located or which agency's website, call center, or office they go to for help. In 2014, all Federal agencies with business-facing capabilities will be participating in integrating and expanding BusinessUSA's capabilities.

DEPARTMENT OF AGRICULTURE

Funding Highlights:

- Provides $22.6 billion in discretionary funding for the Department of Agriculture, roughly equal to the 2012 enacted level.

- Reduces the deficit by $37.8 billion over 10 years by eliminating direct farm payments, decreasing crop insurance subsidies, and targeting conservation programs.

- Supports evidence-based decision-making by aligning program funding with performance measures through the creation of a new rural development grant program, targeting forestry grants and establishing a Chief Evaluation Officer within the Department.

- Invests $4 billion in renewable and clean energy and environmental improvements to make America more energy independent, and drive global competitiveness in the renewable energy sector.

- Increases funding for the Agriculture and Food Research Initiative to $383 million and targets areas that are key to American scientific leadership: human nutrition and obesity, food safety, bioenergy, sustainable agriculture, and climate change.

- Provides $7.1 billion for the Special Supplemental Nutrition Program for Women, Infants, and Children to help ensure good birth outcomes, growth and development for low-income and nutritionally at-risk pregnant and post-partum women, infants, and children up to age five.

- Targets housing and water treatment assistance primarily through lending that has a lower cost to the Government.

- Leverages resources and works with Federal, State, and tribal partners to accelerate voluntary adoption of conservation practices to improve water quality.

The U.S. Department of Agriculture (USDA) provides leadership on issues related to food, agriculture, and natural resources, including energy, based on sound public policy, the best available science, and efficient management. USDA works to expand economic opportunity through the development of innovative practices and research and provides financing needed to help expand job prospects and improve housing, utilities, and community infrastructure in rural America. The Department also works to promote sustainable agricultural production to protect the long-term availability of food. USDA programs safeguard and protect America's food supply by reducing the incidence of food-borne hazards from farm to table. USDA also improves nutrition and health through food assistance and nutrition education. USDA supports agricultural and economic development in developing countries through research and technical assistance to combat chronic hunger and achieve global food security. Finally, USDA manages and protects America's public and private lands by working cooperatively with other levels of government and the private sector to preserve and conserve the Nation's natural resources through restored forests, improved watersheds, and healthy private working lands.

The 2014 Budget provides $22.6 billion in discretionary funding to support this important mission, roughly equal to the 2012 enacted level. While investments are made in renewable energy, rural development, and key research areas, the Budget makes tough choices to meet the current discretionary caps. Deficit reduction savings are achieved by eliminating direct farm payments, decreasing crop insurance subsidies, and better targeting conservation funding.

Supports Evidence-Based Decision-Making

Encourages Job Creation in Rural Communities. The Budget proposes $55 million for a new economic development grant program designed to target small and emerging private businesses and cooperatives in rural areas. The program will be designed to utilize evidence on what works best to create jobs and foster growth. This new program will award funding to grantees that agree to be tracked against performance targets and will improve upon the agency's current grant allocation and evaluation process. In addition, funding is also requested for food hubs that are designed to strengthen the link between rural producers and regional food systems.

Evaluates Business Technical Assistance. In 2014, USDA, along with the Department of Commerce and the Small Business Administration, will continue to participate in an interagency group designed to evaluate the impact of Federal business technical assistance programs. USDA will look at the Rural Business-Cooperative Service business programs with the goal of developing a standard methodology for measuring the impact of technical assistance programs across the Federal Government.

Strengthens Targeting of State Forestry Resource Grants and Public Land Restoration Funds. The Budget strengthens resource management on non-Federal lands by incorporating better data on grantee accomplishments and natural resource outcomes to help guide future Federal investment in State forestry grants. This approach advances the recent shift toward cross-program and competitive-based grant allocations already underway by institutionalizing better data collection and rewarding innovative projects that increase natural resource outcomes, including benefits to water quality from improved forest stewardship and innovative uses of urban forestry in emerging green infrastructure approaches. It also supports Integrated Resource Restoration pilots on Federal land that improve agency efficiency and forest restoration outcomes by enabling cross-disciplinary planning and execution.

Establishes a Chief Evaluation Officer. To support evidence-based policy-making, the Budget provides support for the establishment of a Chief Evaluation Officer within USDA to work closely with program offices and agencies to develop and implement evaluation agendas and priorities set by policy officials.

Fosters Innovation and Job Growth

Promotes Development of Rural Renewable Energy. The Budget proposes $4 billion in loans to rural electric cooperatives and utilities that will support the transition to clean-energy generation. Specifically, this funding will be targeted to decrease America's reliance on fossil fuels and promote renewable and clean energy at electric generation, transmission, and distribution sites in rural communities. In addition, the Budget proposes a program level of $238 million for the Rural Energy for America Program to assist agricultural producers and rural small businesses in developing renewable energy systems, energy efficiency improvements, and renewable energy development.

Spurs American Innovation by Advancing Priority Research. USDA research has played a key role in spurring innovation and advancing technology that has allowed American agriculture to experience increases in efficiency, sustainability, and profitability. At the same time, the Administration recognizes that continued fiscal constraint requires trade-offs to focus resources on the most important priorities. Therefore, the Budget proposes $383 million—a $119 million increase above the 2012 enacted level—for competitive research grants made through the Agriculture and Food Research Initiative. The Budget also increases in-house research in select areas such as crop protection, sustainable agriculture, climate change, childhood obesity, and food safety by $148 million; which includes a reallocation of $125 million from lower priority projects. The Budget also continues funding for the Census of Agriculture. The Budget provides $155 million for design and construction of a new Athens, Georgia poultry lab, the highest USDA laboratory construction priority. The Southeast Poultry Research Laboratory, which it will replace, is the Department's only laboratory specially designed to conduct research on highly infectious diseases of poultry.

Conserves Landscapes. For the first time ever, the Budget proposes mandatory funding for Land and Water Conservation Fund (LWCF) programs in the Departments of the Interior and Agriculture. These funds will assist in conserving lands for national parks, refuges, and forests, including collaborative projects for Interior and the U.S. Forest Service to jointly and strategically conserve the most critical landscapes while improving management efficiency. They will also support the President's America's Great Outdoors Initiative to promote job creation and economic growth by strengthening the Nation's natural infrastructure for outdoor recreation.

Prevents Hunger and Supports Healthy Eating

Prevents Hunger. At a time of continued need, the Administration strongly supports the Supplemental Nutrition Assistance Program (SNAP) and the Child Nutrition Programs, which help families improve their nutrition and reduce hunger. SNAP is the cornerstone of the Nation's nutrition assistance safety net, touching the lives of more than 47 million people. The Budget provides $7.6 billion for discretionary nutrition programs, including $7.1 billion to support the 8.9 million individuals expected to participate in the Special Supplemental Nutrition Program for Women, Infants, and Children (WIC), which is critical to the health of pregnant women, new mothers, infants, and young children. The Budget also provides resources for program integrity and reproposes the continuation of certain temporary SNAP benefits.

Supports Healthy Eating. The Budget supports the implementation of the Healthy, Hunger-Free Kids Act of 2010 with $35 million in school equipment grants to aid in the provision of healthy meals and continued support for other school-based resources.

Makes Tough Choices and Targets Reductions

Reduces Direct Housing Loans in Favor of Guarantees. The Budget proposes a significant reduction for the direct single family housing loan program, providing a $360 million loan level for 2014 compared to the $900 million 2012 enacted level. A lower direct loan level is sustainable, and is expected to increase demand on the guarantee loans to the point where USDA obligates the full $24 billion proposed for 2014. This funding favors providing single family housing assistance primarily through loan guarantees. Interest rates are at their lowest level in decades, which allows the Government to support loans through the private credit market with a robust guaranteed single family housing loan level of $24 billion. In addition, improvements and innovations in the banking industry and the pervasiveness of lending through the Internet have reduced significantly the "pockets of need" for credit that once existed in rural America. Relying more on the private banking industry to provide this service, with a guarantee from the Federal Government, is a more cost-efficient way to deliver housing assistance.

Reduces Water and Wastewater Grants. Consistent loan performance and low interest rates have made USDA's rural water and wastewater direct loans less expensive to administer and allows the Budget to propose $1.2 billion in loan level from the $794 million level enacted in 2012. Higher loan levels at lower interest rates means that less grant funding is needed to fund each facility. Therefore, grants are funded at $304 million compared to $433 million in 2012. The combined grant-loan nature of the program ensures that rural communities will continue to receive an overall increase in program level assistance of $278 million in 2014 for their water and wastewater facility needs.

Government Crop Insurance Subsidies

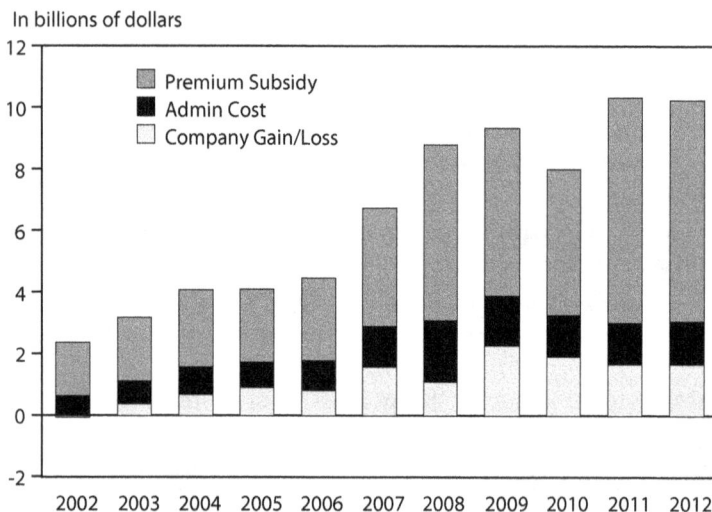

In billions of dollars

Source: USDA Risk Management Agency.

Reforms Farm Programs. The farm sector continues to be one of the strongest sectors of the U.S. economy, with net farm income expected to increase 13.6 percent to $128.2 billion in 2013, which would be the highest inflation-adjusted

amount since 1973. With the value of both crop and livestock production at all-time highs, income support payments based upon historical levels of production can no longer be justified. The Budget, therefore, proposes to eliminate so-called "direct payments," while providing mandatory disaster assistance to producers to protect them from losses. The Budget also proposes to reduce subsidies for crop insurance and to better target conservation programs. As the chart indicates, crop insurance subsidies have risen dramatically in recent years. In total, these proposals will reduce the deficit by $37.8 billion over 10 years.

Improves the Way Federal Dollars are Spent

Protects Communities and Ecosystems from Wildfire Damage. The Budget continues the long-standing practice of fully funding the 10-year average cost of wildland fire suppression operations. It provides an increase of $74 million from the 2012 enacted level for new air tankers and continues to support a modernized aerial retardant delivery capability. In addition, the Budget supports efforts to improve landscape health and wildfire resilience and expand cooperative efforts through the Collaborative Forest Land Restoration program, and proposes a new program to improve public-private partnerships in fire-prone areas to address fire-related risks to municipal watersheds and other public service utilities.

Continues Interagency Collaboration to Improve Water Quality. The United States has made great strides in improving water quality; however, "non-point" source pollution remains a significant economic, environmental, and public health challenge that requires policy attention and thoughtful new approaches. Over the past year, USDA, the Environmental Protection Agency, and State water quality agencies collaborated to select over 150 priority watersheds, where voluntary conservation programs could be targeted to aid in reducing water impairments from non-point source pollution. The Budget builds upon this collaboration by having agencies work with other key Federal partners, agricultural producer organizations, conservation districts, States, Tribes, non-governmental organizations, and other local leaders to implement a monitoring framework and begin collecting baseline performance data to demonstrate that this focused and coordinated approach can achieve significant improvements in water quality.

DEPARTMENT OF COMMERCE

Funding Highlights:

- Provides $8.6 billion for the Department of Commerce, an increase of $1 billion over the 2012 enacted level.

- Increases key investments in research and development to lay the foundation for economic expansion and accelerates advances in manufacturing through targeted research, technical assistance, and support for manufacturing consortia.

- Enhances the competitiveness of U.S. manufacturers by providing $1 billion in mandatory funding to create a network of up to 15 manufacturing institutes across the Nation and creates a $113 million Investing in Manufacturing Communities Fund to provide targeted financial assistance for about five manufacturing communities that have developed comprehensive strategies to strengthen their manufacturing potential.

- Provides $754 million for the National Institute of Standards and Technologies laboratories to accelerate advances ranging from cybersecurity to advanced manufacturing, a $25 million increase for the Hollings Manufacturing Extension Partnership to assist manufacturers in adopting new technologies to improve their competitiveness, and $21 million for the Advanced Manufacturing Technology Consortia to develop road maps that would address common challenges faced by manufacturers.

- Supports continued development of BusinessUSA, a one-stop site for Federal information useful to businesses, including export and business development assistance.

- Supports trade enforcement and promotion activities, invests in underserved markets and regional economic development, and encourages greater investment in the United States through targeted funding increases.

- Increases funding for the National Oceanic and Atmospheric Administration to strengthen support for critical weather satellite programs, Earth observations, and the bureau's other core science and stewardship responsibilities.

- Advances the Administration's efforts to make additional spectrum available for commercial use and improve first responder communication capabilities.

- Continues to support the U.S. Patent and Trademark Office's efforts to accelerate and improve patent processing by providing full access to its fee collections.

- Sustains funding for critical economic and demographic data collection and statistics dissemination activities at the U.S. Census Bureau and the Bureau of Economic Analysis.

The Department of Commerce (Commerce) carries out a wide range of missions, from environmental science and stewardship, to statistical research, to technology and innovation, to domestic economic development and international trade. Overall, Commerce plays a critical role in promoting U.S. economic growth and providing vital environmental information. In total, the Budget provides Commerce with $8.6 billion to support mission areas across its diverse bureaus. Key investments are made in areas such as export promotion and enforcement activities, development of weather satellites, and research and development to support long-term economic growth. At the same time, efficiency gains and reductions in lower-priority activities enable Commerce to achieve administrative savings.

Invests in America's Long-Term Growth and Competitiveness

Strengthens U.S. Manufacturing and Innovation. The Budget includes $1 billion in mandatory funding to establish a national network of manufacturing innovation institutes that will develop cutting-edge manufacturing technologies and capabilities to propel the competitiveness of U.S. manufacturing. The Budget also includes $113 million to create the Investing in Manufacturing Communities Fund, which will be invested in those regions that have created economic development strategies that build on the region's comparative advantages and leverage private-sector resources. These manufacturing investments will fund capital projects such as industrial parks and industry academic centers to promote long-term economic growth in the region in concert with other Federal economic development programs.

The Budget maintains the President's commitment to increase funding for key basic research agencies, including $754 million for National Institute of Standards and Technology (NIST) laboratories as part of the President's Plan for Science and Innovation, $131 million above the 2012 enacted level. This funding will accelerate advances in a variety of important areas, ranging from cybersecurity and smart manufacturing to advanced communications and disaster resilience. The Budget provides a $25 million increase over the 2012 enacted level for the Hollings Manufacturing Extension Partnership to establish Manufacturing Technology Acceleration Centers that would assist manufacturers in adopting new technologies to improve their competitiveness. The Budget also includes $21 million for the Advanced Manufacturing Technology Consortia program, a public-private partnership that will support road maps and research to address common manufacturing challenges faced by American businesses.

Promotes American Exports and Investment in the United States. The Budget proposes $520 million for the International Trade Administration (ITA), a 14 percent increase over the 2012 enacted level, to support the fifth year of the National Export Initiative, a Government-wide strategy to double U.S. exports and add two million export-supported jobs by the end of 2014. Funding for ITA includes $20 million for the Interagency Trade Enforcement Center, an interagency effort to address unfair trade practices and barriers, and $20 million for SelectUSA, which promotes investment in the United States. Other funds support increased export promotion activities in underserved markets around the world and ITA's role in the Administration's BusinessUSA initiative, a one-stop shop to connect businesses with Federal Government resources more effectively and efficiently.

Enhances Export Control Enforcement. The Budget includes $112 million for the Bureau of Industry and Security to sustain export licensing and enforcement activities, as well as to support the bureau's ongoing work under the Administration's Export Control Reform (ECR) initiative. The $11 million increase from the 2012 enacted level will support the bureau's expanded export licensing and export enforcement operations as controlled items shift from the State Department to the Commerce Department's jurisdiction. The Administration's continued efforts to implement the ECR initiative will advance our national security and economic competitiveness by better focusing U.S. controls on transactions to destinations or end users of concern, while facilitating secure trade for controlled items with U.S. allies and close partners.

Promotes Regional Economic Development. The Budget includes $125 million for the Economic Development Administration to support new regional economic development initiatives. As mentioned above, the Budget proposes to use $113 million of these funds to support U.S. manufacturing with the Investing in Manufacturing Communities Fund. The Budget also proposes $12 million to promote regional export strategies with the Regional Export Challenge. The Regional Export Challenge, a competitive grant program, will support those regions that develop and implement sustainable export action plans to proactively identify and support firms and sectors with the greatest export potential.

Invests in Weather Forecasting Improvements. The Budget provides robust support for the National Weather Service, including increases for weather research, weather modeling, and supercomputing capacity to accelerate advancements in weather forecasting. The Budget also provides $2 billion to continue the development of the National Oceanic and Atmospheric Administration's (NOAA's) polar-orbiting and geostationary weather satellite systems, as well as satellite-borne measurements of sea level and potentially damaging solar storms. These satellites are critical to NOAA's ability to provide accurate weather forecasts and warnings that help to protect lives and property.

Strengthens Ocean and Coastal Science and Stewardship. The Budget includes significant investments in NOAA's ocean and coastal research and observing programs, while increasing support for habitat and species conservation activities that are essential to restoring and maintaining healthy, sustainable fisheries. Increased funding for NOAA's research and development and Earth Observations activities will enhance the agency's ability to detect, understand, and forecast global and ecosystem-scale changes and provide sound, science-based information to support decision making and help communities prepare for the consequences of a changing climate. The Budget also supports investments that promote well-coordinated ocean and coastal science and management activities.

Builds on Efforts to Make Additional Spectrum Available and Improve Emergency Communications. The Middle Class Tax Relief and Job Creation Act of 2012 enacted Administration proposals to promote greater wireless broadband deployment by auctioning spectrum and then investing over $7 billion of these proceeds in building a nationwide broadband network for first responders. In total, these actions are expected to contribute nearly $17 billion to deficit reduction over the next 10 years. The Budget builds on this effort by proposing to authorize use of a spectrum license user fee for licenses not allocated via auctions, to promote efficient utilization of spectrum. This fee will raise nearly $5 billion over the next 10 years. In addition, the Budget invests $8 million to monitor spectrum use by Federal agencies in high-priority markets to identify opportunities for repurposing spectrum through auctions.

Sustains Economic Data and Statistics Programs. The Budget provides $1.1 billion for the Census Bureau and the Bureau of Economic Analysis (BEA) to collect economic and demographic data from businesses and households and to produce critical economic statistics. These economic statistics, including gross domestic product, are monitored and used by fiscal and monetary policymakers and businesses in the United States and throughout the world. The Budget includes funding for the last year of the three-year research and testing phase for the 2020 Decennial Census and a BEA initiative that would provide new measures of foreign direct investment and service exports.

Supports Evidence-Based Decision-Making and Achieves Efficiencies

Enhances Evaluation of Technical Assistance Programs. In 2014, Commerce, along with the Small Business Administration and the Department of Agriculture, will continue to participate in an interagency group designed to evaluate the impact of Federal business technical assistance programs. Commerce will look at programs such as ITA's Foreign Commercial Service, with the goal of developing a standard methodology for measuring the impact of this type of technical assistance program across the Federal Government. Also, in response to a Presidential

Memorandum on Accelerating Technology Transfer and Commercialization, NIST is improving and expanding technology transfer metrics and goals to measure the extent that NIST research and development is contributing to the competitiveness of U.S. industry.

Realizes Savings and Efficiencies. The Budget achieves savings of approximately $30 million in 2014 weather satellite development costs, with the potential for more savings over the life-cycle of these programs through reductions to overhead and savings in program content. Additionally, the Administration is taking specific actions to strengthen management of weather satellites, including enhancing satellite systems engineering expertise at NOAA and increasing oversight of these programs. Also, the Budget supports the Administration's Government-wide efforts to consolidate funding for several science, technology, engineering, and mathematics (STEM) programs into the Department of Education and the National Science Foundation, in order to support robust and visible initiatives in K-12 instruction, undergraduate education, and other educational programming.

DEPARTMENT OF DEFENSE

Funding Highlights:

- Provides $526.6 billion in discretionary funding for the base budget of the Department of Defense, a decrease of $3.9 billion, or 0.7 percent, below the 2012 enacted level. This level provides sufficient resources to carry out our national defense strategy.

- Responsibly draws down our military presence in Afghanistan and supports the transition to full Afghan responsibility for their country's own security.

- Following the President's National Security Strategy, makes informed choices to achieve a modern, ready, and balanced force to meet the full range of potential military requirements.

- Supports the Administration's efforts to rebalance diplomatic and military resources to the Asia-Pacific region.

- Invests in the Nation's cybersecurity capabilities by expanding the Cyber Forces led by the United States Cyber Command and increasing funding for cybersecurity information sharing.

- Protects investments in long-term capabilities that support our defense strategy, such as the F-35 Lightning II (the Joint Strike Fighter), the Air Force's KC-46 aerial refueling tanker, littoral combat ships, space systems, and transport helicopters.

- Prioritizes upgrades to existing systems such as the C-130 airlift aircraft, the F-15 fighter aircraft, and the Stryker combat vehicle, to enhance their capability to meet emerging threats.

- Supports the Administration's efforts to reform the Department's acquisition process and to achieve auditable financial statements.

- Enhances the Administration's commitment to maintaining a reliable nuclear deterrent by increasing investments in the nuclear weapons complex and weapon delivery systems.

- Sustains investment in science and technology programs, which drives innovation in the Nation's military, and, through the transfer of this technology, feeds innovation in the civilian economy.

- Provides a one percent military pay raise and protects military pay and benefits. Preserves counseling and educational programs that support servicemembers and their families.

- Takes steps to control rising health care costs without sacrificing quality of care and seeks to improve key needs such as mental health services for servicemembers and their families.

- Enables servicemembers to transition more smoothly and effectively to their lives as civilians and veterans through revamped transition assistance programs that provide information and resources, focusing on servicemembers' individual career goals.

The 2014 Budget provides $526.6 billion for the Department of Defense's (DOD's) base funding in 2014, representing a decrease of $3.9 billion, or 0.7 percent, below the 2012 enacted level. The Budget continues to pursue strategic priorities that reflect our Nation's renewed commitment to our historical role in the Asia-Pacific region. It also targets resources toward other strategic priorities such as increasing our ability to effectively navigate the security challenges and opportunities of cyberspace, continuing to focus funding on research and development, and combatting terrorism. The Budget maintains our commitment to providing servicemembers with the right mix of equipment, infrastructure, and training. It sustains our commitment to the All-Volunteer Force—the backbone of our modern military—and seeks to better support our servicemembers and their families in particular, by helping separating servicemembers transition more effectively to civilian life. It also continues to support DOD's efforts to reform the acquisition process and to achieve auditable financial statements.

Supports Overseas Contingency Operations

The Budget's Overseas Contingency Operations (OCO) funds will continue to support the incremental costs of military operations in Afghanistan, as well as other activities that primarily support Operation Enduring Freedom (OEF). Looking forward to the responsible end of the war in Afghanistan, U.S. forces will gradually draw down and complete the transition to full Afghan responsibility for their country's security by the end of December 2014. OCO funds will support military operations, incremental personnel costs, force protection, repair and replacement of damaged equipment, activities to counter and defeat improvised explosive devices, intelligence activities, support for coalition partners, and the training, equipping, and sustaining of the Afghan National Security Forces. Beyond Afghanistan and OEF, small amounts of funding will continue to support Iraq-related costs, including repair and replacement of equipment and munitions damaged or lost in the war and the operation of the Office of Security Cooperation-Iraq. OCO funds will also continue to fund the portion of temporary Army and Marine Corps end strength that supports current operations in Afghanistan and elsewhere, but that will not be required under the Nation's defense strategy.

Final decisions about the pace of the drawdown in Afghanistan have not yet been made. As a result, the Budget includes a placeholder for DOD's 2014 OCO funding, equivalent to the amount provided in the President's 2013 Budget. The Administration continues to propose a multiyear cap that limits Government-wide OCO funding to $450 billion over the 2013 to 2021 period, including $96.7 billion for OCO-funded activities in 2013. The Administration will submit a Budget amendment to the Congress updating the OCO request after a determination has been made on required force levels in Afghanistan.

Aligns Resources with Strategic Priorities

Rebalances Asia-Pacific Alliances. The United States and its interests are inextricably linked with Asia's economies and security. After more than a decade of war in Iraq and Afghanistan, DOD and other agencies are devoting greater energy and resources to revitalizing

U.S. alliances and economic ties across the Asia-Pacific region. DOD's overarching objective in the region is to sustain a stable security environment and a regional order rooted in economic openness, peaceful resolution of disputes, democratic governance, and political freedom.

The Budget funds critical investments in the region that further this objective. It provides $95 million for Guam military infrastructure to bolster Guam's position as a strategic hub in the western Pacific while taking important steps toward establishing fully capable Marine Air-Ground Task Forces in Japan, Guam, and Hawaii with the intent to rotate forces to Australia. It also provides resources to support up to four Littoral Combat Ships that would maintain a rotational presence in Singapore to improve the ability to counter a range of transnational threats in the region. In addition, the Budget supports increased military-to-military cooperation and training, which will help build the capacity of allies and partners to address security challenges. These and other investments, along with increased engagement with the region, are critical to the Government-wide effort to promote regional security and ensure the free flow of commerce and trade throughout the region.

Improves Cyberspace Operations and Cybersecurity Information Sharing. Cyber attacks targeting the financial industry and the Government demonstrate that no sector, network, or system is immune from cyber penetration by those who seek to make financial gain, to perpetrate malicious and disruptive activity, or to steal commercial or Government secrets and property. Cyber threats are constantly evolving and require a coordinated and comprehensive way of thinking about cyberspace activities. The Budget includes improvements to cyberspace activities, such as:

- *Cyber Forces Led by the U.S. Cyber Command.* Cyber investments will grow in response to emerging threats in cyberspace. Teams of cyber experts—including defensive, intelligence, and analytical—will defend the Nation, as well as DOD infrastructure, by

conducting reconnaissance, surveillance, development, maintenance, and analysis.

- *Cybersecurity Information Sharing.* The Comprehensive National Cybersecurity Initiative Five (CNCI-5) seeks to connect cybersecurity centers and other cybersecurity analytics electronically and in real time. The Budget provides an increase in funding for CNCI-5 to develop a comprehensive coordinated cybersecurity information sharing system that will serve as the foundation for cybersecurity information sharing requirements across the Government. This system will also develop and publish machine-readable interoperable technical standards that will allow for automated information sharing. The goal is for relevant pieces of information to make their way to authorized users throughout the Government, to help connect the dots in identifying cybersecurity threats.

Counters Terrorism. Protecting the United States from terrorism remains a national security priority. The United States and its allies have had many successes against terrorist groups, but the priority of fighting terrorism remains, even as the specific threats have changed. The Budget continues to prioritize this mission by funding investments that are consistent with the four principles of the National Strategy for Counterterrorism, including: combatting terrorism in ways that are consistent with core U.S. values; building the capacity of our partners to fight terrorism; developing systems and capabilities to defend American citizens and deny terrorists safe havens; and preventing terrorists from developing, acquiring, or using weapons of mass destruction.

Invests in Current and Future Capabilities

Funds Military Readiness and Training. The budget environment is challenging both because of fiscal considerations and because we are beginning the difficult process of resetting and restoring our force's ability to conduct the full range of military operations in support of the current defense strategy. The Budget meets these transitional challenges even as the force structure and future funding levels are reduced. Training and readiness are the foundation of ensuring a capable military that provides the President with a range of options to deter or defeat aggression or coercion against the United States and its allies, friends, and interests. The Budget provides $176.2 billion for the operations, training, and supporting activities troops need to defeat current and future threats. The Budget also requests authorization for another Base Realignment and Closure round in 2015 to close or realign excess infrastructure and avoid wasting limited resources maintaining unneeded facilities. The actual closing of any bases would involve a multiyear process that would not start until 2016, after the economy is projected to have more fully recovered.

Provides Needed Weapons Systems for the Challenges of Today and Tomorrow. The Administration is committed to providing servicemembers with the modern equipment they need to defend the Nation. To this end, the Budget provides $166.8 billion to develop and buy weapons systems that can meet emerging threats and that support our defense strategy. For example, the Budget includes $8.4 billion to continue the F-35 Lightning II (Joint Strike Fighter) aircraft program, which is designed to counter threats posed by a sophisticated adversary, and $5.4 billion for the VIRGINIA class submarine to provide asymmetric capabilities, such as improving the Navy's ability to operate in coastal waters and support special operations forces, that are appropriate to our defense strategy. In addition, the Budget proposes $653 million to strengthen the Nation's secure communication links in space by procuring additional Advanced Extremely High Frequency satellites.

While the Administration is committed to continuing its investment in new weapons systems needed to ensure that America's military remains the finest in the world, it is also focused on mitigating the adverse impact of budget constraints on the modernization effort whenever possible by continuing to maintain and upgrade proven existing systems. For example, DOD will continue to use the highly-capable C-130 airlift aircraft rather than procure a new airlifter such as the C-27. In addition, although DOD will also continue to use new Global Hawk Block 30 Unmanned Aerial Vehicles that have already been procured, as well as the proven U-2 reconnaissance aircraft for the critical task of providing intelligence to our troops, it will terminate further procurement of Block 30 Global Hawks. DOD will also retain proven systems such as the F-15 and F-16 fighter aircraft and the B-2 bomber, upgrading them as necessary to enhance their effectiveness, and will field double-v hulls on the Army's Stryker combat vehicles and upgrade the suspension and drive train of Paladin self-propelled howitzers, to improve troop protection, survivability, and mobility.

Modernizes the Nation's Nuclear Deterrent. The Administration remains committed to reducing the number and role of nuclear weapons in support of our national security strategy, to modernizing the Nation's nuclear weapons complex, and to supporting the goals of the Nuclear Posture Review as the United States and Russia implement the New Strategic Arms Reduction Treaty (New START). The Budget proposes $12 billion for strategic offensive forces, $600 million or five percent, less than the 2012 enacted level; the principal reason for the decrease was the two-year slip in the funding profile for the OHIO Class replacement. To ensure that the strategic bomber fleet will be able to conduct future missions, DOD is continuing to develop a new long-range bomber.

DOD continues to review possible reductions in delivery systems to ensure that the New START thresholds are met on schedule. Close cooperation between DOD and the National Nuclear Security Administration (NNSA) at the Department of Energy has resulted in modified weapons system requirements that focus on the highest-priority capabilities. DOD and NNSA continue to ensure that plutonium component production and research capabilities are maintained at required levels, and have increased resources for several programs to extend the service lives of nuclear weapons, as well as for one ongoing major capital asset project, the Uranium Processing Facility. Reflecting their close partnership and shared commitment, DOD continues to provide budgetary support to NNSA.

Funds Research and Development for the Military of the Future. The Administration continues to support strong investment in research and development (R&D) for national security. The Budget provides $67.5 billion for DOD research, development, test and evaluation activities. This funding supports DOD efforts to: evaluate new tactical vehicles; continue to develop the Air Force KC-46 aerial refueling tanker; continue to design the OHIO class ballistic missile submarine replacement; and advance other critical technologies. This research funding also capitalizes on DOD's important role in advanced manufacturing and the development of other forward-looking capabilities, including hypersonics.

The Budget also invests in early-stage science and technology (S&T) programs to support the warfighter. The Administration continues to encourage a strong national investment in R&D, and the Department's R&D activities, especially investments in DOD's S&T program, are a key component of this Government-wide effort. The Budget includes $12 billion for the S&T program. This funding supports basic research, applied research and advanced technology development. The Budget also provides $2.9 billion for the Defense Advanced Research Projects Agency and its breakthrough research, an increase of 1.8 percent above the 2012 enacted level.

Conserves Energy. As one of the largest organizations in the world, DOD consumes almost three-fourths of all energy used by the Federal Government. Consuming that much energy— whether fuel for planes, ships, and tanks, or electricity for bases, commissaries, and schools—has budgetary and strategic impacts. To mitigate those impacts, DOD seeks to be more deliberate about how it uses energy, in line with the Administration's overall approach to energy efficiency, such as by improving the fuel efficiency

of existing equipment, developing and fielding innovative energy technologies, expanding renewable energy sources, and improving the energy efficiency of buildings. The Budget provides $2 billion for initiatives to reduce fuel consumption, and provides $1.2 billion for initiatives to reduce facility energy consumption, including funds to retrofit existing buildings, meet higher energy efficiency standards for new buildings, and develop renewable energy projects. The Budget also includes $150 million for the Energy Conservation Investment Program, which improves the energy efficiency of DOD facilities worldwide, and provides $32 million for the Installation Energy Test Bed Program to demonstrate new energy technologies to reduce risk, overcome barriers to deployment, and facilitate wide-scale commercialization.

Reforms Acquisition Process. The Better Buying Power (BBP) initiative further implements DOD's best practices to strengthen buying power, improve industry productivity, and provide an affordable, value-added military capability to the warfighter. Launched in 2010, BBP encompasses a set of fundamental acquisition principles to achieve greater efficiencies through affordability, cost control, elimination of unproductive processes and bureaucracy, and promotion of competition. Today's constrained funding environment makes it even more important that DOD find effective means to increase its purchasing power for goods and services. New BBP initiatives address current fiscal realities, including enforcing affordability caps, measuring cost performance, and aligning contractor profitability with acquisition goals. DOD has instituted best practices, including applying lessons learned, expanding strategic sourcing, establishing acquisition professional reviews, and instituting peer reviews to ensure effective competition.

Strengthens the All-Volunteer Force

Supports Servicemembers and Their Families. The Administration places a strong focus on military family programs, sustaining funding at $8.5 billion to ensure consistent and effective services across military installations. DOD provides a broad spectrum of programs and services for servicemembers and military families including: mental health and counseling services; deployment assistance; child care and youth programs; morale, welfare, and recreation programs; commissaries; DOD-run schools for military dependents; military spouse employment programs; and many other services. DOD is working to improve its support to the All-Volunteer Force by identifying and discontinuing redundant or less effective military family programs, while increasing support for programs that are proven to serve military families well.

For calendar year 2014, consistent with the views of the uniformed military leadership, the Budget provides a 1.0 percent increase to basic pay, a 4.2 percent increase in the Basic Allowance for Housing, and a 3.4 percent increase in Basic Allowance for Subsistence. This compensation level recognizes the sacrifices made by the men and women in our Armed Forces, while adhering to the current budget constraints faced by DOD.

Promotes Health of Servicemembers and Their Families. To provide quality health care for the Nation's 9.6 million eligible military beneficiaries, the Budget provides $49.4 billion for the DOD Unified Medical Budget that supports the DOD Military Health System. The Budget sustains strong programs that support wounded, ill, and injured servicemembers and their families, and which help servicemembers transition into civilian life and the workforce. In particular, DOD is improving its support for servicemember mental and emotional health by increasing collaboration among suicide prevention programs, working to eliminate the stigma associated with accessing mental health services, and improving the effectiveness of DOD programs. To this end, DOD has started assessing the effectiveness of over 160 DOD psychological health programs and will realign resources by the end of 2014 to support the most effective programs and replace those that are less effective. DOD will sustain funding to improve electronic health record access.

DOD continues to seek efficiencies and cost savings within the Military Health System. The Budget supports adjusted TRICARE cost sharing requirements to address health care cost increases and make the health benefit more sustainable. Survivors of members who died while on active duty and disability retirees and their family members will be exempt from the fee and copay adjustments. DOD and the Department of Veterans Affairs will jointly work on a study to identify best practices and efficiencies within their healthcare systems.

Helps Servicemembers Transition to Civilian Life and Jobs. In the past year and a half, the Administration has worked to make the transition from military to civilian life easier. DOD, along with several other Federal agencies, has focused on creating a "career-ready" military and on increasing veteran employment. The Budget supports the first major redesign of the interagency Transition Assistance Program in over 20 years, which will provide more information and better resources to servicemembers as they begin to navigate civilian life. A new program, entitled Transition GPS (Goals, Plans, Success), will help servicemembers prepare for civilian life by providing pre-separation assessment and individual counseling, a five-day core curriculum, an additional curriculum tailored to the servicemembers' individual career goals, and a capstone event to verify that transitioning servicemembers have met certain standards that show they are ready for their civilian careers. DOD is also working to streamline civilian credentialing for servicemembers and veterans, so that they can better communicate to civilian employers the valuable skills they learned in service to the Nation. For example, the first action of the Military Credentialing and Licensing Task Force, working with manufacturing credentialing agencies, has enabled up to 126,000 servicemembers to gain industry-recognized, nationally-portable certifications for high-demand manufacturing jobs.

NATIONAL INTELLIGENCE PROGRAM

Funding Highlights:

- Provides $48.2 billion in discretionary base funding for the National Intelligence Program. This funding supports our national security goals and reflects a deliberative process to focus funding on the most critical capabilities.

- Continues to better integrate intelligence across the Government to help policy officials make decisions informed by the latest and most accurate intelligence available.

- Strengthens global intelligence capabilities to disrupt terrorism and better understand extremist threats.

- Counters the proliferation of weapons of mass destruction by strengthening collection and analysis capabilities.

- Supports military operations around the world.

- Enhances cyberspace capabilities to help protect Federal networks, critical infrastructure, and America's economy, while improving the security of intelligence networks against intrusion and counterintelligence threats.

- Modernizes the Intelligence Community's information technology infrastructure to remove barriers to collaboration, information sharing, and efficiency.

- Reduces contractors and maintains Government personnel levels in order to sustain other mission critical activities in a constrained fiscal environment.

- Terminates or reduces lower priority programs to enable investments in the most critical National Intelligence Program capabilities.

The National Intelligence Program (NIP) funds Intelligence Community (IC) activities in six Federal departments, the Central Intelligence Agency, and the Office of the Director of National Intelligence. The IC provides intelligence collection, the analysis of that intelligence, and the responsive dissemination of intelligence to those who need it—including the President, the heads of Executive Departments, military forces, and law enforcement agencies. The 2014 President's Budget advances the Administration's national security objectives and the National Intelligence Strategy and plays a critical role in protecting American citizens, safeguarding our economy, and fostering continued economic growth. In addition, it represents a focused effort to address the most critical requirements while accepting and managing risk within a constrained fiscal environment. The Budget strikes a careful balance between addressing critical national security requirements and providing responsible management of taxpayer resources. Savings are achieved by curtailing personnel growth, eliminating legacy capabilities, scaling back operations on lower priority missions, reducing facilities, and implementing new solutions for the delivery of information technology services, as appropriate. Reflecting the Administration's commitment to transparency and open government, the Budget continues the practice begun in the 2012 Budget of disclosing the President's aggregate funding request for the NIP. However, the details regarding the NIP budget remain classified, so the Budget highlights key NIP-funded activities, but does not publicly disclose detailed funding requests for intelligence activities.

Advances National Security Goals

Integrates Intelligence. The IC will continue to improve intelligence integration to more efficiently and effectively harness the strengths and capabilities that are spread across 17 organizations. Through National Intelligence Managers and their associated Unifying Intelligence Strategies, the Director of National Intelligence has drawn together the expertise required to accomplish the goals of the National Security Strategy and the National Intelligence Strategy, as guided by the National Intelligence Priorities Framework. The IC is working to ensure that integrated intelligence information flows anywhere and anytime it is required by any authorized user, from the President to our troops on the ground.

Strengthens Global Intelligence Capabilities to Disrupt Terrorism and Counter Weapons of Mass Destruction. The IC continues to make robust investments to combat terrorism and support the Administration's National Strategy for Counterterrorism. The IC will continue to lead operations to defeat al Qaeda and other violent extremists and disrupt their capabilities; prevent the proliferation of weapons of mass destruction; penetrate and analyze the most difficult targets of interest to U.S. foreign policymakers; identify and disrupt counterintelligence threats; and provide strategic warning to policymakers on issues of geopolitical and economic concern. To protect our national security, the IC will strengthen its collection and analysis capabilities and promote responsible intelligence collaboration and information sharing. The Administration also remains committed to measuring performance to evaluate progress, ensure key intelligence gaps are closed, and create accountability for results across the entire NIP.

Supports the Military Services. The Budget supports the ability of the IC to play a key role in informing military decision-makers at the strategic level, as well as those on the ground. The IC provides situational awareness, particularly as needed for force protection, targeting support, and other timely and actionable intelligence. Planners look to the IC for adversary plans, intentions and capabilities. The Budget balances its focus between current, immediate needs for U.S. military forces engaged in operations with enduring intelligence requirements for potential future military and security needs.

Enhances Cyberspace Operations, Information Sharing, and Safeguards Intelligence Networks. Cyber threats are constantly evolving and require a coordinated and comprehensive way of thinking about cyberspace activities. As we continue to see across our Nation, no sector, network, or system is immune from penetration by those who seek to make financial gain, to perpetrate malicious and disruptive activity, or to steal commercial or government secrets and property. The Budget includes increases and improvements to a full range of cyberspace activities.

The Comprehensive National Cybersecurity Initiative Five (CNCI-5) seeks to connect cybersecurity centers and other cybersecurity analytics electronically and in real time. The Budget provides an increase in funding for CNCI-5 in order to develop a comprehensive, coordinated cybersecurity information sharing system that will serve as the foundation for cybersecurity information sharing requirements across the Government and with appropriate partners. This system will also develop and publish machine readable interoperable technical standards that will allow for automated information sharing. The goal is for relevant pieces of information to make its way to those who need it, regardless of where they are in the Government, within the constraints of policy and law, to connect the dots in identifying cybersecurity threats while protecting individual privacy and civil liberties. In addition, the Budget supports the Senior Information Sharing and Safeguarding Steering Committee, which the President established by Executive Order 13587 in October 2011, to guide and prioritize Government-wide investments in classified networks and to support the Administration's National Strategy for Information Sharing and Safeguarding. The Budget continues to support the protection of these critical networks that facilitate the IC's information sharing and operational requirements.

Modernizes the Information Technology Infrastructure. The IC depends on robust information technology capabilities to support operations and allow for information sharing and collaboration with all authorized users. Management of this information and data is paramount to its usability. Modernization of this infrastructure will develop efficient, interoperable solutions to the IC's storage and data handling challenges. The Budget achieves significant NIP savings by consolidating duplicate information technology infrastructure and applications, and by improving energy efficiency and reducing non-mission critical travel, consistent with Administration policy.

Makes Difficult Cuts and Reforms

Reduces Contractors and Maintains Government Workforce. Consistent with Administration-wide efforts to find savings in the current fiscal environment, the Budget maintains IC Government personnel levels and continues to reduce the IC contractor workforce. The Budget focuses on sustaining the skills in the current IC workforce that have been developed over the past decade.

Achieves Savings Through Reducing or Terminating Lower Priority Programs. Recognizing the challenges of this fiscal environment, the IC has undertaken a comprehensive review of its operational, investment, and infrastructure programs. The NIP budget reflects a deliberative process to ensure that the IC focuses on those programs that have the most significant return and terminates or reduces those considered lower priority or not performing. For example, the Budget includes an initiative to transition to a more efficient space-based architecture that postures the IC for future capabilities.

DEPARTMENT OF EDUCATION

Funding Highlights:

- Provides $71.2 billion in discretionary funding for the Department of Education, which is 4.6 percent, or $3.1 billion, above the 2012 enacted level. This funding builds on the significant gains made through major K-12 reform programs and supports new efforts to help reach the President's 2020 college completion goal.

- Ensures that four-year-olds across the country have access to a high-quality preschool education through a landmark new initiative in partnership with the States.

- Invests $300 million to expand Promise Neighborhoods to improve outcomes for children in high-poverty communities. This investment reflects the President's commitment to create ladders of opportunity in Promise Zones across the country.

- Provides mandatory funding for initiatives to preserve teacher jobs and supports the teaching profession.

- Invests in redesigning high schools to focus on providing students with challenging, relevant learning experiences, and rewarding schools that develop new partnerships with colleges, employers, and non-profit organizations.

- Makes our schools safer by supporting emergency preparedness plans and improving school climates, complementing investments at the Departments of Justice and Health and Human Services to increase school safety and access to mental health services.

- Focuses this year's Race to the Top competition on supporting State efforts to tackle college costs and raise completion levels, while driving innovation and college access through a companion First in the World fund and better leveraging the campus-based aid programs.

- Continues the Administration's strong commitment to maintain historic investments in Pell Grants, while reforming student loan interest rates so they can adjust with the market.

- Places the Department of Education at the center of a major reorganization effort, in partnership with the National Science Foundation and other Federal agencies, to increase the impact of Federal investments in science, technology, engineering, and mathematics education.

Under the leadership of the Department of Education, the Administration has charted a course toward ensuring that every student in America is prepared for college and a career. The Budget pairs new and ongoing K-12 investments with an ambitious new preschool initiative to prepare four-year-olds for learning, and with college cost reforms to improve access, retention, and graduation rates for all students. The Budget also focuses on improving student learning outcomes in mathematics and science, and on preparing students for science, technology, engineering, and mathematics (STEM) career opportunities. Overall, the Budget provides $71.2 billion in discretionary funding for the Department of Education, a 4.6 percent, or $3.1 billion, increase above the 2012 enacted level.

Invests in High-Quality Preschool Education

Enhances the Quality of and Access to Early Childhood Education. The Administration believes that all children should have access to a high-quality preschool education. A child's early years are the most critical for building the foundation needed for success in life. Research has conclusively shown that supporting children at this stage leads to significant benefits in school and beyond. This is particularly true for low-income children, who often start kindergarten academically behind their peers by many months. Providing high-quality early childhood education to all children will enable them to start school ready to learn and realize their full potential. The Budget outlines a proposal to ensure that four-year-olds across the United States have access to high-quality preschool programs, which would be financed through mandatory resources and fully paid for elsewhere in the Budget. This proposal consists of a Federal-State partnership to provide all low- and moderate-income four-year-old children with high-quality preschool, while also providing States with incentives to expand these programs to reach additional children from middle class families and put in place full-day kindergarten policies. To support this effort, the Budget also proposes a $750 million discretionary

investment in Preschool Development Grants in 2014. These grants will ensure that States willing to commit to expanding preschool access are able to make the critical investments necessary to serve their four-year-old children in high-quality programs. The preschool initiative is coupled with a companion investment in the Department of Health and Human Services in voluntary home visiting and high-quality care for infants and toddlers.

Sustains Investments While Ramping up Innovations in Grades K-12

The Department of Education has fueled historic reforms in our education system by rewarding excellence and promoting innovation to help children start school ready to succeed, raise academic standards, ensure that there is an effective teacher in every classroom, and turn around struggling schools. The Budget continues to build on these reforms.

Funds School Turnaround Grants. The Budget provides $659 million for School Turnaround Grants to support the Administration's commitment to help turn around America's persistently lowest-performing schools. This includes $125 million for a new competitive grant program to expand the capacity of school districts to implement effective and sustainable school reform.

Invests in Innovation. One of the Department's trademark programs, Investing in Innovation (i3), uses an evidence-based approach to test new ideas, validate what works, and scale up the most effective approaches. The Budget builds on the success of i3 by providing $215 million, an increase of $66 million above the 2012 enacted level, to support growing the evidence base in high-need areas, including identifying and supporting effective teachers and leaders, improving low-performing schools, and encouraging parent engagement. As part of this investment, i3 will also support up to $65 million for the Advanced Research Projects Agency for Education, which will aggressively pursue technological breakthroughs that transform educational technology and empower teaching and learning similar to the way that the Defense Advanced Research Projects Agency has supported the development of the Internet, GPS, and robotics.

Invests in Promise Neighborhoods. The Budget makes a significant investment in Promise Neighborhoods, funding the program at $300 million, an increase of $240 million over the 2012 enacted level. This initiative supports high-need communities that combine effective, cradle-to-career services for children and families with comprehensive reforms centered on high-quality schools. A portion of these funds will also be targeted to designated Promise Zones—high-poverty communities where the Federal Government will engage more directly with local leaders to break down barriers and help them access and coordinate the resources and expertise they need to create jobs, leverage private investment, increase economic activity, reduce violence, and improve educational opportunities. To further support Promise Zones, the Budget includes companion investments of $400 million in the Department of Housing and Urban Development's Choice Neighborhoods program and $35 million in the Department of Justice's Byrne Criminal Justice Innovation Grants program, as well as tax incentives to promote investment and economic growth.

Supports Teachers and Leaders. Teachers and principals have enormous impacts on students' learning. The Budget continues significant investment to ensure that there is an effective teacher in every classroom through programs such as the Teacher and Leader Innovation Fund and the Effective Teachers and Leaders State Formula Grant program and its 25 percent set-aside for competitive grants. The Administration also recognizes the need to equip school leaders to implement Elementary and Secondary Education Act (ESEA) reforms by providing nearly $100 million for a competition to develop high-quality, large-scale professional development for current school leaders. The Budget also invests $12.5 billion in mandatory funds to help school districts prevent additional teacher layoffs and hire teachers as the economy continues to recover. In

addition, the Budget proposes a $5 billion one-time mandatory investment in the Recognizing Educational Success, Professional Excellence, and Collaborative Teaching (RESPECT) Project, to support States and districts that commit to bold, comprehensive reforms to transform every stage of the teaching profession.

Expands Educational Options. The Budget provides $295 million for the Administration's ESEA reauthorization proposal to increase the supply of high-quality public educational options, especially for students attending low-performing schools. New funds will support the creation and expansion of charter school models shown to be effective in increasing student achievement.

Funds 21st Century Community Learning Centers. The Budget provides $1.3 billion to States and other entities for projects that provide students, particularly those in high-need schools, the additional time, support, and enrichment activities that can improve their achievement. The Budget places a particular focus on programs that support high-quality expanded learning models, which add time to the school day or school year to improve student outcomes.

Maintains Support for Title I and IDEA Grants. The Budget sustains the Department's commitment to supporting education for disadvantaged students and students with disabilities, providing $14.5 billion for ESEA Title I Grants and $11.6 billion for Individuals with Disabilities Education Act (IDEA) Grants to States. These investments provide the resources needed by districts to pay teacher salaries and fund other educational interventions for these groups.

Encourages Smart Reforms by Overhauling Existing Law. The Budget continues to propose reauthorization of ESEA by consolidating a set of existing program authorities into new competitive grant programs that give States and districts more flexibility to use resources where they will have the greatest impact. In the absence of reauthorization, and to build on the successful reforms already underway in States, the Department invited States to apply for ESEA flexibility in exchange for comprehensive State-developed plans designed to increase the quality of instruction and improve educational outcomes for all students. After four rounds of applications, 45 States, the District of Columbia, Puerto Rico, and the Bureau of Indian Education have applied for ESEA flexibility, and of these, 34 States and the District of Columbia have been approved. The Budget maintains investments in key programs that States can use to advance these reforms.

Redesigns High School. The Budget provides $300 million for a new program to strengthen college- and career-readiness by redesigning high school to focus on providing students with challenging, relevant learning experiences, and rewarding schools that develop new partnerships with colleges and employers to support instruction and to help develop the skills students need to be prepared for jobs now and in the future. In addition, the Budget proposes to strengthen and reform career and technical education to better align programs with the needs of employers and higher education.

Makes Our Schools Safer. The President's plan to reduce gun violence and increase school safety requires that we invest not only in preparing our schools for emergencies, but also in creating safe and nurturing climates to prevent future tragedies. The Budget provides $112 million to help schools develop and implement emergency preparedness plans, create safer and more nurturing school climates through evidence-based behavioral intervention practices, provide support and services to children exposed to pervasive violence, collect data on school safety and climate, and highlight best practices regarding school behavioral intervention and discipline policies, including the equitable implementation of these policies. This investment will complement efforts of the Departments of Justice, Health and Human Services, and Homeland Security to support comprehensive school safety strategies and to increase access to mental health services.

Delivers a Quality, Affordable College Education to Millions of Americans

To strengthen our Nation's competitiveness and regain our position of first in the world in our proportion of college graduates, we must open the doors of higher education to more Americans and make sure that students complete their degrees. The Administration has already taken significant strides in making college more affordable. In 2014 more than nine million students will receive Pell Grants, and approximately 11 million borrowers will receive low-cost loans, with new affordable repayment options based on their income after leaving school. This Budget builds on that progress by setting a goal of improved access, increased levels of completion, and better post-graduation outcomes—while reducing costs to students. Key initiatives include:

Tackles College Costs and Helps More Americans Complete College. Although investments in Pell Grants, student financial aid, and higher education tax credits have made higher education more affordable for American families, the rising cost of college continues to be a challenge. Many students struggle to pay their tuition and leave school with significant debt that is difficult to repay. This path is not sustainable. Institutions of higher education have to do their part to rein in costs while delivering a high-value education, and States must continue to invest in higher education and pursue reforms that will make their systems more sustainable in the long run. The investments below are reinforced by the Department's publication of the College Scorecard, which provides students and parents with clear, transparent information they can use to compare schools across cost, completion, earnings, and other metrics.

- *A Higher Education Race to the Top (RTT) Competition.* Building on the success of this program in both early education and K-12 education, the Department of Education will shift the focus of RTT in 2014 to promoting comprehensive reforms in postsecondary education. The Budget provides $1 billion to support competitive grants to States that commit to driving comprehensive change in their higher education policies and practices, while doing more to contain their tuition and make it easier for students to afford a college education. This change establishes RTT as a fund that promotes system-wide reform efforts and can shift its focus each year to support the most promising and comprehensive solutions to strengthen public education and improve outcomes from preschool through college.

- *First in the World Fund.* The Budget provides $260 million for a First in the World fund to spur the development, validation, and scaling-up of cutting-edge innovations to reduce college costs, improve productivity, and boost postsecondary attainment rates. These practices include investing in alternative credentials from new technology-based learning platforms in cases where strong outcomes can clearly be demonstrated. In addition, the First in the World fund will provide new competitive funding to test and expand promising strategies to help low-income high school students prepare for, attend, and succeed at four-year colleges and universities, allowing nonprofits and public and private colleges and universities to explore and implement new ideas and models to promote improved learning and outcomes for high school students.

- *Campus-Based Aid Programs.* The Budget provides more than $10 billion for Supplemental Educational Opportunity Grants, Federal Work Study, and Perkins Loans, including a $150 million increase for the Federal Work Study program to put the program on track to double the number of participants over five years. The Budget also proposes reforms to these programs so that the funds are directed toward institutions that are succeeding in enrolling and graduating students from low-income families, setting a

responsible tuition policy, and demonstrating good value.

Maintains a Strong Pell Grant Program. Since 2008, the Administration has increased the maximum Pell Grant by more than $915, to $5,645. The Budget continues the Administration's strong commitment to the Pell Grant program and to preserving the maximum award, and includes measures that ensure full program funding through the 2015–2016 academic year. The Administration believes that action must be taken to keep the Pell Grant program on a sound footing, and that reforms such as those included in the Budget are necessary to maintain this critical investment in opening the doors of opportunity to all Americans and strengthening our Nation's competitiveness.

Makes Student Loan Interest Rates More Market-Based. Under current law, interest rates on subsidized Stafford loans are slated to rise this summer from 3.4 percent to 6.8 percent. At a time when the economy is still recovering and market interest rates remain low, the Budget proposes a cost-neutral reform to set interest rates so they more closely follow market rates, and to provide students with more affordable repayment options. The rate on new loans would be set each year based on a market interest rate, which would remain fixed for the life of the loan so that student borrowers would have certainty about the rates they would pay. The Budget also expands repayment options to ensure that student borrowers do not have to pay more than 10 percent of their discretionary income on loan payments.

Uses Resources Wisely

Enhances Data and Evaluation to Guide Program Improvements. Leaders at all levels of government are seeking information to help them reform programs and make smarter investments. Recognizing the need for better data across education and human service programs, the Budget provides $85 million, a $47 million increase over the 2012 enacted level, for Statewide Data Systems. The increased funding will support new grants focused on early childhood data systems and projects that enhance States' ability to use data for research and evaluation. To improve Federal data on postsecondary students, the Budget provides $9 million for upgrades to the National Student Loan Data System and $8 million to more frequently survey postsecondary students. These efforts will supply data about who receives student aid, enrollment patterns, and graduation rates for Federal aid recipients. Finally, the Budget includes $67 million in new funding for research and evaluation of Federal student aid. This funding will better harness the Department's data and test innovative strategies for student aid delivery, such as giving aid to students earning college credit while still in high school.

Leads Efforts to Improve the Impact of Federal Investment in STEM Education. The Budget proposes a comprehensive reorganization of STEM education programs to increase the impact of Federal investments in four areas: K-12 instruction; undergraduate education; graduate fellowships; and education activities that typically take place outside the classroom. The reorganization will be implemented with a focus on increasing participation and opportunities for individuals from groups historically underrepresented in these fields. The reorganization involves a consolidation of 90 programs across 11 different agencies and realignment of ongoing STEM education activities to improve the delivery, impact, and visibility of STEM efforts. Nearly $180 million will be redirected from consolidated programs towards the Department of Education, the National Science Foundation (NSF), and the Smithsonian Institution to implement core initiatives in these four priority areas. The Department of Education's role will include developing STEM Innovation Networks to reform STEM instruction and supporting a corps of Master Teachers who can serve as a national resource for improving STEM teaching and learning. NSF will focus on efforts to improve STEM undergraduate education and to reform graduate fellowships so they reach more students and align with national needs. The Smithsonian Institution will improve the reach of informal education activities by ensuring they are aligned with State standards and are relevant to the classroom.

In line with the Government-wide STEM reorganization, the Department will restructure its own existing efforts to lead a cohesive and robust initiative around improving K-12 instruction and working effectively towards the President's goal of generating 100,000 effective STEM teachers over the next decade. The Budget invests $265 million, redirected from within the Department and from other agencies, to support STEM Innovation Networks, which will be districts, or consortia of districts, working in partnership with universities, science agencies, museums, businesses, and other educational entities. These public-private partnerships will work to harness local, regional, and national resources to transform teaching and learning by implementing research-based practices, supporting innovation, and building capacity at both school and district levels. In addition, Networks will leverage the expertise of the Nation's most talented science and math teachers—through a new STEM Master Teachers Corps—to help support and improve instruction in their schools and districts. The new investment also includes $80 million to support the President's goal of preparing 100,000 highly-effective STEM teachers. To reinforce the Department's efforts to improve STEM teaching and learning, the Budget continues support for the joint NSF-Department of Education K-16 Math Initiative.

DEPARTMENT OF ENERGY

Funding Highlights:

- Provides $28.4 billion in discretionary funds for the Department of Energy, an eight percent increase above the 2012 enacted level. This increased funding will position the United States to compete as a world leader in clean energy and advanced manufacturing, enhance our energy security, respond to the threat of climate change, and modernize the nuclear weapons stockpile and infrastructure.

- Maintains the President's commitment to increase funding for key basic research agencies by providing over $5 billion, a 5.7 percent increase over the 2012 enacted level, for the Office of Science for basic research and research infrastructure to lay the foundation for innovation, long-term economic growth, and competitiveness in areas such as foundational science for clean energy and fundamental physics.

- Builds on the Administration's success in reducing our use of oil, promoting energy efficiency, and doubling U.S. renewable electricity generation by increasing funding for the Department's clean energy technology activities by over 40 percent above the 2012 enacted level. Creates new Race to the Top for Energy Efficiency and Grid Modernization awards to support State governments that implement effective policies to increase energy productivity and modernize the grid, and to make progress toward the President's goal of cutting in half the energy wasted by our homes and businesses over the next 20 years.

- Provides $615 million to increase the use and decrease the costs of clean power from solar, wind, geothermal, and water energy.

- Increases the affordability and convenience of advanced vehicles and domestic renewable fuels by investing $575 million in cutting-edge vehicle technologies, $282 million in the next generation of advanced biofuels, and $2 billion of proposed mandatory funding for an Energy Security Trust to transition our cars and trucks off of oil.

- Invests $365 million in advanced manufacturing research and development to strengthen U.S. competitiveness and enable companies to improve product quality and manufacturing processes while cutting production costs by using less energy.

- Achieves savings and efficiencies by eliminating $4 billion in annual unwarranted and unnecessary subsidies to the oil, gas, and coal industries, restructuring the plutonium disposition program, cutting low priority and low performing programs, and increasing utilization of existing facilities and infrastructure.

- Helps consumers and businesses save money and improve their energy efficiency by investing in new technology development, implementing cost-effective appliance standards, and catalyzing private sector investment in more energy efficient buildings through the President's Better Buildings Initiative.

- Invests $16 million—an increase of $10 million—in enhanced energy infrastructure security and energy recovery capabilities.

- Supports modernizing the electricity delivery grid through an investment of $153 million in research and development for smart grid investments, cybersecurity for energy control systems, and permitting, siting, and analysis activities within the Office of Electricity Delivery and Energy Reliability. Advances the technologies and tools for improved clean energy integration onto the grid through an $80 million coordinated effort within the Office of Energy Efficiency and Renewable Energy.

- Increases investments to maintain a safe, secure, and effective nuclear weapons stockpile at levels consistent with planned reductions under the New Strategic Arms Reduction Treaty.

- Strengthens national security by securing, removing, and detecting nuclear and radiological material worldwide.

The Department of Energy (DOE) is charged with advancing the energy, environmental, and nuclear security of the United States, promoting scientific and technological innovation in support of that mission, and ensuring the environmental cleanup of the national nuclear weapons complex. It facilitates many of the President's highest priorities, including cutting carbon pollution, increasing climate preparedness, and supporting clean energy and innovation, which are critical to job creation, long-term economic growth, and national security. In total, the President's 2014 Budget provides $28.4 billion in discretionary funds for DOE to support its mission, an eight percent increase over the 2012 enacted level. It includes $11.7 billion for nuclear security, a six percent increase over the 2012 enacted level. In light of the current discretionary caps, these increases in funding are significant and a testament to the importance of clean energy and innovation to the country's economic future, and the importance of nuclear security to the Nation's safety. While funding has been increased in these critical areas, the Administration has identified areas for savings and efficiency, such as eliminating oil, gas, and coal tax subsidies, restructuring

the plutonium disposition program, and changing the National Ignition Facility's fee structure.

Invests in Clean Energy, Innovation, and Jobs of the Future

Funds Clean Energy Research, Development, and Demonstration to Keep America Competitive and Respond to the Threat of Climate Change. Investing in research and development (R&D) today is critical to leading the clean energy and advanced manufacturing industries of tomorrow. The Budget provides $2.8 billion for the Office of Energy Efficiency and Renewable Energy (EERE) to accelerate research and development, to build on ongoing successes, and to further reduce the costs and increase the use of critical clean energy technologies. Within EERE, the Budget increases funding by 75 percent above 2012 levels for development and demonstration of the next generation of advanced vehicles and by 42 percent for the next generation of advanced biofuels and biorefineries. It increases funding by 29 percent for innovative projects to make clean, renewable power, such as solar energy and off-shore wind, more easily integrated onto the electric grid and as affordable as electricity from conventional sources, without subsidies. It more than doubles funding for energy efficiency and advanced manufacturing activities to help reduce energy use and costs in commercial and residential buildings, in the industrial and business sectors, and in Federal buildings and fleets. These investments will support progress toward the President's goal of cutting in half the energy wasted by our homes and businesses, doubling our energy productivity over the next 20 years. The Budget provides $735 million for the Office of Nuclear Energy, which includes funding for advanced small modular reactors R&D. The Budget also includes $379 million for the Advanced Research Projects Agency–Energy, a program that seeks to fund transformative energy research.

Challenges States to Cut Energy Waste and Support Energy Efficiency and Modernize the Grid. Modeled after a successful Administration approach in education reform designed to promote forward-leaning policies at the State level, the Budget includes $200 million in one-time funding for Race to the Top performance based awards to support State governments that implement effective policies to cut energy waste and modernize the grid. Key opportunities for States include: modernizing utility regulations to encourage cost-effective investments in efficiency, including combined heat and power and demand response resources, and in clean distributed generation; enhancing customer access to data; investments that improve the reliability, security and resilience of the grid; and enhancing the sharing of information regarding grid conditions.

The Administration also continues to call on the Congress to pass HomeStar or similar mandatory funding legislation aimed at creating jobs and spurring economic growth by encouraging Americans to invest in energy saving home improvements. The President's Better Buildings Initiative, launched in 2011, continues to make progress toward a 20 percent improvement in the energy efficiency of commercial and industrial buildings by 2020, including through public-private partnerships under the Better Buildings

Challenge. The Budget also supports increased research and development on innovative building efficiency technologies and the ongoing introduction and enforcement of appliance efficiency standards that save consumers and companies money while improving performance. In addition, the Budget provides $184 million for the Weatherization Assistance Program to help low-income families save hundreds of dollars a year each on their energy bills by making their homes more energy efficient.

Invests in Advanced Energy-Efficient Production Technologies to Strengthen Domestic Manufacturing. The Budget invests in a national effort to develop and commercialize the emerging technologies that will create high quality manufacturing jobs and enhance our global competitiveness. Funding will enable Federal agencies to continue collaboration efforts with the private sector and universities to develop cross-cutting manufacturing technologies. These efforts will speed advancement of ideas from the drawing board to the factory floor, scale up first-of-a-kind technologies, and establish shared facilities and collaborative networks to help small and mid-sized manufacturers innovate and compete. As an integral part of this initiative, the Budget provides DOE with $365 million to expand important efforts on innovative manufacturing processes and advanced industrial materials. These innovations will enable U.S. companies to cut manufacturing costs and reduce the life cycle energy consumption of technologies, while improving product quality and accelerating product development. These activities would include funding to support one or more manufacturing innovation institutes focused on energy and efficiency technologies. These manufacturing R&D centers are part of a larger proposed interagency network aimed at bringing together universities, companies, and the Government to co-invest in solving industry-relevant problems and to create, showcase, and deploy new manufacturing capabilities, products, and processes that can impact large-scale commercial production. The Budget also continues to support the development of competitive new manufacturing processes for advanced vehicles, biofuels, solar energy, wind energy, and other rapidly growing clean energy industries, to help ensure that the technologies developed here are also manufactured here.

Strengthens U.S. Leadership in Advanced Vehicle Development and Production. To lead the world in advanced vehicle development and manufacturing, and to increase the deployment of advanced vehicles, the Budget builds on previous investments supporting electric vehicle and alternative-fuel vehicle manufacturing and adoption in the United States through investments in R&D. The Budget invests $2 billion over the next 10 years from Federal oil and gas development revenue in a new Energy Security Trust that would provide a reliable stream of mandatory funding for R&D on cost-effective transportation alternatives that reduce our dependence on oil. It would be designed to invest in research that will improve and reduce the cost of the technologies of the future—technologies that will allow us to run our cars and trucks on electricity, homegrown biofuels, renewable hydrogen, and domestically produced natural gas. In addition, the Budget advances innovative technologies through $575 million in discretionary funding for vehicle technology activities—an increase of 75 percent over the 2012 enacted level. Funding supports the EV Everywhere initiative, a targeted effort to make electric-powered vehicles as affordable and convenient as gasoline-powered vehicles for the average American family within a decade. This initiative includes accelerated R&D on emerging battery technologies and manufacturing processes to enable production of lower-cost electric vehicles with an improved vehicle range and an increased fast-charging capability. Funding also supports a small number of advanced vehicle deployment communities, which will be competitively selected and will leverage Federal resources to test different real-world approaches to accelerating deployment of advanced vehicles at scale in specific communities.

The Budget continues to promote fuel supply diversification by providing $282 million at DOE to develop and demonstrate conversion technologies to produce cellulosic ethanol and other advanced biofuels, such as algae-derived biofuels and "drop-in" replacements for diesel and jet fuel, for civilian and military uses. In addition, the Budget supports long-term research efforts to promote advanced vehicles, including a battery and energy storage hub, continued fuel cell research, and three Bioenergy Research Centers aimed at developing the scientific understanding underpinning new technological solutions that will enable increased production of advanced biofuels.

Invests in Basic Research and Research Infrastructure to Keep America Competitive. The Budget maintains the President's commitment to increase funding for key basic research agencies, including a 5.7 percent increase over the 2012 enacted level for the Office of Science. To continue the cutting-edge research and development that is essential to U.S. innovation and economic competitiveness, the Budget provides over $5 billion to the Office of Science which funds research grants and unique scientific facilities in several areas of science, including physics, biology, climate and environmental sciences, fusion sciences, computational sciences, materials science, and chemistry. The Budget also includes one-time funding to fully forward fund some five-year awards for new or renewed Energy Frontier Research Centers that conduct basic research aimed at understanding and overcoming the fundamental barriers to transformational advances in many energy technologies. As part of its scientific facilities portfolio, the Office of Science operates U.S. light sources that are used by both biologists and physical scientists to understand the fundamental nature of the world around us, such as the molecular structure of materials and the processes of chemical reactions.

Supports Critical Carbon Capture Research Initiatives. The Budget provides $421 million for the Fossil Energy Research and Development program, including an investment of $266 million in fossil energy R&D primarily dedicated to developing cost-effective carbon capture and storage and advanced power systems. The Budget includes a one-time, $25 million inducement prize for the first natural gas combined cycle power plant to integrate large-scale carbon capture and storage. The Budget also includes $12 million to fund DOE's participation in a multi-agency research initiative aimed at advancing technology and methods to safely and responsibly develop America's natural gas resources. Specifically, DOE, in collaboration with the Environmental Protection Agency and the Department of the Interior, will focus on minimizing the health, safety, and environmental effects of natural gas and oil production from hydraulic fracturing in shale and other geologic formations.

Cuts Wasteful Spending and Improves Efficiency

Eliminates Unnecessary Fossil Fuel Subsidies. As we continue to pursue clean energy technologies that will support future economic growth, we should not devote scarce resources to subsidizing the use of fossil fuels produced by some of the largest, most profitable companies in the world. That is why the Budget proposes to eliminate unnecessary fossil fuel subsidies that impede investment in clean energy sources and undermine efforts to address the threat of climate change. The Budget would repeal over $4 billion per year in tax subsidies to oil, gas, and other fossil fuel producers.

Reduces Energy Use in Federal Buildings. The 270 billion square feet of residential and commercial building space in the United States present an opportunity to realize large gains in energy efficiency. To help the Federal Government lead by example, the Federal Energy Management Program will continue to assist agencies to improve the energy efficiency of Federal buildings (representing over three billion square feet) and to help them implement and monitor performance-based contracts to do so. These contracts provide enough long-term savings in energy costs to more than pay for the up-front investments, achieving savings at no net-cost to the taxpayer.

Enhances Energy Infrastructure Security and Energy Restoration Capabilities. The Budget includes $16 million for new situational awareness investments to be achieved through a DOE regional presence with the Federal Emergency Management Agency, an expanded DOE Emergency Operations Center, and real-time analytic and modeling capabilities to foster a more efficient response to energy emergencies.

Invests in Modernizing the Electricity Delivery Grid. A 21st Century electric grid which is reliable, flexible, efficient, and secure is essential to the Nation's well-being. Within the Office of Electricity Delivery and Energy Reliability, the Budget invests $153 million in R&D and other activities that will further transition to a Smart Grid. This investment seeks to develop real-time situational awareness to improve grid operations, build system-level understanding needed for innovative approaches to technology and regional planning, support advanced visualization analysis and decision support for grid operators leading to predictive response, and enhance security of the grid. It includes $20 million for a new Electricity Systems Hub, which will explore the interface between transmission and distribution systems in the context of a modernized grid. Within EERE, the Budget supports hardware and modeling R&D to improve the integration of clean energy into the electricity distribution grid, including $80 million for a coordinated initiative to develop the technologies and tools to more intelligently, flexibly, and cost-effectively integrate distributed generation, electric vehicles, and residential and commercial buildings loads behind the meter.

Protects Americans from the Threat of Nuclear Harm and Pollution

Modernizes the Nation's Nuclear Deterrent. The Budget proposes $7.87 billion for Weapons Activities, an increase of $654 million, or nine percent above the 2012 enacted level, to maintain a safe, secure, and effective nuclear deterrent as described in the Administration's Nuclear Posture Review (NPR) of 2010. This funding proposal is the result of an unprecedented cooperative analysis and planning process jointly conducted by the National Nuclear Security Administration (NNSA) and the Department of Defense (DOD). The Budget meets the goals of the NPR by funding cost increases for nuclear weapon life extension programs, such as: upgrades to the W76 and B61 nuclear weapons; initiating new upgrades for the W78 and W88 nuclear weapons; improving or replacing aging facilities, such as the Uranium Processing Facility; adding funds for tritium production and plutonium manufacturing and experimentation; and sustaining the existing stockpile by maintaining the underlying science, surveillance, and other support programs. To meet the NPR goals while remaining within the discretionary spending caps currently in place, the Budget proposes to achieve savings by reducing investments in the National Ignition Facility, which failed to achieve ignition in 2012 as scheduled, and by implementing several management efficiencies.

The Budget also proposes $1.25 billion for work on naval reactors, an increase of $166 million, or 15 percent above the 2012 enacted level. This work includes continuing operational support to nuclear powered submarines and aircraft carriers, developing the next generation of reactor for the replacement to the OHIO class ballistic missile submarine, and modernizing the spent nuclear fuel infrastructure.

Further reflecting a close partnership and shared commitment with our Nation's defense, a portion of future funding for NNSA will continue to be included in DOD's outyear budget, providing allocations to NNSA in each budget year.

Prevents the Proliferation of Nuclear Material and Weapons. The Budget proposes $2.14 billion to prevent the proliferation of nuclear weapons. This proposal fully funds Administration priorities to secure and remove nuclear material, develop and field technologies to deter or detect nuclear proliferation, and implement international nonproliferation regulatory controls and safeguards. Decreases to nonproliferation funding are due to the planned December 2013 completion of the domestic uranium enrichment research, development, and demonstration project, and from restructuring the plutonium disposition program. The plutonium disposition program has been building the

Mixed Oxide (MOX) Fuel Fabrication Facility in South Carolina to enable DOE to dispose of plutonium by converting it to MOX fuel and burning it in commercial nuclear reactors. This current plutonium disposition approach may be unaffordable, though, due to cost growth and fiscal pressure. While the Administration will assess the feasibility of alternative plutonium disposition strategies, resulting in a slowdown of MOX Fuel Fabrication Facility construction in 2014, it is nonetheless committed to the overarching goals of the plutonium disposition program to: 1) dispose of excess U.S. plutonium; and 2) achieve Russian disposition of equal quantities of plutonium. The Administration recognizes the importance of the U.S.-Russia Plutonium Management and Disposition Agreement, whereby each side committed to dispose of at least 34 metric tons of weapon-grade plutonium.

Protects the Public from Harmful Exposure to Radioactive Waste and Nuclear Materials at DOE Sites. The Environmental Management (EM) program continues to clean up waste and contamination, focusing on its legally enforceable regulatory commitments. The Budget includes $5.6 billion for EM to ensure that nuclear wastes from the production of weapons during the Cold War are safely processed, secured, and disposed of in a timely manner. The program's cleanup actions include removing radioactive wastes from underground storage tanks, decontaminating and decommissioning old production facilities, and remediating soil and groundwater, primarily at sites in Washington, South Carolina, Idaho, Tennessee, Kentucky, Ohio, and New Mexico.

Securing the Long-Term Disposal of Nuclear Waste

Begins to Implement a New Strategy for the Management and Disposal of Spent Nuclear Fuel and High-Level Radioactive Waste. In 2010, the Administration determined that Yucca Mountain was not a workable solution for disposing of the Nation's spent nuclear fuel and high-level radioactive waste. The Secretary of Energy established the Blue Ribbon Commission on America's Nuclear Future to review options for managing these wastes, and the Commission released its final report in January 2012. After careful consideration of the Commission's recommendations, the Administration released its Strategy for the Management and Disposal of Used Nuclear Fuel and High Level Radioactive Waste in January 2013. The Administration's Strategy supports the principles of the Commission's recommendations and provides a framework for an integrated program for nuclear waste management, including sustainable funding mechanisms. Fundamentals of the Strategy include the creation of a well-defined consent-based facility siting process, implementation of interim storage in the near term, development of geologic disposal as a permanent solution, establishment of a new body to run the program, and an approach to make funds collected to support nuclear waste management more directly available for that purpose. The Budget provides $60 million for transportation, storage, disposal, and siting activities to lay the groundwork for implementing this strategy, as well as related R&D activities.

DEPARTMENT OF HEALTH AND HUMAN SERVICES

Funding Highlights:

- Provides $80.1 billion in discretionary funding for the Department of Health and Human Services, $3.9 billion above the 2012 enacted level. The Budget continues to invest in Administration priorities such as Affordable Care Act implementation, medical research, mental health services, and Head Start. Savings are achieved through difficult trade-offs such as the elimination of the Preventive Health and Health Services Block Grant, and reductions in the Low Income Home Energy Assistance Program and the Community Services Block Grant.

- Supports innovative medical research by providing $31 billion for the National Institutes of Health, including fulfilling the Administration's commitment to enhancing Alzheimer's research.

- Invests in high-quality care for our youngest children, with $1.6 billion in increased discretionary funding for Early Head Start and Child Care and additional funds to expand evidence-based, voluntary home visiting.

- Expands mental health services for youth and families with a $130 million initiative to help teachers and other adults recognize signs of mental illness in young people, provides students with needed services such as counseling to improve mental health services for young people ages 16-25, and trains 5,000 more mental health professionals with a focus on serving students and young adults.

- Supports a nationwide violent death surveillance system and research on the causes and prevention of gun violence with more than $30 million for the Centers for Disease Control and Prevention.

- Supports implementation of the Affordable Care Act's health insurance coverage improvements through the operation, with States, of Health Insurance Marketplaces (also known as Affordable Insurance Exchanges) and the delivery of premium tax credits and cost sharing assistance to make coverage affordable.

- Strengthens Medicare, Medicaid, and other health programs by implementing payment innovations and other reforms that encourage high-quality and efficient care, improve program integrity, and preserve the fundamental compact with seniors, individuals with disabilities, and low-income Americans these programs represent. These improvements will save approximately $400 billion over the next decade.

- Improves access to health care services for American Indians and Alaska Natives by funding additional medical services and staff at new facilities.

- Invests over $3.2 billion, an increase of $30 million above the 2012 enacted level, in discretionary HIV/AIDS prevention and treatment activities across the Centers for Disease Control and Prevention and Health Resources and Services Administration to expand access to affordable health care, prevention, and treatment services and continue to align activities with the National HIV/AIDS Strategy.

- Bolsters food and medical product safety activities by increasing the Food and Drug Administration's total funding by $821 million above the 2012 enacted level and supporting an effort to improve food and drug import safety.

- Strengthens national preparedness for threats to public health, including naturally occurring threats and deliberate attacks, through funding the development and acquisition of next generation medical countermeasures against chemical, biological, radiological, and nuclear threats, and pandemic influenza.

- Eliminates the Preventive Health and Health Service Block Grant because some of these activities can be more effectively implemented through targeted programs within the Centers for Disease Control and Prevention.

- Reinforces our Nation's ability to more quickly detect infectious disease outbreaks through a new Advanced Molecular Detection Initiative and maintains strong epidemiologic and laboratory expertise at the Centers for Disease Control and Prevention.

- Improves access to reproductive and primary health care services for nearly five million low-income individuals through a $327 million investment in family planning.

- Strengthens families by removing financial deterrents to marriage for low-income couples and by modernizing the child support enforcement program to encourage fathers working and engaging with their children.

- Assists vulnerable populations by investing in efforts to reconnect children with family members and supporting the prevention of human trafficking and direct services for domestic victims.

- Targets Low Income Home Energy Assistance Program assistance on the Nation's most vulnerable households with high energy burdens.

The Department of Health and Human Services (HHS) is the principal Federal agency charged with protecting the health of all Americans and providing essential human services. The 2014 Budget includes $80.1 billion to support HHS's mission, $3.9 billion above the 2012 enacted level. Within this level, the Department is carrying out significant responsibilities such as implementing the Affordable Care Act and strengthening program integrity across programs. The Budget also invests in early childhood development, biomedical research, mental health services, and health care for American Indians and Alaska Natives. These increases are offset by tough cuts to programs like the Community Services Block Grant and the Preventive Health and Health Services Block Grant.

Improves Health Care Access, Research, and Quality of Services

Drives Down Health Care Costs by Implementing the Affordable Care Act. The Affordable Care Act took historic and significant steps toward putting the Nation back on a sustainable fiscal course while laying the foundation for a higher-quality, more efficient health care system. In its most recent analysis, the Congressional Budget Office estimated that the Affordable Care Act will reduce the deficit by more than $100 billion over the first decade and by more than $1 trillion in the second decade. At the same time, the Affordable Care Act has the potential to fundamentally transform our health system into one that delivers better care at lower cost. The Affordable Care Act will also ensure that every American can access high-quality, affordable coverage, providing health insurance to nearly 30 million Americans who would otherwise be uninsured. The Affordable Care Act does this by establishing Health Insurance Marketplaces (also known as Affordable Insurance Exchanges), that act as competitive marketplaces to provide millions of Americans and small businesses with "one-stop shopping" for affordable coverage beginning in 2014. It also provides premium tax credit and cost sharing assistance to make coverage affordable and increased Federal support to States expanding Medicaid coverage for low-income adults. Efficiently and effectively implementing these coverage improvements is one of the Administration's highest priorities. The Budget provides resources in support of these efforts, including the operations of the Marketplace to help individuals enroll in the best health insurance coverage option for themselves and their families. The Budget proposes small, targeted reductions in select HHS direct health care programs (e.g., immunizations and cancer screenings) because these services will now be financed through expanded insurance coverage and increased reimbursements for safety net providers beginning in 2014. The Budget also supports entities such as Public Health Departments and Community Based Organizations to develop the capacity to bill third party payers for covered services (e.g., HIV testing, immunizations, and substance abuse treatment).

Supports Biomedical Research at the National Institutes of Health (NIH). Biomedical research contributes to improving the health of the American people, as well as the economy. The Budget includes $31 billion for NIH to support research on-campus and at academic and independent research institutions across the United States, including delivering on the Administration's commitment to enhance investment in Alzheimer's research. Tomorrow's advances in health care depend on today's investments in basic research on the fundamental causes and mechanisms of disease, new technologies to accelerate discoveries, advances in translational sciences, and new investigators and new ideas. The Budget will increase focus on research that aims to increase understanding of the brain, improve the clinical trials network, and enhance the development of new therapeutics to treat diseases and disorders that affect millions of Americans. NIH will implement new policies to collect better data on trainees and institutions' administrative costs.

Improves Mental Health Services. The Budget includes a new $130 million initiative to expand mental health treatment and prevention services, including: $55 million for Project AWARE (Advancing Wellness and Resilience in Education) to provide Mental Health "First Aid" training in schools and communities and to help school districts and their communities work together to ensure that students with mental health issues are referred to the services they need; $50 million to train 5,000 new mental health professionals to serve students and young adults, including social workers, counselors, psychologists, and other mental health professionals; and $25 million for Healthy Transitions, a new competitive grant to help support transitioning youth (ages 16-25) and their families access and navigate behavioral health treatment systems.

Supports Gun Violence Prevention Research. The Budget includes an additional $20 million for the National Violent Death

Reporting System to expand the surveillance system to all States in 2014 to improve our understanding of violence. The Budget also includes $10 million within the Centers for Disease Control and Prevention (CDC) to support research on the causes and prevention of gun violence.

Strengthens the Health Workforce. Strengthening the primary care workforce is critical to reforming America's health care system. Increasing access to primary care health providers can help prevent disease and illness, ensure all Americans have access to high-quality care, and reduce costs by decreasing the need for more invasive treatment that could have been prevented through early care. To increase access, the Budget provides increased resources for primary care training programs and support for health care providers who choose to train and practice in medically-underserved areas. The Budget includes funding that will support over 8,800 health care professionals practicing in underserved areas. In addition, the Budget initiates investments that will help train more than 2,800 additional primary care providers estimated to enter the workforce over the next five years.

Continues Funding for Health Centers. Health centers are a key component of the Nation's health care safety net. To ensure Americans receive comprehensive, high-quality, primary and preventive health care services regardless of their ability to pay, the Budget invests $3.8 billion for health center services in 2014 to support services to an estimated 22 million patients. The Affordable Care Act provides the Health Center program with a total of $9.5 billion through 2015. Health centers will continue to be a critical element of the health system, largely because they can provide an accessible and dependable source of primary care services in underserved communities.

Strengthens Primary Care and Reproductive Health Services for Women. The Budget includes $327 million for the Title X Family Planning program, an increase of $33 million above the 2012 enacted level, to expand access to primary care and reproductive health services for low-income women in historically underserved communities.

Maintains Continuity of Coverage for Low-Income Individuals. The Budget continues to fund Transitional Medical Assistance, which provides continued Medicaid eligibility for low-income adults transitioning to work. States that adopt the Affordable Care Act Medicaid expansion will be able to opt out of Transitional Medical Assistance. It also maintains funding for the Qualified Individuals program, which pays Medicare Part B premiums for qualified low-income seniors.

Improves Access to Health Care for American Indians and Alaska Natives (AI/ANs). The Budget includes $4.4 billion for the Indian Health Service (IHS) to strengthen Federal, tribal, and urban programs that serve over two million AI/ANs at over 650 facilities in 35 States. The Budget provides increased resources to purchase health care services provided outside of the Indian health system when services are not available at IHS-funded facilities. In addition, the Budget funds construction of new and replacement hospitals and health clinics, and staff and operating costs at new and replacement facilities, to increase access to health care services and improve the Indian health system. The Administration has prioritized funding for health care for AI/ANs by proposing increases to the IHS budget of over $800 million in the last four years, which has led to expanded medical services in Indian Country. These budget increases have enabled Tribes to expand self-determination contracts and compacts and have funded associated administrative costs, known as Contract Support Costs (CSC), which Tribes receive from both IHS and the Bureau of Indian Affairs (BIA).

Funding for CSC is an important part of self-determination, but it must be balanced with funding for health care services. In 2012, the Supreme Court ruled in *Salazar v. Ramah Navajo Chapter* that past appropriations language was not sufficiently constructed to execute the longstanding policy of managing CSC costs. The Court identified five legislative remedies, ranging from changing payments for CSC through amendments to underlying self-determination authorities, to enacting line-item appropriations for each contract, to appropriating the full estimates for CSC. Consistent with the Supreme Court ruling, the Budget proposes a new approach for CSC, along with a funding increase, for IHS and BIA to continue the policy of supporting self-determination while protecting funding for health care services for AI/ANs. The Administration looks forward to working with the Tribes and the Congress to develop a balanced, long-term solution.

Expands Access to HIV/AIDS Treatment, Care, and Prevention. The Budget expands access to HIV/AIDS prevention and treatment activities and supports the goals of the National HIV/AIDS Strategy to reduce HIV incidence, increase access to care and optimizing health outcomes for people living with HIV, and reduce HIV-related health disparities. By providing resources for the Affordable Care Act implementation, the Budget will support increased health care coverage for thousands of people living with HIV/AIDS. The Budget increases funding for the Ryan White HIV/AIDS program by $20 million, including an additional $10 million for the AIDS Drug Assistance Program to ensure that individuals living with HIV can access their medications, and an additional $10 million for HIV medical clinics to expand access to care and improve systems for connecting individuals to care and retain them in care over time. The Budget includes an increase of $10 million for CDC HIV/AIDS prevention activities to expand surveillance activities and improve timeliness of data. The Budget also redirects $40 million from less effective activities to support a new $40 million initiative to improve systems that link persons recently diagnosed with HIV to care.

Strengthens the Safety of U.S. Food and Medicines. The Budget includes $2.6 billion in budget authority and $4.7 billion in total program resources for the Food and Drug Administration (FDA). It includes $10 million in new resources to improve the safety of food and medical product imports to the United States through a greater FDA presence in foreign countries such as China.

The Budget includes new user fee programs to support implementation of key elements of the Food Safety Modernization Act. To better protect public health in response to natural or intentional threats, the Budget also invests in FDA's efforts to advance regulatory science and support the review of new medical countermeasures for chemical, radiological, biomedical, and nuclear threats.

Strengthens National Preparedness for All Hazards, Including Naturally Occurring Threats and Intentional Attacks. The Budget includes $415 million to enhance the advanced development of next generation medical counter-measures against chemical, biological, radiological, and nuclear threats, including resources to establish the Strategic Investor, an independent venture capital entity in the Office of the Assistant Secretary for Preparedness and Response. The Budget continues funding for both the NIH Concept Acceleration Program to assist investigators with developing promising new countermeasures, and the FDA's Medical Countermeasures Regulatory Science Initiatives. The Budget also provides $250 million to replenish the BioShield Special Reserve Fund, to provide resources through annual appropriations, renewing the Government's long-term commitment to the acquisition of new medical countermeasures against chemical, biological, nuclear and radiological threats. To further support this long-term commitment, the Budget provides a new, flexible contracting authority. HHS has invested over $10 billion since 2005 to enhance America's ability to rapidly respond to an influenza pandemic. The Budget provides an additional $140 million to continue support for these high-priority activities, including the licensure of influenza vaccines that provide the same protection with a smaller dose, and to support international vaccine production capacity.

Bolsters Effective Prevention and Public Health Programs. The Budget invests $40 million for a new Advanced Molecular Detection initiative (AMD) to allow CDC to more quickly determine where emerging diseases come from, whether microbes are resistant to antibiotics, and how microbes are moving through a population. The AMD initiative will strengthen CDC's epidemiologic and laboratory expertise to effectively guide public health action. The Budget strengthens core public health programs at CDC through an increase of $12 million to reduce health care associated infections in more than 1,800 additional facilities and an increase of $16 million to implement the Food Safety Modernization Act, integrate and enhance national food safety surveillance systems, and improve the ability to attribute illnesses to specific foods. The Budget focuses on detection and elimination of infectious diseases globally through an increase of $15 million to end wild polio virus transmission by the end of 2014. The Budget also allocates the Prevention and Public Health Fund to improve health outcomes through effective public health prevention programs across the United States.

Invests in Behavioral Health Prevention and Treatment. The Budget includes $3.6 billion for the Substance Abuse and Mental Health Services Administration to support the Nation's behavioral health prevention and treatment infrastructure. The Budget maintains the Community Mental Health Services Block Grant and increases the Substance Abuse Prevention and Treatment Block Grant to support States in an effective transition in the first year of the Affordable Care Act that will include expanded coverage for mental health and substance abuse treatment services. The Budget also proposes funding within the Block Grants to encourage States to build provider capacity to bill public and private insurance and to promote the adoption of evidence-based programs.

Invests in Electronic Health Records. The number of health care providers adopting electronic health records (EHRs) is growing rapidly. According to the CDC's National Center for Health Statistics, the percentage of office-based physicians that use an EHR increased from 48 percent in 2009 to 72 percent in 2012. With EHR adoption rising, it is increasingly important that health information technology (IT) investments aim to advance EHR standards, program integrity, and technology to support interoperable

exchange of health data. Furthermore, exchange of health data with appropriate privacy protections, will support new payment and delivery models designed to create value based on quality instead of volume. The Budget provides $26 million for the Office of the National Coordinator for Health IT to support work to advance EHR technology and standards.

Accelerates the Issuance of State Innovation Waivers. The Budget empowers States to develop their own innovation strategies to ensure their residents have access to high-quality, affordable health insurance, achieving the same outcomes as those achieved through the Affordable Care Act. Similar to legislation previously introduced in the Senate and endorsed by the President, the Budget proposes to make "State Innovation Waivers" available starting in 2014, three years earlier than under current law. These State strategies would provide affordable insurance coverage to at least as many residents as would have been covered without the waiver and must not increase the Federal deficit. The Administration is committed to the budget neutrality of these waivers.

Improves Conditions for Vulnerable Populations

Invests in High-Quality Infant and Toddler Care. Research has shown that effective early childhood programs help children succeed in school and beyond. Increasing Federal investments in high-quality early education is a key part of a broader education agenda that will strengthen the Nation's competitiveness and help every child reach his or her potential. The Budget invests $1.4 billion in new Early Head Start-Child Care Partnerships to support States and communities in expanding the availability of high-quality learning opportunities for our youngest children. The Budget also provides an additional $200 million for States to support high-quality child care in 2014 and $7 billion over the next 10 years to maintain the availability of child care subsidies. In addition, the Budget invests $15 billion over the next 10 years to extend and expand evidence-based, voluntary home visiting. These investments will be paired with a new initiative in the Department of Education to expand preschool to all low- and moderate-income four-year-olds.

Promotes Responsible Fatherhood and Strong Families. The Budget proposes policy changes to modernize the Child Support Enforcement Program, which touches the lives of one-quarter of the Nation's children. These policy changes will encourage non-custodial parents to take greater responsibility for their children while maintaining rigorous enforcement efforts. The Budget supports States in providing access and visitation services that can improve a non-custodial parent's relationship with his or her family and increases support for States that pass child support payments through to families rather than retaining them. The program will continue to evaluate the effectiveness of providing employment services aimed at increasing child support payments from non-custodial parents. In addition, the Budget provides $35 million for States to test strategies to overcome financial deterrents to marriage.

Provides Services for Vulnerable Populations. The Administration continues to support flexible funding through waivers that allow States to test innovative approaches to child welfare service delivery and financing, which may help shape future reforms. The Budget provides $45 million over three years to reauthorize grants that help children reconnect with family members. The Budget also includes $10 million for a new initiative to prevent and address domestic human trafficking. This initiative will provide direct services to domestic victims of trafficking, train service providers, and invest in data collection, research, and evaluation.

Provides Targeted Energy Assistance to Low-Income Families. The Budget provides $3 billion for the Low Income Home Energy Assistance Program (LIHEAP) to help struggling families with residential heating and cooling expenses. The Budget targets funds to States with vulnerable households facing high home heating costs. The Budget includes $50 million for competitive grants to help reduce energy burdens for LIHEAP households that rely on persistently high-cost systems.

Cuts and Reforms the Community Services Block Grant (CSBG). CSBG provides funding for the important work of community action agencies, but the program's current structure does too little to hold these agencies accountable for outcomes. The Budget provides $350 million for CSBG and proposes to use competition to target the funds to high-performing agencies that are most successful in meeting important community needs.

Improves the Way Federal Dollars are Spent and Strengthens Long-Term Viability of Current Programs

Reduces Waste, Fraud, and Abuse in Medicare, Medicaid, and the Children's Health Insurance Program (CHIP). Progress has been made in reducing the Medicare fee-for-service improper payment rate and in implementing the Affordable Care Act's anti-fraud provisions. The Budget builds on this progress through a robust set of proposals to strengthen Medicare, Medicaid, and CHIP program integrity. The Budget proposes $640 million in combined mandatory and discretionary program integrity funding to implement activities that reduce payment error rates, prevent fraud and abuse, target high-risk services and supplies, and enhance civil and criminal enforcement for Medicare, Medicaid, and CHIP. For example, the Budget proposes to authorize civil monetary penalties or other intermediate sanctions for providers who do not update enrollment records and permit exclusion of individuals affiliated with entities sanctioned for fraudulent or other prohibited actions from Federal health care programs. The Budget also expands authorities to investigate and prosecute allegations of abuse or neglect of Medicaid beneficiaries in additional health care settings and affirms Medicaid's position as a payer of last resort when another entity is legally liable to pay claims for beneficiaries. These new resources and authorities will better enable the Administration to minimize improper payments and provide greater value for program expenditures to beneficiaries and taxpayers.

Supports Permanent, Fiscally Responsible Reform to Medicare's Payments to Physicians. Medicare payments to physicians are determined under a formula, commonly referred to as the "sustainable growth rate" (SGR). This formula has called for reductions in physician payment rates since 2002, which the Congress has consistently overridden for over 10 years. Under the SGR, physician payment rates would be reduced by about 25 percent in 2014. The Administration is committed to working with the Congress to reform Medicare physician payments to provide predictable payments that incentivize quality and efficiency in a fiscally responsible way. Failing to address this issue creates uncertainty about beneficiaries' access to care. The Administration supports a period of payment stability lasting several years to allow time for the continued development of scalable accountable payment models. Such models can take different forms, but all will have several common attributes such as encouraging care coordination, rewarding practitioners who provide high-quality, efficient care, and holding practitioners accountable through the application of financial risk for consistently providing low quality care at excessive costs. HHS will welcome input from physicians and other professionals in designing these models. Following the period of stability, practitioners will be encouraged to partner with Medicare by participating in an accountable payment model, and over time, the payment update for physician's services would be linked to such participation. Those that successfully participate could receive larger payments under Medicare, while those who provide lower quality, inefficient care would receive lower payments. To complement these changes, the Administration also supports immediate reforms to improve the accuracy of Medicare's current physician payment system.

Improves Medicare's Sustainability by Encouraging High-Quality, Efficient Care. The Budget contains proposals that build on initiatives included in the Affordable Care Act to help extend Medicare's solvency while encouraging provider efficiencies and improved patient care. Specifically, the Budget modifies payments to certain providers to address payments that exceed patient care costs. For example, the Budget proposes to align Medicare payments for drugs with Medicaid rebate policies for low-income beneficiaries. It continues to crack down on fraud, proposing among other policies greater scrutiny over payment for power wheelchairs, and it incentivizes skilled nursing homes to prevent hospital readmissions. These, along with other Medicare proposals, would extend the solvency of the Hospital Insurance Trust Fund by approximately four more years.

Encourages Beneficiaries to Seek High-Value Services. The Budget includes structural changes that will help encourage Medicare beneficiaries to seek high-value health care services. To help improve the financial stability of the Medicare program, the Budget reduces the Federal subsidy of Medicare costs for those beneficiaries who can most afford them, and also introduces a modified Part B deductible for new beneficiaries beginning in 2017. To encourage appropriate use of home health services that are not preceded by inpatient care, new beneficiaries beginning in 2017 would be responsible for a modest copayment for home health services in certain cases. Research indicates that beneficiaries with Medigap plans that provide first dollar or near-first dollar coverage have less incentive to consider the costs of health care services, thus raising Medicare costs and Part B premiums for all beneficiaries. The Budget applies a premium surcharge for new beneficiaries beginning in 2017 if they choose such Medigap coverage. In addition, the Budget alters prescription cost-sharing levels to encourage low-income beneficiaries to choose generic medications when clinically appropriate.

Streamlines Systems and Lowers Drug Costs for Medicare Beneficiaries. The Budget proposes to implement a streamlined, single beneficiary appeals process for managed care plans that integrate Medicare and Medicaid payment and services and serve Medicare-Medicaid enrollees to address the sometimes conflicting requirements in each program. The Budget also proposes to permanently authorize a demonstration that provides retroactive drug coverage for certain low-income Medicare beneficiaries through a single plan, establishing a single point of contact for beneficiaries seeking reimbursement for claims. In addition, the Budget proposes to close the donut hole in the Part D benefit by 2015, rather than 2020, for brand drugs by increasing the discounts offered by the pharmaceutical industry.

Enhances Accountability in the Medicaid Program. Medicaid is critically important to providing health care coverage to the neediest Americans, and the Administration strongly supports State efforts to expand Medicaid with the increased Federal funding provided in the Affordable Care Act. The Budget seeks to preserve the existing partnership between States and the Federal Government while making Medicaid more efficient and sustainable through sensible, targeted, Medicaid reforms. For example, the Budget helps States and the Federal Government leverage more efficient reimbursement rates for durable medical equipment based on Medicare rates. The Budget also better aligns Medicaid Disproportionate Share Hospital (DSH) payments with expected levels of uncompensated care by beginning the scheduled reductions in 2015, and bases future State DSH allotments on States' actual DSH allotments as reduced by the Affordable Care Act. In addition, the Budget would improve rebate and payment policies for Medicaid prescription drugs. These proposals are projected to save approximately $16.9 billion over 10 years.

DEPARTMENT OF HOMELAND SECURITY

Funding Highlights:

- Provides $39 billion in discretionary funding for the Department of Homeland Security, a decrease of 1.5 percent, or $615 million, below the 2012 enacted level. The Budget funds critical capital needs and continues a commitment to core homeland security functions, such as transportation security, cybersecurity, and border security. Estimated savings of more than $1.3 billion are created by reducing administrative costs and streamlining professional services. To improve disaster preparedness, the Budget reforms homeland security grants by allocating resources based on risk reduction.

- Protects our citizens and agricultural economy from future threats by investing $714 million in a new, state-of-the-art laboratory to develop countermeasures for diseases originating from large animals that can be transmitted to humans.

- Allocates $44 million in new funding in support of the expansion of the Comprehensive National Cybersecurity Initiative Five to develop a comprehensive and coordinated system that will foster cybersecurity information sharing across the Government while protecting individual privacy and civil liberties.

- Eliminates duplicative, stand-alone Federal Emergency Management Agency grant programs, consolidating them into a new homeland security grants program to better develop, sustain, and leverage core capabilities across the United States to support national preparedness.

- Focuses immigration detention resources on priority aliens such as criminals, repeat immigration law violators, recent border entrants, and immigration fugitives, and expands resources for electronic monitoring and supervision.

- Provides $114 million to support, expand, and enhance the E-Verify system to build additional system capacity, enhance fraud-prevention and detection capabilities, and improve individuals' ability to ensure their employment eligibility records are accurate.

- Promotes innovation and economic growth by providing $494 million to fund important research and development advances in cybersecurity, explosives detection, and chemical/biological response systems.

- Supports job growth and expansion of the U.S. economy with $221 million to add 1,600 new Customs and Border Protection officers and mobile equipment that will result in faster processing and inspecting of passengers and cargo at U.S. ports of entry, as well as more seizures of illegal items, such as drugs, guns, and counterfeit goods.

The Department of Homeland Security's (DHS) mission is to ensure that America is safe, secure, and resilient against terrorism and other hazards. DHS has responsibility for leading all levels of government and working with the private sector to prepare for and respond to natural disasters and other threats. To ensure fiscal sustainability in a complex world of threats and hazards, DHS leverages its investment through risk-based decision making. DHS promotes information sharing and collaborative planning between Federal, State, local, and tribal partners. The President's 2014 Budget includes $39 billion to support the Department, $615 million less than the 2012 enacted level. The Budget reflects an estimated savings of more than $1.3 billion from efficiencies implemented in administrative categories including travel, strategic sourcing, overtime pay, and fleet management.

Protects the Homeland

Invests in New Facilities for Health Security. The Budget includes $714 million for a new National Bio and Agro-Defense Facility (NBAF) to study large animal zoonotic diseases and develop countermeasures to protect our citizens and agricultural economy from future threats. This facility will replace the Plum Island Animal Disease Center, which will soon reach the end of its useful life.

Continues Strong Support for Cybersecurity Initiatives. The Budget includes $810 million to support the National Protection and Programs Directorate's efforts to protect Federal computer systems and networks from cyber attack, disruptions, and exploitations, strengthen State and local governments' cybersecurity capacity, and support private sector efforts to protect critical infrastructure. The Budget also sup-

ports the development of a concept of operations to co-locate key civilian cybersecurity agencies to promote a whole of government approach to cybersecurity incident response. New funding of $44 million will foster cybersecurity information sharing across the Government while protecting individual privacy and civil liberties.

Sustains Essential Fire and Emergency Response Coverage. The Budget provides over $1 billion in assistance to States and local governments for the retention, rehiring, and hiring of firefighters and emergency management personnel in 2014.

Sustains Aviation Security. The Budget includes $4.8 billion for the Transportation Security Administration to sustain critical investments in aviation security that will continue to protect the American traveling public from terrorist threats.

Makes Smart Choices to Balance Priorities

Streamlines and Restructures FEMA Grant Programs. First responders are at the forefront of addressing natural disasters and other threats. The Budget provides $2.1 billion for State and local programs to hire, equip, and train first responders and build preparedness capabilities. To better target these funds, the Budget proposes eliminating duplicative, stand-alone grant programs, consolidating them into the National Preparedness Grant Program. This initiative is designed to build, sustain, and leverage core capabilities as established in the National Preparedness Goal. Using a competitive risk-based model, the National Preparedness Grant Program will apply a comprehensive process that identifies and prioritizes deployable capabilities, ensures grantees put funding to work

---

FEMA Response to Hurricane Sandy

Hurricane Sandy struck in late October 2012, devastating the East Coast from North Carolina to Maine. Thousands of individuals were displaced, millions were left without power, businesses were shuttered, and fuel distribution was severely disrupted in one of the most costly natural disasters in U.S. history.

Building on lessons learned from Hurricane Katrina, the Federal Emergency Management Agency (FEMA) prepositioned teams and supplies in the path of the storm before it made landfall. At the peak of the response effort, FEMA deployed over 7,000 individuals to assist impacted communities, including the first-ever activation of FEMA Corps, an innovative new partnership with the Corporation for National and Community Service that brings young people interested in careers in emergency management into public service. FEMA opened over 70 Disaster Recovery Centers, and provided food, blankets, and other needed commodities to thousands of survivors in New York, New Jersey, and the other impacted States. FEMA has provided over $3.5 billion to help return individuals to their homes, repair public infrastructure, and invest in mitigation efforts to prepare for future severe weather events.

FEMA continues to work with States, local communities, other Federal agencies, and thousands of volunteers to help the impacted areas recover and rebuild. In 2014, the Budget supports the recovery of States and communities that have been devastated by disasters and emergencies by replenishing FEMA's Disaster Relief Fund with $6.2 billion.

---

more quickly, and requires grantees to regularly report progress in the acquisition and development of these capabilities.

Keeps Capital Investment on Track. The Budget provides $3.4 billion for the major asset acquisitions planned in 2014. In addition to funding NBAF and cybersecurity investments, the Budget continues to fund border surveillance technology to improve the security of our borders.

Aligns Immigration Detention and Alternatives to Detention Capabilities with Risk. Under this Administration, the U.S. Immigration and Customs Enforcement (ICE) has focused its immigration enforcement efforts on identifying and removing priority aliens such as criminals, repeat immigration law violators, recent border entrants, and immigration fugitives. To ensure the most cost-effective use of Federal dollars, the Budget aligns ICE capabilities to place priority and mandatory detainees in detention, while allowing low-risk, non-mandatory detainees to enroll in lower cost parole-like alternatives to detention programs, which may include electronic monitoring and supervision. As ICE continues to focus on priority cases, it will work to reduce the time removable aliens spend in detention custody. To achieve this goal, ICE is working with the Department of Justice to expedite removal of convicted criminal aliens to reduce costly stays in U.S. immigration detention prior to deportation.

Enhances the Administration's Employment Eligibility Verification System, E-Verify. In order to assist U.S. employers with maintaining a legal workforce, the Budget proposes $114 million to support, expand, and enhance E-Verify. The President's proposal invests in improvements to the system's fraud-prevention and detection capabilities, modernizes E-Verify customer service to improve ease of use, and invests in additional capacity to support continued expansion. More than 430,000 employers are currently enrolled in E-Verify and the program continues to grow by approximately 1,500 new employers each week.

Although E-Verify is primarily a service for employers, the Budget also enhances the E-Verify

Self Check service, the first online E-Verify service offered directly to workers. Self Check offers individuals a tool to check their own employment eligibility status, as well as guidance on how to correct their eligibility records. This provides U.S. workers with the opportunity to ensure employment authorization records are accurate before getting a job and improves employee understanding of the employment eligibility process.

Promotes Secure Long-Term Growth

Supports Individuals on the Path to Citizenship. The Budget proposes $10 million to assist individuals on the pathway to naturalization and increases support for local programs that develop innovative techniques to improve citizenship education and share best-practices for integrating new citizens into American communities.

Invests in Research and Development in Homeland Security. To continue progress in enhancing homeland security technology, the Budget proposes $494 million for research and development activities. This funding will target opportunities in cybersecurity, explosives detection, and chemical and biological detection.

Strengthens Travel and Trade. The Budget proposes $221 million to add 1,600 Customs and Border Protection (CBP) officers and more inspections equipment and technology at U.S. ports of entry. This funding will help CBP process increased travel and trade arriving at our air, land, and sea ports. These investments will reduce wait times and speed the flow of trade and tourism. Additionally, this funding will result in the seizure of more illegal items, including counterfeit and fraudulent goods, further protecting U.S. businesses.

DEPARTMENT OF THE INTERIOR

Funding Highlights:

- Provides $11.7 billion in discretionary funding for the Department of the Interior, an increase of over four percent above the 2012 enacted level. This funding level reflects an ongoing commitment to protect critical landscapes and infrastructure, partially paid for with savings achieved through administrative efficiencies.

- Promotes job creation and economic growth by conserving landscapes and promoting outdoor recreation in national parks, refuges, and on other public lands through the America's Great Outdoors initiative.

- Proposes for the first time a dedicated source of long-term funding—reaching $900 million by 2015—for Land and Water Conservation Fund programs to support land conservation and resource protection, in collaboration with Federal, State, and local partners.

- Invests in the safety, reliability, and efficiency of America's water infrastructure and in the protection and restoration of fragile aquatic ecosystems.

- Continues efforts to manage and promote the ecological sustainability and resilience of ecosystems on a landscape and watershed scale such as the California Bay-Delta, the Everglades, the Great Lakes, Chesapeake Bay, and the Gulf Coast.

- Proposes oil and gas management reforms to save $2.5 billion over 10 years by building on the Administration's efforts to encourage diligent development of Federal energy resources while improving the return to taxpayers from royalty reforms.

- Provides robust support for energy development on Federal lands and waters and continues investments to strengthen safety oversight for offshore oil and gas operations.

- Supports tribal priorities in Indian Country by increasing funding for public safety and justice, natural resources, and assistance for Tribes that assume responsibility for managing Federal programs.

- Reforms oversight of mining on Federal lands and reduces the environmental impacts of coal and hardrock mining by dedicating and prioritizing funds to reclaim abandoned mines.

- Invests in science to support decision-making in the Department's resource management and trust responsibilities.

- Saves over $200 million from 2010 levels through administrative efficiencies and reduced spending in travel, printing, supplies, and advisory services.

The Department of the Interior's (DOI's) mission is to protect America's natural resources and cultural heritage; manage development of energy and mineral resources on Federal lands and waters; provide scientific and other information about those resources; and honor its trust responsibilities and special commitments to American Indians, Alaska Natives, and Insular areas. In support of this mission, the Budget provides $11.7 billion for DOI, a four percent increase over the 2012 enacted level. The Budget represents an unprecedented commitment to America's natural heritage by proposing mandatory funds for Land and Water Conservation Fund (LWCF) programs. This funding will provide the stability needed for agencies and States to make strategic, long-term investments in our natural infrastructure and outdoor economy to support jobs, preserve natural and cultural resources, bolster outdoor recreation opportunities, and protect wildlife. The Budget also includes legislative proposals that will save taxpayers more than $3 billion over the next 10 years, including reforms to fees, royalties, and other payments related to oil, gas, coal, and other mineral development on Federal lands and waters.

Promotes Economic Growth by Investing in Our Natural and Energy Resources

Creates Jobs Through Conservation and Recreation. The America's Great Outdoors (AGO) initiative supports Federal, State, local, and tribal conservation efforts, while reconnecting Americans, particularly young people, to the outdoors. Investments for AGO programs support conservation and outdoor recreation activities nationwide that create and maintain millions of jobs, generate hundreds of millions of dollars in tax revenue, and spur billions in total national economic activity. For the first time ever, the Budget proposes mandatory funding for LWCF programs in the Departments of the Interior and Agriculture, including $200 million in mandatory funds out of $600 million overall for LWCF programs in 2014. Starting in 2015, the Budget proposes $900 million annually in mandatory funding, which is equal to the amount of oil and gas receipts deposited in the LWCF each year. In 2014, $356 million is proposed to conserve lands in or near national parks, refuges, forests, and other public lands, including $169 million in collaborative LWCF funds for DOI and the U.S. Forest Service to jointly and strategically conserve the most critical landscapes. The Budget also proposes $15 million in LWCF funding to revive the Urban Parks Recreation and Recovery Program, which can help revitalize urban parks and increase access to trails, green space, and other recreational areas in the most underserved urban communities. Other AGO programs include grant programs that assist States, Tribes, local governments, landowners, and private groups (such as sportsmen) in preserving wildlife habitat, wetlands, historic battlefields, regional parks, and the countless other sites that form the mosaic of our cultural and natural legacy. They also include funds for operating national parks, refuges, and public lands, which are critical for conserving natural and cultural resources, protecting wildlife, and drawing recreational tourists from across the United States and the world.

Protects and Restores Water Resources and Infrastructure. The Budget invests in the safety, reliability, efficiency, and ecological sustainability of our water infrastructure, to ensure the continued delivery of water and power to millions of customers and serve as a foundation for a healthy economy, especially in the arid West. The Budget continues investments in the protection and restoration of fragile aquatic ecosystems, such as California's Bay-Delta and the San Joaquin River, to ensure that such environmental treasures are available for future generations. These investments are made possible by making difficult choices elsewhere, finding savings and consolidations, and reaping the benefits of smart choices made in previous years. Examples of difficult choices include severely curtailing the study of new projects and construction of ongoing projects, proposing to merge the Central Utah Project Completion Act Office with the Bureau of Reclamation, and emphasizing water reuse, recycling, and conservation programs over new construction.

Makes Public Lands Available for Clean Energy Infrastructure Projects. To enhance energy security and create green jobs in new industries, the Budget proposes key funding increases for DOI renewable energy development activities and related transmission infrastructure. This funding includes $100 million to maintain capacity to review and permit new renewable energy projects on Federal lands and waters.

Continues Support for Responsible Development of the Nation's Oil and Gas Resources. The Budget proposes $169 million and $222 million, respectively, to fund the Bureau of Ocean Energy Management and the Bureau of Safety and Environmental Enforcement, which share responsibility for overseeing development of oil and gas resources on the Outer Continental Shelf (OCS). The current OCS five-year leasing program will make more than 75 percent of estimated undiscovered technically recoverable oil and gas resources on the OCS available for development. Funding increases will support continued reforms to strengthen oversight of industry operations following the 2010 Deepwater Horizon oil spill, with an additional emphasis on ensuring the safe and responsible development of Arctic OCS resources.

The Budget also provides robust support for onshore energy permitting and oversight on Federal lands, with a more than 20 percent increase over the 2012 enacted level in discretionary funding for the oil and gas program of the Bureau of Land Management (BLM). Combined with an extended and revamped permitting pilot office authority and ongoing administrative efforts, these resources will facilitate improved responsiveness to permit requests and will strengthen oversight and enforcement of industry operations. BLM's costs would be partially offset through new inspection fees totaling $48 million in 2014, requiring the onshore industry to bear a greater share of the cost of managing the program from which it benefits, just as the offshore industry does.

Protects Communities and Ecosystems from Wildfire Damage. The Budget continues the long-standing practice of fully funding the 10-year average cost of wildland fire suppression operations. The Budget also targets funding for reducing hazardous fuels near communities where these treatments are most effective at reducing risks. Priority is given to projects in communities that have met "Firewise" standards (or the equivalent), identified acres to be treated, and invested in local solutions to protect against wildland fire. In response to last year's severe fire season, the Budget increases funding for burned area rehabilitation.

Strengthens Tribal Nations. The Administration supports the principle of tribal self-determination and improved outcomes with a $10 million increase over the 2012 enacted level to assist Tribes when they manage Federal programs themselves under self-determination contracts and self-governance compacts. Funding for Contract Support Costs (CSC) is an important part of self-determination, but it must be balanced with funding for other tribal program services. In 2012, the Supreme Court ruled in *Salazar v. Ramah Navajo Chapter* that past appropriations language was not sufficiently constructed to execute the longstanding policy of managing CSC costs. The Court identified five remedies, ranging from changing payments for CSC through amendments to underlying self-determination authorities, to enacting line-item appropriations for each contract, to paying the full estimates for CSC. Consistent with one of the remedies identified in the Supreme Court ruling, the Budget proposes a short-term approach for CSC, along with funding increases for the Bureau of Indian Affairs and the Indian Health Service, to continue the policy of supporting self-determination while protecting funding for other tribal program services. The Administration looks forward to working with Tribes and the Congress to develop a balanced, long-term solution.

Administration efforts to combat crime in Indian Country through cooperation between Federal, State, and tribal entities are making progress, as demonstrated by a pilot program to reduce violent crime on selected reservations. The Budget builds on this progress with increased funds for operating tribal courts, staffing new detention centers, and coordinating community policing programs to reduce crime. The Budget also includes increases to meet needs due to growing enrollment at tribal colleges and to promote economic development and job growth in Indian Country through technical and scientific support for natural resources management and renewable energy potential.

Improves Oversight and Use of Federal Dollars

Reforms Federal Oil and Gas Management. The U.S. Treasury received over $9 billion in 2012 from fees, royalties, and other payments related to oil and gas development on Federal lands and waters. A number of recent studies by the Government Accountability Office and DOI's Inspector General have found that taxpayers could earn a better return through policy changes and more rigorous oversight. The Budget proposes a package of legislative reforms to bolster administrative actions being taken to reform the management of DOI's onshore and offshore oil and gas programs, with a key focus on improving the return to taxpayers from the sale of these Federal resources and on improving transparency and oversight. Proposed statutory and administrative changes fall into three general categories: advancing royalty reforms; encouraging diligent development of oil and gas leases; and improving revenue collection processes.

Royalty reforms include establishing minimum royalty rates for oil, gas, and similar products; increasing the standard onshore oil and gas royalty rate; piloting a price-based sliding scale royalty rate; and repealing legislatively-mandated royalty relief. Diligent development requirements include shorter primary lease terms, stricter enforcement of lease terms, and monetary incentives to get leases into production (e.g., a new per-acre fee on nonproducing leases). Revenue collection improvements include simplification of the royalty valuation process, elimination of interest accruals on company overpayments of royalties, and permanent repeal of DOI's authority to accept in-kind royalty payments. Collectively, these reforms will generate roughly $2.5 billion in net revenue to the Treasury over 10 years. Many States will also benefit from higher Federal revenue sharing payments as a result of these reforms.

Reforms Mining Operations and Reduces the Environmental Impacts of Mining. The Budget addresses the environmental impacts of past mining by dedicating and prioritizing funds to clean up abandoned mines. Currently, DOI collects from the coal industry an abandoned mine lands (AML) fee for cleaning up abandoned mines. The Budget proposes to establish a new AML fee on hardrock mining, with receipts used by States, Tribes, and Federal agencies to restore the most hazardous hardrock AML sites on both public and private lands. For non-Federal lands, each State and Tribe would select its own priority projects according to national criteria, similar to how coal AML funds are allocated. A hardrock AML fee would hold the hardrock mining industry accountable for legacy sites in the same manner as the coal mining industry is held accountable today.

Eliminates Wasteful Spending and Provides a Fair Return to Taxpayers from Mineral Development. The Budget proposes a number of other actions that eliminate wasteful spending and ensure taxpayers receive a fair return from mining on Federal lands, including:

- Charging a royalty on select hardrock minerals, such as silver, gold and copper;

- Terminating unwarranted payments to coal-producing States and Tribes that no longer need funds to clean up abandoned coal mines;

- Extending net receipts sharing, where States receiving mineral revenue payments help defray the costs of managing the mineral leases that generate the revenue; and Reauthorizing the Helium Fund and encouraging the development of a fair-market price for helium sales.

Increases Investments in Science and Evaluation to Support Decision-Making. The Budget provides strong support for basic and applied science in support of decision-making, including over $960 million for research and development, an 18 percent increase over the 2012 enacted level. This funding supports scientific monitoring, research, and analysis to assist decision-making in resource management and the special trust responsibilities of DOI and other federally mandated and nationally-significant programs. Specific activities supported include energy permitting, ecosystem management, oil spill restoration, Earth observations (such as water and wildlife monitoring), and tribal natural resource management.

The Budget also funds four independent evaluations to increase the use of evidence and analysis to promote rigor, transparency, and independence in decision-making at DOI. The Bureau of Indian Education (BIE) will commission an independent evaluation to examine the role of BIE and guide future reforms to improve educational opportunities for Native American children. DOI will also conduct a comprehensive evaluation of Federal policy and engagement on Indian water rights issues that analyzes options to improve policies, programs, and budgetary coordination. This evaluation will help to strengthen the oversight, management and analytical capabilities of the Indian Water Rights Office and other bureaus and offices that work on these issues. The Budget supports the Bureau of Reclamation's in-house analytical capabilities to allow for more rigorous economic and evidence-based evaluation of Reclamation's programs, projects, and operations. Finally, DOI will commission an independent, public evaluation of the Payments in Lieu of Taxes (PILT) program, which expires at the end of 2013 and is proposed for a one-year extension. The evaluation will look at PILT—in both concept and practice—with a goal of developing options to put the program on a sustainable long-term funding path.

DEPARTMENT OF HOUSING AND URBAN DEVELOPMENT

Funding Highlights:

- Provides $47.6 billion for Department of Housing and Urban Development (HUD) programs, an increase of $4.2 billion, or 9.7 percent, above the 2012 enacted level. Over 90 percent of this funding increase is used to maintain current levels of rental and homelessness assistance for vulnerable families. The Budget also makes investments to revitalize high-poverty neighborhoods, reduce blight in communities hardest hit by the foreclosure crisis, and support sustainable economic development. Savings are achieved through reduced funding for new affordable housing construction and reforms to the Department's rental assistance programs that do not reduce the number of families served.

- Includes $37.4 billion to provide rental housing assistance to 4.7 million low-income families and $2.4 billion to continue progress toward the Administration's goal to end chronic homelessness and homelessness among veterans and families.

- Provides $400 million to transform neighborhoods with distressed HUD-assisted housing and concentrated poverty into opportunity-rich, mixed-income neighborhoods. This investment reflects the President's commitment to creating ladders of opportunity in high-poverty Promise Zones across the United States.

- Maintains support for housing counseling services, including assistance for families in danger of foreclosure, and continues to offer loss mitigation solutions for Federal Housing Administration-insured borrowers. The Budget also includes actions to reduce the Federal Housing Administration's exposure to risk and proposes reforms to strengthen its programs, which continue to play a critical role in the national mortgage market.

- Provides $3 billion for the Community Development Block Grant program and neighborhood stabilization activities, including $200 million in new competitive funding to further reduce and repurpose vacant and blighted properties and create jobs in communities hardest hit by the foreclosure crisis. The Budget also continues to support an investment of $15 billion for the Project Rebuild program to bring neighborhood stabilization to national scale.

- Includes $75 million to help communities develop comprehensive housing and transportation plans that increase transit-accessible housing, reduce energy consumption and greenhouse gas emissions, and expand economic opportunities.

- Expands the Moving to Work Program to test innovative, locally-driven rental assistance policies to achieve positive outcomes for families, streamline program administration, and reduce Federal costs. To build evidence of what works, this expansion is accompanied by rigorous reporting and evaluation requirements.

- Provides $726 million to address the housing needs of Native American Tribes and $332 million for a modernized Housing Opportunities for Persons with AIDS program that will target funds to areas with the highest need.

- Reduces funding for the HOME Investment Partnerships program. The Budget mitigates this reduction by providing $1 billion to capitalize the Housing Trust Fund to expand the supply of housing targeted to very-low income families.

- Reduces costs in HUD's core Rental Assistance programs by simplifying administration of the medical expense deduction, better targeting rental assistance to the working poor, and setting more equitable Public Housing rents.

The Department of Housing and Urban Development (HUD) supports home ownership, access to affordable housing free from discrimination, and community development. The President's Budget provides $47.6 billion for HUD programs to support these efforts, an increase of $4.2 billion over the 2012 enacted level. Increases are provided to protect vulnerable families and support community-centered investments, including funding to revitalize neighborhoods with distressed HUD-assisted housing and concentrated poverty. To build evidence of what works, State and local public housing authorities are offered program flexibilities in exchange for designing and rigorously evaluating innovative programs and policies. The constrained fiscal environment also forced tough choices, including funding reductions to programs that increase the supply of affordable housing.

Provides Housing Assistance to Vulnerable Families

Supports Affordable Rental Housing for 4.5 million Families. The Budget includes $20 billion for the Housing Choice Voucher program to help more than 2.2 million low-income families afford decent housing in neighborhoods of their choice. This funding level supports all existing vouchers and provides 10,000 new vouchers targeted to homeless veterans. The Budget also includes $10.3 billion for the Project-Based Rental Assistance program to maintain affordable rental housing for 1.2 million families, and provides $6.6 billion in operating and capital subsidies to preserve affordable public housing for an additional 1.1 million families. An additional $10 million for the Rental Assistance Demonstration will be targeted to Public Housing properties in high-poverty neighborhoods, including designated Promise Zones, where the Administration is also supporting comprehensive revitalization efforts.

Makes Progress on the Federal Strategic Plan to Prevent and End Homelessness. The Budget provides $2.4 billion for Homeless Assistance Grants, $480 million above the 2012 enacted level. This funding maintains the approximately 325,000 HUD-funded beds that assist the homeless nationwide and expands rapid re-housing and permanent supportive housing. Backed with new data and emerging best practices across the United States, this evidence-based investment will make further progress toward the goals laid out in the Federal Strategic Plan.

Supports the Housing Sector and Invests in High-Poverty Communities and Sustainable Economic Development

Transforms Distressed HUD-Assisted Housing and High-Poverty Neighborhoods. The Budget provides $400 million for Choice Neighborhoods to continue to transform neighborhoods of concentrated poverty into opportunity-rich, mixed-income neighborhoods. This funding level, which is $280 million above 2012 enacted, will be used to revitalize HUD-assisted housing and surrounding neighborhoods through partnerships between local governments, housing authorities, nonprofits, and for-profit developers. A portion of these funds will be targeted to designated Promise Zones—high-poverty communities where the Federal Government will work with local leadership to invest and engage more intensely to create jobs, leverage private investment, increase economic activity, reduce violence and expand educational opportunities. To further support Promise Zones, the Budget includes companion investments of $300 million in the Department of Education's Promise Neighborhoods program and $35 million in the Department of Justice's Byrne Criminal Justice Innovation Grants program, as well as tax incentives to promote investment and economic growth.

Supports the Mortgage Market and Helps Borrowers Who are at Risk of Foreclosure. The Administration projects that the Federal Housing Administration (FHA) will insure $178 billion in mortgage loans in 2014, supporting new home purchases and refinanced mortgages that significantly reduce borrower payments. FHA financing was used for 27 percent of home purchase loans in 2011, including an estimated 41 percent of first-time homeowners. FHA's loss mitigation program minimizes the risk of financially struggling borrowers going into foreclosure, and since the start of the mortgage crisis, it has helped more than a million homeowners. Recent increases in FHA premium levels will boost FHA's capital reserves and increase Federal revenues. The Budget also includes $132 million for housing and homeowner counseling through HUD and the Neighborhood Reinvestment Corporation (NeighborWorks). Over half of these funds are dedicated to foreclosure assistance. NeighborWorks' National Foreclosure Mitigation Counseling program has assisted over 1.4 million households since its inception in 2008.

Invests in Community Development and Neighborhoods Most Affected by Foreclosures. The Budget provides $3 billion for the Community Development Block Grant (CDBG) program and neighborhood stabilization activities, and proposes reforms to better target CDBG investments to address local community development goals. This funding level includes $200 million in new competitive funds to continue mitigating the impacts of the foreclosure crisis. This funding will provide essential new resources to help communities hardest hit by the foreclosure crisis while creating jobs through rehabilitating, repurposing, and demolishing vacant and blighted properties. The Budget also continues to support the $15 billion Project Rebuild program, which will leverage private capital to bring the benefits of neighborhood stabilization to national scale.

Supports Strategic Housing and Infrastructure Planning and Investments. As part of the Administration's multiagency partnership between HUD, the Department of Transportation, and the Environmental Protection Agency, the Budget provides $75 million in Integrated Planning and Investment Grants to create incentives for communities to develop and implement comprehensive housing and transportation plans, such as updates to building codes, land use and zoning ordinances, that result in more resilient economic development, reduce energy consumption and greenhouse gas emissions, and increase affordable housing near public transit. This funding will support about 30 additional regional and neighborhood planning and implementation grants to enable communities to align public and private investments in housing, transportation, and infrastructure. These efforts also align with a broader Administration commitment to help communities improve their resilience to extreme weather and other climate change impacts through direct technical assistance, data and tools on projected impacts, and other support.

Improves the Way Federal Dollars are Spent and Builds Evidence of What Works

Expands the Moving to Work (MTW) Program with Strong Reporting and Evaluation Requirements. The Budget proposes to scale up the MTW program, which gives high-performing state and local Public Housing Authorities (PHAs) various flexibilities in their use of Housing Choice Voucher and Public Housing funds. In exchange for this flexibility, PHAs will help design and test innovative policies to support self-sufficiency and other positive outcomes for families, streamline and consolidate program delivery, and reduce long-term costs. In addition, PHAs will report on outcomes associated with their MTW activities, and those that choose to implement work requirements, time limits on assistance, or major rent reform initiatives will participate in rigorous evaluations.

Reforms the Housing Opportunities for Persons with AIDS (HOPWA) Program. The Budget proposes to update the HOPWA program to better reflect the current case concentration and understanding of HIV/AIDS and ensure that funds are directed in a more equitable and effective manner. This modernization includes a new formula that will distribute HOPWA funds based on the current population of people living with HIV/AIDS, fair market rents, and poverty rates in order to target funds to areas with the most need. It also makes the program more flexible, giving local communities more options to provide targeted, timely, and cost-effective interventions. The Budget's $332 million investment in HOPWA, in combination with the proposed modernization, will assist local communities in keeping individuals with HIV/AIDS housed, making it easier for them to stay connected to treatment, and therefore improving health outcomes for this vulnerable population.

Supports a New Source of Funding for Innovative Homeless Programs. The Administration's proposed Civilian Property Realignment Act will help consolidate, reduce, and realign the Federal civilian real estate footprint, as well as expedite the disposal of properties. At the same time, acknowledging the long-standing role of homeless assistance in real property management, the Administration supports the use of revenue created by the proposed Board's action to help prevent and end homelessness. One way to accomplish this would be to allocate up to five percent of the future profits from these real estate sales toward innovative homelessness programs. These funds could potentially be aligned with and distributed through HUD's existing Continuum of Care structure, and could be used in a variety of ways, including possible "Pay for Success" projects that would make Federal payments only upon achievement of clearly defined outcomes.

Makes Tough Choices

Reduces Funding for the HOME Investment Partnerships Program. The Budget provides $950 million for the HOME Investment Partnerships Program, five percent below the 2012 enacted level. At this funding level, HOME will provide grants to State and local governments to supply almost 40,000 additional units of affordable housing for low-income families. This funding reduction is mitigated by the investment of $1 billion in mandatory funding for the Housing Trust Fund to finance the development, rehabilitation, and preservation of affordable housing for extremely-low income families.

Limits Funding for New Housing Construction. The Budget provides a total of $526 million for the Housing for the Elderly and Housing for Persons with Disabilities programs, $14 million below the 2012 enacted level. This funding level will support all 150,000 existing units in these programs, and includes $40 million for additional supportive housing units.

These investments also directly support research that will build our understanding of the intersection between supportive housing and health care costs, and help identify what works best in allowing seniors to age-in-place.

DEPARTMENT OF JUSTICE

Funding Highlights:

- Provides $27.6 billion in discretionary funding for the Department of Justice, an increase of 3.1 percent above the 2012 enacted level. Essential Government programs, including law enforcement, litigation, and prisons and detention, are funded at three percent above 2012 levels.

- Invests $395 million in new resources to combat gun violence and ensure that those who are not eligible to purchase or possess guns are prevented from doing so. The Budget also provides funding to improve criminal history records information and increase inspections of the firearms industry.

- Includes $93 million in cybersecurity enhancements and ensures that critical investments in cybersecurity are made in a whole-of-government manner and that cross-agency priorities receive attention.

- Contributes to the Department's national security duties by providing more than $3.5 billion for the Federal Bureau of Investigation and National Security Division programs that are critical to mitigating and countering the threat of terrorism.

- Funds activations of recently constructed or acquired prisons, including the Thomson, Illinois correctional facility. The Budget also provides additional contract beds to address growth by alleviating crowding throughout the prison system.

- Sustains efforts to combat major drug trafficking organizations and targets transnational organized crime syndicates.

- Increases funding for general legal activities, including civil rights, intellectual property, and financial fraud enforcement.

- Improves reentry initiatives by expanding Second Chance Act programs and works to reduce recidivism rates by providing drug treatment, increasing alternatives to incarceration, and strengthening family and parental ties.

- Supports additional immigration judge teams and system improvements to address the immigration case backlog. Expanding the Department's capacity to process immigration cases is a crucial part of current immigration policy, as well as commonsense immigration reform efforts to fix the broken immigration system so that everyone plays by the same rules.

- Increases by 10 percent above the 2012 enacted level State and local criminal justice assistance by making critical investments in programs that promote public safety.

- Ensures that Federal funds flow to evidence-based activities by making additional resources available for alternatives to incarceration, gun safety initiatives, police hiring, and other evidence-based initiatives to improve the targeting and effectiveness of grant assistance.

The Department of Justice (DOJ) is responsible for enforcing laws and defending the interests of the United States; protecting the public against foreign and domestic threats; providing Federal leadership in preventing and controlling crime; punishing those guilty of unlawful behavior; and ensuring fair and impartial administration of justice for all Americans. The President's Budget supports these commitments and protects the progress that has already been made in key areas, while continuing to reflect the need to operate within fiscal constraints.

Enforces Laws and Protects U.S. Interests

Improves Law Enforcement's Ability to Implement and Enforce Gun Safety Measures. To better protect American communities from gun-related violence and mass shootings, the Budget includes an increase of $173 million above the 2012 enacted level to help Federal law enforcement continue to combat gun violence. These funds will support DOJ's ability to perform additional background checks, increase the frequency of inspections of federally-licensed firearms dealers, improve tracing and ballistics analysis, and keep guns out of the hands of dangerous criminals and other prohibited persons.

Promotes Cybersecurity Initiatives. Cyber threats are constantly evolving and require a coordinated and comprehensive plan for protection and response. As we continue to see across the Nation, no sector, network, or system is immune from penetration by those who seek to make financial gain, to perpetrate malicious and disruptive activity, or to steal commercial or Government secrets and property. The Budget,

therefore, identifies and promotes cross-agency cybersecurity initiatives and priorities, including improving cybersecurity information sharing while protecting individual privacy and civil liberties and enhancing State and local capacity to respond to cyber incidents.

Preserves National Security and Counters the Threat of Terrorism. Battling the threat of terrorism and preserving national security, while remaining true to our values, continues to be a top priority for DOJ. The Budget maintains funding related to the High-Value Detainee Interrogation Group, the Joint Terrorism Task Forces, and the Federal Bureau of Investigation (FBI) intelligence gathering and surveillance capabilities, as well as other critical counterterrorism and counterintelligence programs housed within the FBI and the National Security Division.

Maintains Safe and Secure Prison Capacity. The Budget proposes $8.6 billion, a 4.3 percent increase over the 2012 enacted level, for Federal prisons and detention facilities. These funds are provided to continue activation of newly completed or acquired prisons, and to provide additional contract beds to address growth by alleviating crowding in low security facilities and system-wide. Opportunities to reduce the prison population, with a focus on non-violent offenders, will continue to be explored.

Sustains Drug Enforcement Efforts and Targets Transnational Organized Crime. The Budget provides $2.6 billion for drug enforcement and organized crime targeting programs. This funding includes an increase of $3 million for the International Organized Crime Center to help further implement strategies to combat major drug trafficking organizations and transnational organized crime syndicates.

Combats Financial Fraud, Promotes Innovation, and Protects Civil Rights. Ensuring honest and fair competition and protecting the rights and property of citizens are paramount to our economy and American competitiveness. As a result, the Budget provides an additional $55 million to continue supporting aggressive efforts to investigate and prosecute financial, mortgage, and other fraud, while also continuing to counter intellectual property crimes. Additionally, the Budget provides enhancements to ensure the protection of civil rights, including enforcing Federal prohibitions against racial and ethnic discrimination.

Improves the Way Federal Dollars are Spent

Enhances Reentry and Recidivism Initiatives. The Administration is committed to a comprehensive strategy to contain incarceration costs over the long term by assisting inmates with reentering society and reducing the population of individuals who return to prison after being released, while improving public safety. To do this, the Budget provides $15 million for the Bureau of Prisons to expand the Residential Drug Abuse Program and $6 million to expand alternatives to traditional incarceration, including home monitoring programs. Additionally, through State and local assistance programs, the Budget provides $119 million for the Second Chance Act Grant program to reduce re-offending and help ex-offenders return to productive lives, $19 million for Residential Substance Abuse Treatment in the Nation's prisons and jails to help break the cycle of drug offending, and $10 million to expand Hawaii's HOPE Probation project with "swift and certain" sanctions to other sites. The Budget also addresses the needs of children of incarcerated persons by including funding to expand children and family visitations, develop and disseminate information about child support rules and regulations, and evaluate arrest policies to minimize the impact on children.

Addresses the Immigration Case Backlog. A key component of any immigration policy is ensuring that immigration cases are processed efficiently and fairly. The Budget, therefore, provides enhancements to the Executive Office for Immigration Review to add 30 new immigration judge teams, expand the successful Legal Orientation Program, and establish a pilot program to implement additional efficiencies in the immigration court system. Together, these proposals will help increase efficiency in the immigration courts.

Invests in State and Local Public Safety Initiatives That Work

Promotes Smart Crime Strategies That Protect the Public and Reduce Incarceration. The Budget also invests in several programs to promote better public safety and help reduce State and local corrections system costs. For example, the Budget invests $44 million in Problem-Solving Grants, which support drug courts, mentally ill offender assistance, and other problem solving approaches to work with special needs offenders while minimizing costly incarceration. The Justice Reinvestment Initiative, funded at $85 million, works with States to reduce unnecessary incarceration and reinvest the savings in efforts that promote public safety. In coordination with the Department of Education's School Climate Transformation Grants, the Budget also proposes $20 million for a Juvenile Justice and Education Collaboration Assistance program to help reduce juvenile arrests (and the "school-to-prison pipeline") while improving school safety. With 2.3 million individuals in U.S. prisons, 1 in 32 American adults under correctional supervision, and 71,000 juveniles held in juvenile facilities, these programs aim to achieve improved public safety using evidence-based strategies and data-driven approaches.

Prioritizes Evidence-Based Practices That Work at the State and Local Level. The Budget bolsters the Administration's efforts to ensure that more Federal grant funding flows to evidence-based activities and helps to advance knowledge of what works in State and local criminal justice. To accomplish this objective, the Budget increases set-asides for research, evaluation, and statistics; couples the formula Byrne Justice Assistance Grant and Juvenile Accountability Block Grant programs with competitive incentive grants that provide "bonus" funds to States and localities for better, evidence-based use of formula funds; expands the Pay for Success initiative; adopts a more evidence-based, data-driven use of competitive grant funds; and invests in the expansion of *CrimeSolutions.gov*, a "what works" clearinghouse for best practices in criminal justice, juvenile justice, and crime victim services.

Expands Gun Safety Initiatives and Works to Prevent Mass Casualty Violence. The Budget includes $222 million to help State and local governments continue implementing the Administration's proposals for increasing firearms safety and supporting programs that help keep communities safe from mass casualty violence. Included in these initiatives are $150 million for the Comprehensive School Safety Program, $55 million in grants to improve the submission of State criminal and mental health records to the National Instant Criminal Background Check System, $15 million to improve police officer safety, and $2 million to develop better gun safety mechanisms to prevent the use of firearms by unauthorized users.

Renews Efforts to Promote Juvenile Justice and Fight Youth Violence. The Budget provides $332 million for the Department's Juvenile Justice Programs and includes evidence-based investments to prevent youth violence, including $25 million to fund the Community-Based Violence Prevention Initiative, which would provide grants to replicate successful community-based interventions to control shootings and other serious gang violence, and $4 million for the National Forum on Youth Violence Prevention, which provides assistance for selected communities across the Nation to develop and implement youth violence strategies. The Budget also includes $20 million for the Juvenile Justice

Realignment Incentive Grants, which, in tandem with the $30 million reserved for Juvenile Accountability Block Grants, will assist States that are pursuing evidence-based, juvenile justice system alignment to foster better outcomes for young people, less costly use of incarceration, and increased public safety. Further, the Budget makes available $23 million for research and pilot projects focused on developing appropriate responses to youth exposed to violence.

Promotes Community Policing. The Budget provides $440 million to support evidence-based community policing in the Nation's local law enforcement agencies. While a portion of this funding will support the Comprehensive School Safety Program and be used to hire school resource officers and mental health professionals and make other investments in school safety, $257 million is provided for the hiring and retention of police officers and sheriffs' deputies across the United States, and includes a preference for the hiring of post-9/11 military veterans and school resource officers. Of the total, $35 million is set aside for Tribal Law Enforcement to help ensure the safety and security of our tribal partners. The Budget also includes $4 billion in immediate assistance for the retention, rehiring, and hiring of police officers, as requested by the President in his proposed American Jobs Act.

Continues Efforts to Combat Violence Against Women. The Budget provides $413 million to reinforce efforts to combat and respond to violent crimes against women. These grants play a critical role in helping to create a coordinated community response to this problem. As a result of prior investments in this area, civil and criminal justice systems are more responsive to victims. Crimes of violence committed against women have declined in recent years. Yet, reducing such violence and meeting the needs of the almost 1.3 million women victimized by rape and sexual assault annually, and the nearly seven million victims of intimate partner violence each year, remains a critical priority.

DEPARTMENT OF LABOR

Funding Highlights:

- Provides $12.1 billion in discretionary funding for the Department of Labor, an increase of more than $20 million from the comparable 2012 level. The Budget continues critical investments in training and resources for job seekers. It also includes savings from projected reductions in workload for the Unemployment Insurance program and administrative efficiencies.

- Improves services for workers and job seekers by modernizing the Federal job training system, including through the creation of a Universal Displaced Worker program. Invests $150 million in a competitive Workforce Innovation Fund to engage States and localities in identifying effective models and establishes a Community College to Career Fund to invest in successful job training partnerships between community colleges and business.

- Ensures that Americans who have lost their jobs have the help they need to develop their skills and return to work and creates employment opportunities for the long-term unemployed and low-income adults and youth.

- Strengthens Job Corps by improving its outcomes and cost-effectiveness and creating stronger oversight.

- Provides improved re-employment services to newly-separated veterans and focuses resources on veterans with disabilities or other significant barriers to employment.

- Maintains support for agencies that protect workers' wages, benefits, health and safety, and invests in preventing and detecting the misclassification of employees as independent contractors.

- Assists workers who need to take time off to care for a child or other family member by helping States launch paid leave programs.

- Safeguards workers' pensions by encouraging companies to fully fund their employees' promised benefits and assuring the long-term solvency of the Federal pension insurance system.

- Improves the solvency of the Unemployment Insurance system by encouraging States to fully fund their programs and works to reduce improper payments in the Unemployment Insurance program to improve program integrity and cost-effectiveness.

- Protects workers who suffer injuries and fatalities while on the job and their families by modernizing and improving the operation of Federal workers' compensation systems.

- Builds knowledge about which programs work, including through new approaches to reducing recidivism and increasing employment for young ex-offenders.

The Department of Labor (DOL) is charged with promoting the welfare of American workers, job seekers, and retirees, a mission that is critical to the Nation's continued economic recovery and long-term competitiveness. To support this mission, the Budget provides more than $12.1 billion in discretionary funding for DOL. This funding level allows substantial investments to support workers and is coupled with significant reforms to better help people gain skills, regain their footing after a job loss, and find new employment opportunities. The Budget also makes investments to bolster the enforcement of critical wage and hour, whistleblower, and worker safety laws.

Invests in a Competitive Workforce

Promotes New Approaches to Job Training and Employment Services. As the economy changes, training and employment programs must continually innovate and adapt to effectively help American workers gain the skills they need to find new jobs and careers.

- *Modernizes, Streamlines, and Strengthens the Delivery of Training and Employment Services.* Today more than 40 programs at 11 Federal agencies deliver job training and employment services. The Administration believes we should be doing everything we can to make it easier for people who need help to find a job or build their skills for a better one, and for employers who need to find well-qualified workers. The Administration is exploring opportunities to revisit how the Federal Government funds job training and employment services, including the possibility of reorganizing some of the existing training programs that serve overlapping populations. For example, the Budget proposes a Universal Displaced Worker program that will reach up to a million workers a year with a set of core services, combining the best elements of two more narrowly-targeted programs. Any reform must ensure that the needs of particularly vulnerable job-seekers and workers continue to be met and ensure greater accountability and transparency about the performance of federally supported job training providers and programs. The Administration looks forward to working with the Congress and other stakeholders on job training reform in the coming year.

- *Drives Innovation.* To spur innovation, the Budget provides $150 million for the Workforce Innovation Fund. The Fund tests new ideas that States and regions bring forward to implement systemic reforms and replicate evidence-based strategies for training and helping workers find jobs. DOL will continue to administer the Fund, working closely with agencies that support educational, employment, and related services. Within the Fund, $10 million is dedicated to building knowledge about which interventions are most effective for disconnected youth. The Budget also provides $80 million to increase the set-aside for governors in the Workforce Investment Act formula grants from 5 percent to 7.5 percent in order to boost States' capacity to engage in program improvements and reform. In addition, the Budget provides $25 million to support new, evidence-informed efforts to improve employment outcomes for older Americans.

- *Strengthens Community Colleges to Train Workers for Available Jobs.* Too often, employers struggle to find workers with the skills they need, even as millions of Americans look for work. The Budget funds an $8 billion Community College to Career Fund jointly administered by DOL and the Department of Education to support State and community college partnerships with businesses to build the skills of American workers. The Fund will build on the Trade Adjustment Assistance Community College and Career Training Grants, for which 2014 is the final year of funding.

Helps the Unemployed and Low-Income Adults and Youth. As we work to strengthen and rebuild our economy from the worst economic downturn since the Great Depression, it is critical to provide a helping hand and a viable path back to work for those who have had their lives disrupted by unemployment. Unemployment Insurance (UI) benefits have helped American families stay afloat, keeping 2.3 million individuals—including 600,000 children—from falling into poverty in 2011 alone. With Emergency Unemployment Compensation extended through the end of 2013, the Administration is focused on helping the long-term unemployed get back to work. The Budget proposes a $4 billion Reemployment NOW program, which incorporates a number of reforms to help UI claimants and other long-term unemployed individuals get back to work more quickly. The Budget also includes a $12.5 billion Pathways Back to Work Fund to make it easier for workers to remain connected to the workforce and gain new skills for long-term employment. This initiative will support summer and year-round jobs for low-income youth, subsidized employment opportunities for unemployed and low-income adults, and other promising strategies designed to lead to employment. In addition, the Budget builds upon the demonstration authority that was included in the Middle Class Tax Relief and Job Creation Act of 2012, providing $25 million to encourage innovative States to come forward with new and better strategies for getting UI beneficiaries back to work.

Reforms Job Corps. The Budget continues the Administration's commitment to improving and reforming the Job Corps program, which provides comprehensive services and support to some of the Nation's most disadvantaged youth. These reforms include closing a small number of Job Corps centers that are chronically low-performing, identifying and seeking to replicate the practices of high-performing centers, and adopting cost-saving reforms. In addition, the Budget proposes steps to strengthen financial and contract oversight, so the program can continue to provide valuable services to disadvantaged youth while maintaining strong internal controls and ensuring that its contracts are procured at the lowest risk and the best value to the Federal Government.

Improves Career Transitions for Newly-Separated Veterans. Over the past 18 months, the President has announced a series of actions to combat the high levels of veterans' unemployment and to provide greater support for servicemembers seeking to transition to civilian education and employment. Although the number of unemployed veterans remains too high, especially for post-9/11 veterans, over the past year there has been an encouraging downward trend in the overall veterans' unemployment rate, consistent with the decline in the national unemployment rate. DOL, in partnership with the Departments of Defense and Veterans Affairs, is implementing the first major redesign of transition assistance services in over 20 years. This new program, Transition Goals, Plans, Success (Transition GPS), will help servicemembers more effectively transition to civilian life and find employment that capitalizes on the skills they have developed through their service. DOL is also providing increased access to intensive reemployment services for post-9/11 veterans, helping employers take advantage of tax credits for hiring veterans, and continuing its work to connect veterans with available jobs. The Budget builds on these efforts and will fully fund the cost to DOL of meeting the expected level of military separations and refocus its grants to serve veterans with disabilities or other significant barriers to employment. In addition, the Workforce Innovation Fund includes $50 million for projects to address the employment needs of veterans—including recently separated veterans—and to improve employment services for military families and members of the Guard and Reserves who face unique challenges in the civilian workforce because of their military commitments.

Maintains Strong Support for Worker Protection. The Budget includes nearly $1.8 billion for DOL's worker protection agencies, putting them on sound footing to meet their responsibilities to protect the health, safety, wages, working conditions, and retirement security of American workers. The Budget preserves recent investments in rebuilding DOL's enforcement capacity and makes strategic choices to ensure funding is used for the highest priority activities.

- *Strengthens Enforcement of Wage and Hour and Family Leave Laws.* The Budget provides an increase of $3.4 million for the Wage and Hour Division (WHD) for increased enforcement of the Fair Labor Standards Act and the Family and Medical Leave Act, which ensure that workers receive appropriate wages, overtime pay, and the right to take job-protected leave for family and medical purposes. The Budget also provides $5.8 million for WHD to develop a new integrated enforcement and case management system to allow investigators to capture higher quality and more timely data to analyze trends in labor law violations, target investigations and compliance assistance efforts, and evaluate the impact and quality of enforcement.

- *Promotes Worker Health and Safety.* The Budget provides $571 million for the Occupational Safety and Health Administration (OSHA), allowing OSHA to inspect hazardous workplaces and work with employers to help them understand and comply with safety and health regulations. The Budget includes an additional $5.9 million to bolster OSHA's enforcement of the 21 whistleblower laws that protect workers and others who are retaliated against for reporting unsafe and unscrupulous practices.

- *Protects the Health and Safety of the Nation's Miners.* The Budget provides $381 million for the Mine Safety and Health Administration (MSHA), including additional funding for MSHA's enforcement programs to enforce and promote mine safety and health laws and to implement recommendations from the Internal Review conducted in the wake of the Upper Big Branch mine disaster.

- *Detects and Deters the Misclassification of Workers as Independent Contractors.* When employees are misclassified as independent contractors, they are deprived of benefits and protections to which they are legally entitled, such as minimum wage, overtime, unemployment insurance, and anti-discrimination protections. Misclassification, together with the underreporting of cash income for those paid as independent contractors, also costs taxpayers money in lost funds for the Treasury and in Social Security, Medicare, the Unemployment Trust Fund, and State programs. The Budget includes approximately $14 million to combat misclassification, including $10 million for grants to States to identify misclassification and recover unpaid taxes and $4 million for personnel at WHD to investigate misclassification.

Provides Greater Security for American Workers and Retirees

Encourages State Establishment of Family Leave Initiatives. Too many American workers must make the painful choice between the care of their families and a paycheck they desperately need. While the Family and Medical Leave Act allows many workers to take job-protected unpaid time off, millions of families cannot afford to use unpaid leave. A handful of States have enacted policies to offer paid family leave, but more States should have the chance to follow their example. The Budget includes a $5 million State Paid Leave Fund to provide technical assistance and support to States that are considering paid leave programs.

Promotes Equal Pay for Equal Work. According to the latest Census statistics, full-time working women earn 77 cents to every dollar earned by men, and the gap is significantly more for women of color. The Budget makes important investments to help ensure that women receive equal pay for equal work. It provides additional resources to strengthen the pay discrimination enforcement efforts of DOL's Office of Federal Contract Compliance Programs and the Equal Employment Opportunity Commission, agencies that work to secure equal employment opportunities for all workers.

Strengthens the Pension Benefit Guaranty Corporation to Protect Worker Pensions. The Pension Benefit Guaranty Corporation (PBGC) acts as a backstop to insure pension payments for workers whose companies have failed. Currently, PBGC's pension insurance system is itself underfunded, and PBGC's liabilities exceed its assets. PBGC receives no taxpayer funds and its premiums are currently much lower than those a private financial institution would charge for insuring the same risk. The Budget proposes to give the PBGC Board the authority to adjust premiums and directs PBGC to take into account the risks that different sponsors pose to their retirees and to PBGC. This reform will both encourage companies to fully fund their pension benefits and ensure the continued financial soundness of PBGC. In order to ensure that these reforms are undertaken responsibly during challenging economic times, the Budget would require a year of study and public comment before any implementation and the gradual phasing in of any premium increases. This proposal is estimated to save $25 billion over the next decade.

Establishes Automatic Workplace Pensions and Expands the Small Employer Pension Plan Startup Credit. Currently, 78 million working Americans—roughly half the workforce—lack employer-based retirement plans. The Budget proposes a system of automatic workplace pensions that will expand access to tens of millions of workers who currently lack pensions. Under the proposal, employers who do not currently offer a retirement plan will be required to enroll their employees in a direct-deposit Individual Retirement Account (IRA) that is compatible with existing direct-deposit payroll systems. Employees may opt out if they choose. To minimize burdens on small businesses, those with 10 or fewer employees would be exempt. Employers would also be entitled to a tax credit of $25 per participating employee—up to a total of $250 per year—for six years. To make it easier for small employers to offer pensions to their workers in connection with the automatic IRA proposal, the Budget will increase the maximum tax credit available for small employers establishing or administering a new retirement plan from $500 to $1,000 per year. This credit would be available for four years.

Strengthens the UI Safety Net and Improves Program Integrity. The combination of chronically underfunded reserves and the economic downturn has placed a considerable financial strain on States' UI operations. Currently, 23 States owe more than $28 billion to the Federal UI trust fund. As a result, employers in those States are now facing automatic Federal tax increases, and many States have little prospect of paying these loans back in the foreseeable future. At the same time, State UI programs have large improper payment rates. It is important to put the UI system back on the path to solvency and financial integrity while maintaining benefits for job seekers. The Budget provides immediate relief to employers to encourage job creation now, reestablishing State fiscal responsibility going forward, and working closely with States to eliminate improper payments. Under this proposal, employers in indebted States would receive tax relief for two years. To encourage State solvency, the proposal would also raise the minimum level of wages subject to unemployment taxes in 2016 to a level slightly less in real terms than it was in 1983, after President Reagan signed into law the last wage base increase. The higher wage base would be offset by lower tax rates to avoid a Federal tax increase.

The Administration has also taken a number of steps to address program integrity in States that have consistently failed to place enough emphasis on combating improper payments in their UI programs. The Administration's aggressive actions have given States a number of tools to prevent improper payments, and reducing State UI error rates remains an Administration priority. The Budget includes several additional proposals to help States combat improper payments in their UI programs, including providing funds for the recently established UI Integrity Center of Excellence and mandating State participation in the Treasury Offset Program, State Information Data Exchange System, and the Prisoner Update Processing System.

Modernizes Workers' Compensation Systems. The Budget includes legislative proposals to reform two workers' compensation programs, authorized by the Federal Employees' Compensation Act (FECA) and the Defense Base Act (DBA). FECA covers Federal civilian employees and DBA covers Federal contract employees working overseas on military bases and public works projects. Both reforms would produce Government-wide savings, and improve the operation of these programs for workers and families who suffer injuries and fatalities in the line of duty.

- *FECA Reform.* FECA has not been substantially updated since 1974. FECA benefits typically exceed Federal retirement benefits, which creates an incentive for beneficiaries to remain on FECA beyond their normal retirement age. In addition, while State workers' compensation systems have waiting periods for benefits to discourage less serious claims, FECA has a three-day waiting period for non-Postal employees that is imposed too late in the claims process to be effective. The Budget acts on longstanding recommendations from the Government Accountability Office, the Congressional Budget Office, and DOL's Inspector General, as well as numerous Securing Americans Value and Efficiency (SAVE) Award nominations, to amend FECA to convert future retirement-age beneficiaries to a retirement annuity-level benefit, impose an up-front waiting period for benefits for all beneficiaries, permit DOL to recapture compensation costs from responsible third parties, give DOL additional tools to reduce improper payments, and make other changes to improve the program. These reforms would generate Government-wide savings of more than $500 million over 10 years.

- *Defense Base Act Reform.* The growth in Federal contractors working overseas has brought into sharp focus the need for a more efficient approach to the DBA. The Budget proposes a new Government-wide fund to replace the patchwork of contract coverage now in effect under the DBA. Since 2002, the DBA caseload has increased by almost 2,600 percent, from 430 in 2002, to over 11,600 in 2011. DOL has experienced a number of administrative challenges in the wake of the increased workload, including difficulties in obtaining necessary documentation from foreign workers and delays in processing cases originating from war zones. In addition, under the program's current structure, the costs of DBA insurance—which agencies pay through individual contracts—exceed actual benefits by a significant margin. Over the past several years, DOL, the Department of Defense, the Department of State, and the U.S Agency for International Development have been working closely together to reform and improve the operation of the program, and the Budget reflects the culmination of those collaborative efforts. The proposal would replace the current DBA program with a new Government-wide benefit program—modeled on FECA—under which benefits would be paid directly from a Federal fund administered by DOL, and agencies would be billed only for their share of benefits and administrative costs.

Supports Evidence-Based Decision-Making and Achieves Efficiencies

Boosts Funding for Program Evaluation. During this Administration, DOL has made a significant commitment to the evaluation of its programs, which over time will allow it to drive more investments toward practices that achieve better outcomes at lower costs. The Budget builds on this commitment by increasing to one percent the amount of program dollars that can be set aside for evaluation, complementing funds provided to the Chief Evaluation Office and helping to support rigorous evaluations.

Builds Knowledge About What Works to Increase Employment for Ex-Offenders. The Budget devotes $50 million to test and replicate innovative and evidence-based strategies for young ex-offenders. For example, the Budget seeks to test if non-violent youth will reap the same benefits from the National Guard's Youth ChalleNGe program that other at-risk youth do such as higher rates of employment, high school or GED completion, and earning college credit. To further spur innovation and direct funding to effective programs, the Budget also dedicates $10 million to Pay for Success programs designed to improve employment and reduce recidivism among ex-offenders.

DEPARTMENT OF STATE AND OTHER INTERNATIONAL PROGRAMS

Funding Highlights:

- Provides a total of $47.8 billion in discretionary funding for the Department of State and U.S. Agency for International Development, a decrease of six percent from the 2012 enacted level, due to lower Overseas Contingency Operations activity.

- Advances the President's Global Health Initiative by supporting the Administration's ambitious targets for preventing and treating HIV/AIDS; maintaining the U.S. contribution to the Global Fund for AIDS, Tuberculosis, and Malaria at $1.65 billion; fully funding the Administration's pledge to the Global Alliance for Vaccines and Immunization; and scaling up proven child survival interventions to accelerate progress toward the goals of the Child Survival Call to Action.

- Proposes major reforms to make food aid more cost-effective and have greater impact, while maintaining robust levels of emergency food assistance and related development assistance and creating a new $75 million Emergency Food Assistance Contingency Fund.

- Continues a multi-year plan for Feed the Future to make strategic investments addressing the root causes of hunger and poverty to help prevent crises such as the recent famine in the Horn of Africa and food insecurity crisis in the Sahel.

- Provides $909 million for strategic investments to support low-emission, climate-resilient development, promote investment from the private sector in clean energy and low carbon infrastructure, and reduce greenhouse gas emissions.

- Responds to continuing challenges to stability in the Middle East and North Africa by providing $580 million to assist countries in transition and create incentives for long-term economic, political, and trade reforms, building on substantial investments since the Arab Spring.

- Provides over $4 billion to secure overseas personnel and facilities, including sufficient funding for the State Department to increase embassy security construction to $2.2 billion, as recommended by the Benghazi Accountability Review Board.

- Includes $6.8 billion for the frontline states of Iraq ($2.1 billion), Afghanistan ($3.4 billion), and Pakistan ($1.4 billion), including $3 billion in base funding and $3.8 billion in Overseas Contingency Operations funding. The Budget prioritizes core diplomatic and development activities to ensure strong, lasting partnerships with these countries and to promote stability.

- Rebalances diplomatic and assistance resources to the Asia-Pacific region.

- Provides $2.9 billion to the Department of the Treasury for U.S. commitments to the multilateral development banks and for international environmental, food security, and technical assistance activities.

- Provides $447 million to strengthen efforts at five international trade and investment agencies to promote international trade, enforce trade agreements, and help meet the goals of the National Export Initiative.

- Includes provisions to enact the December 2010 International Monetary Fund agreement, leaving the overall U.S. level of financial participation in the Fund unchanged while instituting important reforms.

The Department of State, the U.S. Agency for International Development (USAID), and other international programs advance the national security interests of the United States by helping to build and sustain a more democratic, secure, and prosperous world. Investing in civilian diplomacy and development fosters stability around the world, supports the goals of the President's Policy Directive on Global Development, reduces poverty, and promotes universal values, which in turn helps to protect our national security. International programs also support economic development and job creation in the United States by increasing trade and expanding access for U.S. businesses to international markets.

The President's 2014 Budget proposes $47.8 billion for the Department of State and USAID, including costs for Overseas Contingency Operations (OCO), a six percent decrease from the 2012 enacted level, which is largely driven by a $7.4 billion reduction in OCO funding. The Administration continues to prioritize funding for global health to achieve the vision of an AIDS-free generation, for food security to reduce extreme poverty and malnutrition and to foster sustained and inclusive growth, and for combatting climate change by supporting clean energy and energy efficiency, reducing deforestation, and building climate-resilience in developing countries. The Budget continues the long standing support of our allies built through security partnerships that promote regional and global stability. The

Budget also continues to support transitioning countries in the Middle East and North Africa by investing in economic and political reform in the wake of the Arab Spring. The Budget provides the necessary base resources to maintain critical diplomatic and development efforts around the world, including diplomatic operations and assistance in Iraq, Afghanistan, and Pakistan. At the same time, the Department of State and USAID are committed to finding efficiencies and cutting waste, allowing savings to be refocused on the highest priorities worldwide.

Maintains U.S. Global Leadership

Supports Global Health by Investing in High-Impact Interventions. The Administration is investing in proven interventions to accelerate progress toward the goals of achieving an AIDS-free generation and an end to preventable child and maternal deaths. The Budget supports the achievement of aggressive HIV/AIDS prevention and treatment targets as announced by the President on World AIDS Day in 2011, and continuing progress toward eliminating pediatric AIDS. The Budget builds on the momentum of the Child Survival Call to Action by increasing investments in proven child survival interventions, including those addressing malaria, malnutrition, pneumonia, and complications in childbirth. In recognition of the Global Fund to Fight AIDS, Tuberculosis, and Malaria's key role as a multilateral partner and its progress in instituting reforms, the Budget provides $1.65 billion to leverage pledges from other donors and accelerate progress against these three diseases. In addition, the Budget fully funds the balance of the Administration's pledge to the Global Alliance for Vaccines and Immunization.

Reforms Food Aid for More Cost-Effective Use of Taxpayer Resources. The Budget proposes a major reform of the Nation's largest food aid program to make it more cost effective and increase its impact, while maintaining robust levels of food and development assistance. The Budget shifts funding from the P.L. 480 Title II (Title II) account to the International Disaster Assistance (IDA) account for emergency food needs and to the Development Assistance account for development programs. With respect to emergencies, a majority of IDA food aid funding would be used to purchase and ship food from the United States. IDA funding would also be used to purchase food from markets near crises, or for interventions such as cash transfers and vouchers. In the case of development programs, non-governmental organizations that receive Title II development resources would be funded directly, rather than through the proceeds from selling U.S. food abroad (monetization) and, in the case of non-emergency direct feeding programs, food would be sourced locally, or from the United States, as appropriate. Early experience with IDA emergency food aid has shown that it has not only saved money and time, among other benefits, but that it has also been invaluable for addressing needs in several difficult crises such as Syria and the recent famine in the Horn of Africa. The Budget redirects $75 million of the funding reallocated from Title II to fund a new Emergency Food Assistance Contingency Fund to address above-trend emergency food needs.

The Budget also provides $25 million per year through the Department of Transportation's Maritime Administration for additional targeted operating subsidies for militarily-useful vessels and incentives to facilitate the retention of mariners. Worker adjustment assistance would be available for remaining eligible mariners.

Fights Hunger by Improving Food Security. As part of a multi-year plan to address the root causes of hunger and poverty, the Budget increases funding for agriculture development and nutrition programs. The recent famine in the Horn of Africa has underscored the need for targeted programs to help prevent future famines and crises in the region and elsewhere. Administration programs are intended to reduce extreme poverty, increase food security, and reduce malnutrition for millions of families by 2015. The Budget provides bilateral assistance for Feed the Future, including the New Alliance for Food Security and Nutrition, and funding for the multi-donor Global Agriculture and Food Security Program. These programs direct funding to poor countries that commit to policy reforms and strong country-led strategies to address internal food security needs. Assistance helps countries increase agricultural productivity, improve agricultural research and development, expand markets and trade, and increase resilience to help prevent recurrent crises. The Budget also maintains strong support for food aid and other humanitarian assistance, including over $4.1 billion to help internally displaced persons, refugees, and victims of armed conflict and natural disasters.

Combats Global Climate Change by Promoting Low-Emission, Climate-Resilient Economic Growth. Building on our robust investment to date, the Budget provides $909 million in 2014 to promote efforts to combat the drivers of climate change by supporting clean energy, reducing deforestation, and enhancing low-emission, climate-resilient development. The Administration is working in partnership with national and local governments, and the private sector, to make effective investments in three key programmatic areas: 1) multilateral institutions and bilateral activities that focus on energy efficiency, renewable energy, and energy sector reforms; 2) sustainable land use to combat unsustainable forest clearing for agriculture and illegal logging, and to promote forest governance; and 3) programs to build resilience of the communities and countries most vulnerable to climate change, and reduce the risk of damage, loss of life, and broader instability that can result from extreme weather and climate events.

Assists Countries in Transition and Promotes Reforms in the Middle East and North Africa. Building on the Administration's significant and continuing response to the transformative events in the Middle East and North Africa region, the Budget supports the economic and security sectors in this region. The Budget continues, or expands, our bilateral economic support in countries such as Egypt, Tunisia, and Yemen where transitions are ongoing. In addition, the Budget includes $580 million for regional programs and the Middle East and North Africa Incentive Fund, which will support countries in transition and provide incentives for long-term economic and political reforms. This fund builds upon several initiatives the United States is supporting to respond to regional developments since the beginning of the Arab Spring, including Enterprise Funds, fiscal stabilization support through cash transfers and loan guarantees, and various initiatives through the G8's Deauville Partnership, including technical assistance, trade, and asset recovery initiatives. In addition, base funding for diplomatic operations in the region is increased by $39 million, supporting both increased engagement and measures to protect diplomatic personnel.

Invests in Security Upgrades. The Budget provides $4 billion for Department of State security programs, including security staff, construction, and infrastructure upgrades. With additional funds, the Department of State will increase Diplomatic Security staff by five percent and provide targeted security upgrades at critical locations that face heightened threats in the wake of the attacks on September 11, 2012. The Budget funds a program level of $2.2 billion for capital security construction, as recommended by the Benghazi Accountability Review Board.

Invests in Long-Term Partnerships in Iraq, Afghanistan, and Pakistan. The Budget continues to support U.S. security, diplomatic, and development goals in Afghanistan, Pakistan, and Iraq while scaling down funding for opera-

tions and assistance, consistent with U.S. policy. Ongoing resources requested to support strong, long-term partnerships with these countries include core diplomatic and development operational support funding, as well as economic development, health, education, governance, security, and other assistance programs necessary to reinforce development progress and promote stability. OCO funding provides for near-term development assistance related to stabilization and counterinsurgency programs, extraordinary costs of operating in a high-threat environment, protection of civilian personnel, and oversight activities of the Special Inspector General for Afghanistan Reconstruction.

Promotes Gender Equality and Women and Girls Empowerment. The Administration has made it clear that advancing the rights of women and girls is critical to the foreign policy of the United States. In January, the President acted to elevate and integrate a strategic focus on the promotion of gender equality and the advancement of women and girls globally. This is a matter of national security as much as it is an issue of morality and fairness. The Budget supports the promotion of gender equality and advancement of the political, economic, social, and cultural status of women and girls.

Leverages International Organizations to Support Cooperation and Security. The Budget continues to support the President's vision of robust multilateral engagement as a tool in advancing U.S. national interests, accomplished through our contributions to the United Nations, peacekeeping, and international organizations. Our contributions enable U.S. participation in over 40 international organizations that maintain peace and security, promote economic growth, provide humanitarian aid, and advance human rights around the world. These peacekeeping resources fund activities to promote the peaceful resolution of conflict.

Continues Investments in Nonproliferation and Counterterrorism Programs. The Budget continues to support the President's vision of a world without nuclear weapons by providing key investments for nonproliferation programs at the Department of State. The Budget provides resources for flagship counterterrorism programs that develop partner capabilities to prevent terrorist attacks on the United States and other countries and to prevent the development, acquisition, trafficking, and use of weapons of mass destruction by terrorists.

Rebalances Diplomatic and Assistance Resources to the Asia-Pacific Region. The Budget provides over $1.2 billion to support the Presidential priority of advancing security, prosperity, and human dignity across the Asia-Pacific region by supporting programs such as the Lower Mekong Initiative to foster sub-regional cooperation and capacity-building among Cambodia, Laos, Thailand, Vietnam, and Burma. The Budget also provides significant resources for economic and security assistance to the region.

Makes Contributions to Economic Growth, National Security, and Multilateral Poverty Reduction Efforts. The Budget provides $2.9 billion to the Department of the Treasury for economic growth, national security, and multilateral poverty reduction efforts. These resources fund all annual general capital increase and replenishment commitments to the multilateral development banks, as well as critical contributions to international environmental, food security, and technical assistance activities. These programs leverage the resources of other donors to support U.S. and multilateral objectives in key international institutions. The Budget continues to pursue a multi-year strategy to meet our existing commitments, clear our arrears, and promote U.S. leadership in international financial institutions.

Encourages Economic Growth Through Support for the National Export Initiative and Tourism Promotion. A critical component of stimulating domestic economic growth is ensuring that U.S. businesses can actively participate in international markets and increase their exports of goods and services. The Administration launched the National Export Initiative (NEI) in 2010 to improve the private sector's ability to export American goods and services. The NEI advances the Administration's goal of doubling exports over five years by working to remove trade barriers abroad, helping firms—especially small businesses—overcome the hurdles to entering new export markets, assisting with trade financing, and pursuing a Government-wide approach to export advocacy abroad. The Budget provides targeted increases for agencies involved in trade promotion and financing, development finance, and trade enforcement in support of the NEI. The Budget includes $307 million for the U.S. Trade and Development Agency, Office of the U.S. Trade Representative, U.S. International Trade Commission, and the Overseas Private Investment Corporation (a combined $46 million increase over the 2012 enacted level), as well as $131 million for the Export-Import Bank's administrative expenses and Inspector General, a $37 million increase over the 2012 enacted level. These investments will strengthen international trade promotion and enforcement efforts.

Promotes Global Financial Stability and U.S. Leadership in the International Monetary Fund (IMF). The Budget includes provisions to implement the December 2010 IMF agreement by increasing the U.S. quota in the IMF by approximately $63 billion and simultaneously reducing by an equal amount U.S. participation in the New Arrangements to Borrow (NAB), in addition to instituting other reforms that the United States has sought. The NAB is a set of standing IMF borrowing arrangements with 38 members and institutions to supplement IMF resources as needed to respond to financial crises that threaten the stability of the global financial system. The 2010 agreement results in no overall change in U.S. financial participation in the IMF, while preserving U.S. veto power and restoring the primacy of the IMF's quota-based capital structure in which the United States has the largest share.

Transitions International Broadcasts to Digital Transmission Technologies. The Budget builds upon the Broadcasting Board of Governors' efforts to evolve international broadcasts from shortwave radio into more effective and less expensive digital tools (satellite and Internet radio, mobile phone technologies, and Internet-based social media) that reach today's technologically savvy audiences. To maintain U.S. global leadership, our international broadcasts must reach tomorrow's leaders in key regions, such as in the fast growing and technologically-connected middle class of China and the youth populations that rose up in support of democracy during the Arab Spring. Shortwave radio broadcasts will continue in regions that lack access to digital technologies, such as in Darfur, North Korea, and Tibet.

Improves Efficiency and Transparency

Enhances Transparency of Foreign Assistance. In September 2012, the Office of Management and Budget released a Bulletin that institutionalizes the U.S. Government's commitment to aid transparency and directs all Federal agencies to provide timely and detailed data on foreign assistance. These data are being published on the Foreign Assistance Dashboard (*www.foreignassistance.gov*)—which provides a visual presentation of U.S. Government foreign assistance funds that enables the public to examine, research, and track aid investments in a standard and easy-to-understand format. Consistent with the Bulletin's guidance, the Dashboard will continue to add more comprehensive data going forward.

Reforms Contract Procurement. USAID will continue to increase the efficiency of U.S. foreign assistance through the Implementation and Procurement Reform Initiative, which streamlines procurement policies, procedures, and processes, increases the use of small business and host country systems, and strengthens the local capacity of partner countries.

Fosters Innovation. USAID will continue direct programming for innovation through the Office of Innovation and Development Alliances and throughout the agency through Development Innovation Ventures. USAID will accelerate the adoption of mobile banking and related solutions, and gain more development results through highly focused and leveraged public-private partnerships.

Improves the Management of Information Technology Projects. The Department of State will continue to strengthen the Chief Information Officer's authorities and increase the oversight and management of information technology projects across the agency. The agency is developing plans to move data centers, bandwidth, enterprise licensing, hardware, project overhead, and other new services or technologies into the Department's Working Capital Fund to enable more effective and efficient technology in support of the Department's mission.

DEPARTMENT OF TRANSPORTATION

Funding Highlights:

- Provides a total of $76.6 billion in discretionary and mandatory budgetary resources for the Department of Transportation, an increase of 5.5 percent, or $4 billion, above the 2012 enacted level.

- Jumpstarts job creation with an additional $50 billion in immediate investments in 2014 to support critical infrastructure projects, improving America's roads, bridges, transit systems, border crossings, railways, and runways. This includes $40 billion in "Fix-it-First" investments for improving existing infrastructure assets and $10 billion to help spur State and local innovation in infrastructure development.

- Proposes a five-year, $40 billion rail reauthorization proposal to significantly improve existing intercity passenger rail services, develop new high speed rail corridors, and strengthen the economic competitiveness of our freight rail system.

- Fully funds the authorized funding levels provided in the Moving Ahead for Progress in the 21st Century Act (MAP-21) for surface transportation programs.

- Reserves funding after the expiration of MAP-21 in 2015 for a robust, long-term reauthorization of surface transportation programs, including a 25 percent increase from current funding levels.

- Supports a more robust, rigorous, and data-driven pipeline safety program to ensure the highest level of safety for America's pipeline system.

- Invests nearly $1 billion in the Next Generation Air Transportation System, a revolutionary modernization of our aviation system.

- Pays for the rail and surface transportation proposals with savings from ramping down overseas military operations. Because rebuilding the Nation's transportation infrastructure is an immediate need, the Budget uses near-term savings from reduced overseas operations to fully offset the long-term reauthorization proposals.

- Maintains reduced funding for Airport Grants, focusing Federal support on smaller airports, while giving commercial service airports additional flexibility to raise their own resources.

A well-functioning transportation system is critical to America's economic future. Whether it is by road, transit, air, rail, pipeline, or waterway, Americans rely on our transportation system to move people and goods safely, facilitate commerce, attract and retain businesses, and support jobs. The President's 2014 Budget provides a total of $76.6 billion in discretionary and mandatory funding for the Department of Transportation, plus an additional $50 billion to jumpstart economic growth and job creation through immediate infrastructure investment.

Invests in Infrastructure Critical for Long-Term Growth

Creates Jobs Now. To spur job growth and allow States to initiate sound multi-year investments, the Budget provides an additional $50 billion for transportation investments in 2014. Although infrastructure projects take time to get underway, these investments would create hundreds of thousands of jobs in the first few years and in industries suffering from protracted unemployment. This includes $40 billion in "Fix-it-First" investments to improve existing infrastructure assets most in need of repair and $10 billion to help spur States and local innovation in infrastructure development. These funds will be leveraging State, local, tribal, and private funds. Of the innovation-spurring proposal, $200 million will fund communities that include enhanced resilience to extreme weather and other impacts of climate change in their planning efforts, and that have proposed, or are ready to break ground on, infrastructure projects to improve resilience. Planning by these communities will be supported by a broader Administration commitment to help communities improve their resilience through direct technical assistance, provision of useful data and tools on projected impacts, and support for planning. Making infrastructure investments now will put workers back on the job and support local transportation programs in the near-term, but the return on investment for Federal taxpayers will benefit from historically low interest rates and construction costs. To help these funds flow into communities without delay, key

Federal agencies have been directed to find ways to expedite the permitting and approvals for infrastructure projects.

Proposes Dedicated Funding for High Speed Rail Investments. The Budget provides $40 billion over five years to fund the development of high-speed rail and other passenger rail programs as part of an integrated national transportation strategy. This system will provide 80 percent of Americans with convenient access to a passenger rail system, featuring high-speed service, within 25 years. The proposal also benefits freight rail and significantly restructures Federal support for Amtrak, to increase transparency, accountability, and performance.

Fully Supports MAP-21. On July 6, 2012, the President signed MAP-21, which reauthorized Federal Aid Highways, Transit formula grants, and highway safety programs through 2014. The Budget provides $50.1 billion in obligation limitations for these programs, equal to the contract authority levels authorized by MAP-21.

Includes a Reserve for Surface Transportation Reauthorization. While MAP-21 provided much needed certainty to transportation funding and enacted a number of important reforms, the Administration strongly believes that more needs to be done to maintain, improve, and expand the Nation's transportation systems. Much of the country's transportation infrastructure was built decades ago and is in urgent need of repair to meet current and future economic demands. Given this, the Budget includes an allowance beginning in 2015 to support additional investments in surface transportation under the next reauthorization. The Administration looks forward to working with the Congress to secure these critical investments.

Enhances Pipeline Safety. In order to ensure the highest safety standards for the U.S. pipeline system, the Budget proposes a Pipeline Safety Reform initiative to both enhance and revamp the Department's Pipeline Safety program. The Budget maintains the size of the State Pipeline Safety Grant program and institutes several reforms to the Federal program. It funds the first phase of a multi-year effort to more than double the number of Federal pipeline safety inspectors. There are currently only 135 inspectors responsible, in collaboration with State partners, for inspecting segments of 2.6 million miles of pipeline and ensuring incident investigations following explosions occur promptly. In addition, the Budget modernizes pipeline data collection and analysis, improves Federal investigation of pipeline accidents of all sizes, and expands the public education and outreach program.

Modernizes the Nation's Air Traffic Control System. The Budget provides nearly $1 billion in 2014 for the Next Generation Air Transportation System (NextGen). NextGen is the multi-year effort currently underway to improve the efficiency, safety, capacity, and environmental performance of the aviation system. These funds would continue to support the transformation from a ground-based radar surveillance system to a more accurate satellite-based surveillance system; the development of 21st Century data communications capability between air traffic control and aircraft to improve efficiency; and the improvement of aviation weather information.

Pays for Transportation Investment Using Overseas Military Operations Savings. The President is committed to working with the Congress to ensure that funding increases for surface transportation do not increase the deficit. Because rebuilding our transportation infrastructure is an urgent need, the Budget uses savings from ramping down overseas military operations to fully offset baseline Highway Trust Fund solvency needs, the out-year surface transportation reauthorization allowance, and the rail reauthorization proposal. Beyond the reauthorization window, the Budget assumes that the President and the Congress will work together to develop other fiscally responsible solutions.

Improves the Way Federal Funds are Spent

Maintains Reduced Funding in Targeted Areas. In support of the President's call for spending restraint, the Budget lowers funding for the airport grants program to $2.9 billion offset in part by eliminating guaranteed funding for large hub airports. The Budget focuses Federal grants to support smaller commercial and general aviation airports that do not have access to additional revenue or other outside sources of capital. At the same time, the Budget would allow larger airports to increase non-Federal passenger facility charges, thereby giving larger airports greater flexibility to generate their own revenue.

DEPARTMENT OF THE TREASURY

Funding Highlights:

- Provides $14.2 billion in discretionary funding for the Department of the Treasury, including a program integrity initiative. Excluding investments in the Internal Revenue Service, spending across other Treasury bureaus is reduced by 2.3 percent from the 2012 enacted level, while select investments are made in high-priority programs.

- Implements the Wall Street Reform Act to protect consumers in the financial marketplace.

- Supports small business lending and protects vulnerable homeowners.

- Continues to responsibly wind-down the Troubled Asset Relief Program.

- Promotes community development through capital, credit, and financial services to low-income communities.

- Supports innovative, evidence-based public-private partnerships that yield Federal, State, and local savings.

- Implements the Affordable Care Act tax provisions that become effective in 2014 and supports efforts to effectively respond to the expected increase in public inquiries pertaining to the law.

- Improves program integrity in tax enforcement, generating $32.7 billion in net savings to reduce the deficit over the next 10 years. The multi-year initiative to narrow the gap between taxes owed and paid, increases tax revenues through enhanced compliance efforts.

- Invests in financial management innovations through online reporting and transparency platforms and Government-wide shared service reforms.

The Department of the Treasury (Treasury) supports a strong U.S. economy by promoting economic growth, building a comprehensive financial regulatory framework, and identifying and addressing domestic and international economic threats. The Department also carries out many functions that are essential to the financial integrity of the Federal Government such as collecting revenue, managing finances, distributing payments, and producing currency. To support Treasury's mission, the President's Budget provides $14.2 billion; a 7.7 percent increase above the 2012 enacted level. Excluding the Internal Revenue Service (IRS) where the Budget proposes a program integrity initiative to increase revenues, Treasury funding is reduced by $31 million, or 2.3 percent, from the 2012 enacted level.

Strengthens Financial Market Stability, Promotes Economic Growth, Improves Healthcare Coverage, Supports Homeowners, and Improves Financial Management

Protects Consumers and Supports Continued Implementation of Wall Street Reform. The Administration continues to support financial regulators' efforts to effectively implement the Wall Street Reform Act, enacted three years ago to improve market transparency and operations, strengthen financial institutions, and increase consumer protections. Through the Financial Stability Oversight Council chaired by the Treasury Secretary, the Administration supports efforts to identify, monitor, and respond to emerging threats to U.S. financial stability. The Administration also continues to vigorously support the protection of American consumers and investors, including through the new Consumer Financial Protection Bureau's efforts to protect consumers and penalize bad actors in the financial services marketplace, as well as through the Securities and Exchange Commission and the Commodity Futures Trading Commission, whose funding in the Budget increases 27 percent and 54 percent, respectively.

Encourages Small Business Lending. The Small Business Lending Fund (SBLF) and the State Small Business Credit Initiative (SSBCI), both created by the Small Business Jobs Act of 2010, have committed over $5 billion to facilitate the restoration of credit markets and financing options for small businesses for years to come. The SBLF has provided over $4 billion to 332 banks and community development loan funds across the United States, supplying low-cost capital to small and community banks to enable them to increase their small business lending. The SSBCI, which boosts State-sponsored small business loan funds, has approved funding for 47 States, five U.S. territories, four municipalities, and the District of Columbia, and is expected to spur at least $15 billion in new lending. The Budget provides $2 million to enable the SSBCI to expand technical assistance provided to program participants beginning in 2013. These funds will focus on assistance tailored to each of these State-sponsored programs, designed to increase the effectiveness of the program to boost small business and entrepreneurial capital and create jobs.

Responsibly Winds-Down the Troubled Asset Relief Program. The Treasury's authority to enter into new financial commitments through the Troubled Asset Relief Program (TARP) program ended on October 3, 2010. The Budget continues to support the effective, transparent, and accountable winding down of TARP programs that have helped stabilize the financial system, preserve jobs in the American automotive industry, and restart markets critical to financing American households and businesses. Moreover, TARP's banking programs have generated a positive return for taxpayers, with over $268 billion recovered for taxpayers as of December 31, 2012, compared to the $245 billion originally invested in banks. The progressing economic recovery and the Administration's prudent management have resulted in an estimated lifetime TARP cost of $47.5 billion, significantly lower than the $341 billion cost originally estimated for the program in its first year.

Supports Struggling Homeowners. The Administration continues to implement ongoing TARP and other activities to assist homeowners threatened by foreclosure, including unemployed homeowners and those with negative home equity. As of December 31, 2012, over 1.1 million borrowers have received permanent modifications through the Home Affordable Modification Program (HAMP), which amounts to an estimated $17.3 billion in realized aggregate savings for these homeowners. The Administration's TARP housing programs have also been a catalyst for private sector mortgage modifications. Between April 2009 and the end of November 2012, HAMP and the private sector HOPE NOW alliance initiated over 6.1 million mortgage modifications and loss mitigation interventions, approximately double the number of foreclosure completions that were executed in the same period. Furthermore, the Administration has allocated $7.6 billion to eligible States through the Housing Finance Agencies' Hardest Hit Fund to implement innovative housing programs that stabilize local housing markets and meet the unique needs of communities.

Invests in Community Development. The Budget increases funding for the Community Development Financial Institutions (CDFI) Fund, which provides financing to increase economic and community development and job opportunities in poor and underserved communities. It also expands the Fund's Healthy Food Financing Initiative that promotes the development of healthy food outlets in areas known as "food deserts"—low-income areas where a substantial number of residents have limited access to a supermarket or large grocery store. In addition, the Budget supports improvements in the Bank Enterprise Awards program that will better incentivize banks to invest in distressed communities. The Administration is dedicated to improving the CDFI Fund's effectiveness by investing in data collection and program analysis that will foster a better understanding of the impact of CDFI programs on poverty reduction and development investment in underserved communities.

Invests in Partnerships and Innovation. The Budget also creates a $300 million Pay for Success Fund within Treasury. Non-profit intermediaries and State and local governments will be able to leverage the Fund to provide credit enhancements and success-based payments to investors in public programs that impact families and communities and generate Federal savings. The Fund is designed to encourage innovation and accelerate the use of evidence-based approaches by lowering the risk associated with initial investments.

Supports Implementation of the Affordable Care Act. The Affordable Care Act will ensure that every American can access high-quality, affordable health care coverage, providing health insurance to nearly 30 million Americans who would otherwise be uninsured. Tax provisions play an important role in the health care law's implementation, and many of its provisions are scheduled to take effect in 2014. The Budget provides funding for the IRS to implement these tax provisions and to respond effectively to public inquiries about the Affordable Care Act's new benefits and standards.

Invests in Financial Management Innovation and Leadership. To help Federal agencies respond to the current fiscal realities, the Administration is focused on maximizing the effectiveness of Government-wide financial management practices. Increasing shared services among agencies, modernizing information systems, plans, and requirements, and facilitating Government-wide operational capabilities will improve the efficiency of the Federal Government— accomplishing more while spending less. To aid such efforts, the Budget invests in Treasury's leadership capacity to support implementation of several Government-wide financial innovation initiatives, including management of a simplified financial reporting system and expanding the use of Federal shared service arrangements to support future financial management needs.

Improves and Expands Government Transparency. The Budget capitalizes on Treasury's extensive financial expertise by having the Department assume responsibility for operating and expanding *USASpending.gov*. Treasury will increase the transparency of Government-wide programs by improving the publicly-accessible database that communicates financial information to the public and agencies. This program transfer from the General Services Administration is consistent with recommendations from the Government Accountability and Transparency Board to transition assets built by the Recovery Accountability and Transparency Board into the Federal Government's overall financial management framework.

Makes Necessary Cuts and Saves Taxpayer Money

Cuts Administrative Overhead. The Budget proposes over $350 million in reduced Treasury administrative costs through technology consolidations, teleworking implementation, efficiency initiatives, and other overhead reductions that are consistent with the President's Campaign to Cut Waste.

Modernizes and Streamlines U.S. Currency Production. The Budget proposes legislation to grant the U.S. Mint and Bureau of Engraving and Printing increased flexibility to share services and engage in cooperative actions, in order to gain efficiency savings by reducing unnecessary duplication of effort. The Budget also proposes legislation to provide the Secretary flexibility to change the composition of coins to more cost-effective materials, given that the current cost of making the penny is two cents and the cost of making the nickel is 11 cents. Treasury is taking additional actions to improve the efficiency of coin and currency production efforts. For example, the Budget includes proposals that will save $22 million from information technology efficiencies and reduced labor costs for currency production.

Invests in and Modernizes Tax Administration to Prevent Evasion and Cheating. The Budget funds IRS at nearly $12.9 billion, roughly $1 billion above the 2012 enacted level. More than $400 million of this total is provided through a program integrity cap adjustment. This investment pays for itself several times over, with strong tax enforcement returning $4 or more in revenue for each additional IRS dollar spent. The Budget also continues to support the IRS's major technology investment program that will yield substantial benefits to taxpayers by fundamentally changing how the IRS does business, vastly improving both the taxpayer experience and the effectiveness of the agency through faster taxpayer refunds and more accurate issue resolution.

Improves Efforts to Collect Debt. The Budget proposes common sense debt collection reforms that will significantly increase Federal collections from individuals and businesses that have failed to pay their taxes or repay Government loans, and will help States collect a portion of the sizable State income tax debt owed by former residents. These proposals will increase collections by approximately $1 billion over the next 10 years and help enforce a tax system in which everyone pays their share.

DEPARTMENT OF VETERANS AFFAIRS

Funding Highlights:

- Provides $63.5 billion in discretionary funding for the Department of Veterans Affairs, an 8.5 percent increase over the 2012 enacted level, to provide needed care and other benefits to veterans and their families. In addition, the Budget includes $3.1 billion in estimated medical care collections, for a total budget authority of approximately $66.5 billion.

- Includes $54.6 billion for veterans' medical care, supporting continuing improvements in the delivery of mental health care, the development of telehealth technologies, specialized care for women veterans, and benefits for veterans' caregivers.

- Requests $55.6 billion in 2015 advance appropriations for medical care programs, to ensure continuity of veterans' health care services.

- Provides $1.4 billion to support the Administration's ongoing efforts to combat veteran homelessness.

- Invests $586 million for medical and prosthetic research efforts to advance the care and quality of life for veterans.

- Provides $799 million to ensure timely activation of new and renovated medical facilities already under construction.

- Improves the Department's efficiency by investing $136 million in a Veterans Claims Intake Program, continuing to implement the paperless claims system, and undertaking additional efforts to provide faster and more accurate benefits claims processing and improve veterans' access to benefits information.

- Provides $104 million through a new Transition Assistance Program called "Transition GPS" to help separating military servicemembers better transition to civilian life.

- Supports three new national cemeteries for veterans in Florida and Nebraska.

Our Nation has a solemn obligation to take care of our veterans and to honor them for their service and sacrifice on behalf of the United States. To deliver on this commitment, the 2014 President's Budget provides $63.5 billion in discretionary funding for the Department of Veterans Affairs (VA), an 8.5 percent increase above the 2012 enacted level. In addition, the

Budget includes $3.1 billion in estimated medical care collections, for a total budget authority of approximately $66.5 billion. This funding will continue to drive improvements in efficiency and responsiveness at VA, enabling the Department to better serve veterans and their families at a time when much is being asked of our men and women in uniform. The Budget supports efforts to ensure we meet the needs of today's veteran population, and invests in the continued modernization of VA to meet 21st Century challenges.

Sustains and Strengthens Services for Veterans

Protects Critical Funding for VA Medical Care. The Budget provides $54.6 billion for VA medical care, a 7.9 percent increase above the 2012 enacted level, to provide high-quality and timely health care services to veterans and other eligible beneficiaries. These services include innovative programs to educate and support veterans' caregivers, enhance veterans' access to care via telehealth technologies, and support the provision of equitable, high-quality care for women veterans in a sensitive and safe environment. In addition, the Budget proposes $55.6 billion in advance appropriations for the VA medical care program in 2015, which will provide timely and predictable funding for VA's medical care to prevent our veterans from being adversely affected by appropriations delays.

Strengthens Mental Health Care Services. The Budget provides nearly $7 billion, a 15.4 percent increase above the 2012 enacted level, to continue VA's focus on expanding and transforming mental health services for veterans to ensure accessible and patient-centered care, including treatment for Post-Traumatic Stress Disorder and Military Sexual Trauma. This funding will allow VA to continue its collaborative efforts with the Departments of Defense (DOD) and Health and Human Services, as directed in the President's executive order on veterans' mental health, to help veterans receive timely access to mental health services, including through enhanced partnerships with community providers.

Combats Veteran Homelessness. The Budget invests $1.4 billion to provide VA services for homeless and at-risk veterans. These funds will help combat veterans' homelessness through collaborative partnerships with local governments, non-profit organizations, and the Departments of Housing and Urban Development, Justice, and Labor.

Supports Medical and Prosthetic Research. As part of the largest integrated health care system in the United States, the VA research program benefits from clinical care and research occurring together, allowing discoveries to be directly coordinated with the care of veterans. In particular, the Budget includes $586 million in funds for medical and prosthetic research.

Activates New and Improved Health Care Facilities. The Budget includes $799 million to help VA provide the best possible specialized care for veterans in new or renovated facilities. These funds will support the staff and equipment at VA facilities across the Nation, including improved polytrauma and spinal cord injury units.

Improves Health Care Delivery for Our Nation's Veterans. The Budget includes funding for VA to further assess and develop efficiencies and successful practices by analyzing the delivery and reimbursement of health care within other Federal health programs, such as Defense Health Programs and Medicare. This assessment will help to drive future innovation as VA strives to continually improve health outcomes, quality of care, and access to services while responsibly managing public resources.

Continues Implementation of the Paperless Claims System. The Budget includes $136 million for a Veterans Claims Intake Program that will allow VA to directly receive and convert paper evidence, such as medical records, into a digital format for increased efficiency in claims processing. The Budget also supports transformation initiatives, including the continued development of a digital, near-paperless environment that allows for greater exchange of information and increased transparency for veterans. Specifically, the Budget includes $155 million for the Veterans Benefit Management System, designed to reduce the processing time and the claims backlog, facilitate quality improvements through rules-based calculators that provide claims processors better capabilities to assign accurate service-connected evaluation, and automate claims tracking. These overall efforts support VA's pursuit of eliminating the claims backlog and achieving VA's goal of processing all claims within 125 days with 98 percent accuracy in 2015.

Supports Veteran Employment and Transition Assistance. The Budget provides $104 million to help our Nation's servicemembers transition to civilian life after over 10 years of war. The Budget supports the enhancement of the inter-agency Transition Assistance Program, designed by the Veterans Employment Initiative Task Force, by creating a new program called Transition GPS (Goals, Plans, Success). The Transition GPS program will help separating servicemembers prepare for their civilian life by providing pre-separation assessments and individual counseling, a five-day core curriculum, an additional curriculum tailored to the servicemembers' individual career goals, and a capstone event to verify that transitioning servicemembers have met certain standards that show they are ready for their civilian careers. For example, Transition GPS will provide servicemembers with comprehensive benefits briefings, additional training on VA education programs, and facilitated access to other government agencies to ensure that servicemembers can fully utilize available education and employment services as they prepare to separate.

Improves Access to Comprehensive Services and Benefits. The Budget supports VA's efforts to ensure consistent, personalized, and accurate information about services and benefits, especially in the delivery of compensation and pension claims processing. In order to improve the speed, effectiveness, and efficiency of benefits service delivery, the joint DOD/VA eBenefits web portal provides veterans with the critical self-service capabilities to manage their VA, military and personal information, apply online for benefits, and check the status of a claim.

Expands Access to National Veterans Cemeteries. In 2011, VA reduced the population threshold used to determine where new national veterans cemeteries should be built from 170,000 to 80,000 veterans living within 75 miles of a potential location. Under this lower threshold, VA will develop five new cemeteries, providing a nearby national cemetery option to at least 550,000 additional veterans and resulting in 94 percent of all veterans having a veterans cemetery burial option within a reasonable distance from their homes. The Budget provides funding to construct and open the first three of these five new national cemeteries which would be located in St. Augustine, Florida, Tallahassee, Florida, and Omaha, Nebraska.

CORPS OF ENGINEERS—CIVIL WORKS

Funding Highlights:

- Provides $4.7 billion for the Army Corps of Engineers civil works program, a 5.5 percent decrease from the 2012 enacted level. The Budget achieves savings by focusing on investments that will yield high economic and environmental returns or address a significant risk to public safety.

- Continues efforts to restore significant aquatic ecosystems such as the California Bay-Delta, the Chesapeake Bay, the Everglades, the Great Lakes, and the Gulf Coast, helping to promote their ecological sustainability and resilience.

- Continues to provide priority funding for the operation and maintenance of high performing projects, such as navigation on the Mississippi and Ohio Rivers and the Illinois Waterway.

- Reforms the way that the Federal Government finances capital investments in support of navigation on the inland waterways including a new user fee.

- Supports a high level of investment in maintenance work and related activities at the most heavily used commercial harbors in the Nation.

- Increases the organizational efficiency and improves the management, oversight, and performance of ongoing programs to meet water resources needs and achieve additional savings.

The Army Corps of Engineers civil works program (Corps) develops, manages, restores, and protects water resources primarily through construction of projects, operation and maintenance, studies of potential projects, and its regulatory program. Working with other Federal agencies, the Corps also helps communities respond to and recover from floods and other natural disasters.

To support this work, the President's 2014 Budget provides $4.7 billion, a $276 million, or 5.5 percent decrease from the 2012 enacted level. The Budget focuses on the highest priority work within the agency's three main missions— flood and storm damage reduction, commercial navigation, and aquatic ecosystem restoration.

Invests in Our Water Resources to Spur Competiveness and Protect the Environment

Emphasizes Investments in Construction Projects with High Economic and Environmental Returns While Addressing Public Safety. The Budget proposes $1.35 billion for high-return construction projects in the three main mission areas of the Corps: flood and storm damage reduction; commercial navigation; and aquatic ecosystem restoration. The Budget emphasizes funding for projects that address a significant risk to public safety, including investments to repair high-risk dams. The Administration's Task Force on Ports is developing a national strategy for investment leading to a network of ports and related infrastructure that is more efficient, safe, secure, resilient, and environmentally sustainable. The strategy will be informed by stakeholder input. As a first step, the Task Force is proposing a set of principles to guide investment decisions. The principles envision a series of targeted investments over time that would be highly cost-effective when viewed together, and would encourage better alignment of investment decisions.

Restores High-Priority Aquatic Ecosystems. The Budget proposes funding to restore significant aquatic ecosystems based on sound science and adaptive management. Funds are provided for work on priority aquatic ecosystems, including the California Bay-Delta, Chesapeake Bay, Everglades, Great Lakes, and Gulf Coast. Funds are also provided for other aquatic ecosystem efforts, such as restoring Puget Sound and improving environmental outcomes in the Upper Mississippi River and the Missouri River.

Invests in Existing Water Resources Infrastructure. The Budget focuses on the operation of existing infrastructure and improving its reliability. The Budget gives priority to funding the operation and maintenance of key infrastructure, including navigation channels that serve our largest coastal ports and the inland waterways with the most commercial use.

Improves Funding and Management

Reforms Inland Waterways Financing. The Administration has proposed legislation to reform the laws governing the Inland Waterways Trust Fund, including establishing an annual per vessel fee to increase the amount paid by commercial navigation users sufficiently to meet their share of the costs of activities financed from this fund. The additional revenue would help finance future capital investments in these waterways to support economic growth. The amounts collected would reflect the actual costs incurred, so any cost savings would translate over time directly into lower fees.

Modernizes Federal Water Resources Management. The Administration has already proposed several major actions to modernize the policies and procedures of the Army Corps of Engineers, and other Federal water resources agencies, so that the Federal Government, in partnership with its non-Federal partners, can make better use of our Nation's water resources to generate economic growth, environmental improvements, and social benefits. These include revising the 25-year old principles and guidelines for planning water resources projects, proposing a user fee to help finance inland waterways capital investments, and establishing an Infrastructure Bank that would help finance port deepening, levees, and other major water resources development activities. The Administration is also considering proposals to improve the ability of the Corps to invest in and manage its assets and to enhance non-Federal leadership in water resources, including removing unnecessary obstacles and streamlining procedures for non-Federal parties to move forward on their own with important water resources activities, while ensuring appropriate Federal interests are maintained.

Increases Organizational Efficiency. The Administration is also working to improve the responsiveness, accountability, and operational oversight of the civil works program in order to best meet current and future water resources challenges. This effort will improve performance and free up resources for other uses and deficit reduction.

ENVIRONMENTAL PROTECTION AGENCY

Funding Highlights:

- Provides $8.2 billion for the Environmental Protection Agency, a decrease of $296 million, or 3.5 percent, below the 2012 enacted level.

- Builds on prior information technology advancements and efforts to streamline regulations by investing in the E-Enterprise Initiative to assess and reformulate business processes, transition from paper-based to electronic reporting, and develop an interactive portal for regulatory transactions with States and the business community. This investment will improve the quality of data used for decision-making and allow the Agency and States to regulate and enforce compliance more effectively and efficiently.

- Modernizes the Agency by consolidating positions and restructuring the workforce to ensure the Agency has the necessary skills for the current era of environmental protection, and supports investment in the E-Enterprise Initiative as a means of using data and evidence to improve program performance.

- Increases support to States and Tribes by $47 million for implementation of delegated authorities, including those for air quality management and water pollution control programs.

- Continues efforts to restore significant ecosystems such as the Great Lakes, Chesapeake Bay, California Bay-Delta, Everglades, and the Gulf Coast, by helping to promote their ecological sustainability and resilience.

- Reduces funding for Drinking Water and Clean Water State Revolving Funds by a combined $472 million, while focusing assistance on small and underserved communities and the use of green infrastructure.

- Limits new Hazardous Substance Superfund remedial action project starts while maintaining emergency preparedness and response programs.

The Environmental Protection Agency's (EPA) mission is to protect human health and the environment. Due to the current fiscal environment, the 2014 President's Budget includes $8.2 billion to continue to deliver on this mission, a decrease of $296 million, or 3.5 percent, from the 2012 enacted level. This funding supports the E-Enterprise Initiative, designed to transform the way the Agency does business, and increases core priorities, such as grants to support State and tribal implementation of delegated environmental programs. The Budget provides $1.9 billion for the annual Federal contribution to State Revolving Funds, a reduction of $472 million that will still allow for robust financing by State programs, while emphasizing small, underserved communities and the use of green infrastructure to leverage resources. The Budget also reduces the Hazardous Substance Superfund account by $33 million, and eliminates $54 million in outdated, underperforming, and overlapping programs.

Supports a 21st Century EPA

Moves EPA Forward by Investing in the E-Enterprise Initiative. By developing an interactive portal for environmental protection transactions, including processing permit applications and providing updated regulations and relevant compliance information to industry, E-Enterprise will enable EPA and the States to more efficiently and effectively implement programs. The E-Enterprise Initiative will start by assessing and updating current business processes and implementing the information technology systems needed to transition from paper to electronic reporting, which will reduce the reporting burden on industry, as well as encourage greater transparency and compliance. This initiative capitalizes on ongoing investments made by EPA and the States to share data through the Central Data Exchange, and promotes a data infrastructure that will be used to gather evidence and apply lessons learned to improve programs and realize efficiencies. E-Enterprise builds on efforts such as e-Manifest for hazardous waste, which will allow for one-stop reporting and save industry the costs of completing thousands of pages of paper reports that cannot easily be used for tracking and managing shipments.

Begins Transforming the Workforce for the Modern Era. The Budget restructures the workforce, focusing on matching the right skills with program implementation and utilizing best management practices. Some positions will be consolidated and reconfigured to reflect the current era of environmental protection that increasingly relies on advanced monitoring tools and information technology for data-driven analyses and targeted enforcement and compliance activities. This restructuring will support the implementation of the E-Enterprise Initiative.

Reduces the Agency's Physical Footprint. The Budget continues to support EPA's efforts to shrink its physical footprint through reconfiguring and consolidating workspace, and disposing of underutilized properties and satellite offices.

Fosters Progress on a Clean Energy Economy

Supports Efforts to Address Climate Change. The President has set a goal to reduce domestic greenhouse gas emissions 17 percent below 2005 levels by 2020, and EPA has taken steps to help make significant progress toward this goal. For example, when fully implemented, the Administration's national program of fuel economy and greenhouse gas standards for cars and light trucks alone will save consumers an average of $8,000 in fuel costs, cut oil use by approximately 12 billion barrels and prevent six billion metric tons of greenhouse gas emissions over the lifetimes of the vehicles sold through model year 2025. In 2014, EPA will continue to implement existing regulations to reduce emissions from light duty and heavy duty mobile sources. EPA will continue to collaborate with Federal and State agencies, the private sector, and other stakeholders, to explore other cost-effective strategies to reduce greenhouse gas emissions. The Budget also maintains funding levels for partnership and voluntary programs like ENERGY STAR, which help reduce energy waste and cut household utility bills. To help prepare the Nation for climate change impacts that cannot be avoided, EPA programs will also support local community efforts to improve resilience to extreme weather and other climate change impacts. These efforts are consistent with a broader Administration commitment to help communities improve their resilience to climate change through direct technical assistance, useful data and tools on projected impacts, and other support.

Strengthens the Economy Through Environmental Investments

Promotes Economic Growth with Funding for Brownfields. Brownfields are lightly contaminated sites, many in economically hard-hit areas, where the presence or potential presence of contamination may keep these sites from being used productively. The Budget leverages funding from across the Federal Government, as well as State, local, and private investment in order to promote job creation and economic growth in these communities through initiatives such as the Urban Waters Federal Partnership, the Partnership for Sustainable Communities, and Strong Cities, Strong Communities. In order to support these initiatives and communities around the Nation while recognizing fiscal constraints, the Budget increases funding for technical assistance, but slightly reduces competitive grant funds.

Continues to Fund the Great Lakes Restoration Initiative. The Budget proposes to maintain funding for the Great Lakes Restoration Initiative at $300 million, which will allow for continued ecosystem restoration efforts while exercising fiscal restraint. This EPA-led interagency effort to restore the Great Lakes focuses on priority environmental issues such as cleaning up contaminated sediments and toxics, reducing non-point source pollution, mitigating habitat degradation and loss, and addressing invasive species.

Supports Restoration of the Chesapeake Bay. Funding for Chesapeake Bay restoration is increased by $16 million to support Bay watershed States as they implement their plans to reduce nutrient and sediment pollution in an unprecedented effort to restore this economically important ecosystem. EPA and Federal partners will continue to coordinate with States, municipalities, and industry to restore the integrity of this national treasure.

Supports State and Tribal Environmental Programs. The Budget proposes $1.1 billion for grants to support State and tribal implementation of delegated environmental programs. The support includes $257 million in State grant funding for air programs, an increase of $22 million to assist States in addressing additional responsibilities associated with greenhouse gas reduction efforts and other air pollutants, and $259 million in State water pollution control grants, a $20 million increase, including $15 million to improve nutrient management. The Budget also proposes to increase funding for the Tribal General Assistance Program (Tribal GAP) by $5 million. Tribal GAP funding builds tribal capacity and assists Tribes in leveraging other EPA and Federal funding to contribute to a higher level of environmental and health protection.

Enhances Interagency Efforts to Improve Water Quality. The United States has made great strides in improving water quality; however non-point source pollution remains a significant economic, environmental, and public health challenge that requires policy attention and thoughtful new approaches. Key Federal partners, along with agricultural producer organizations, conservation districts, States, Tribes, non-governmental organizations, and other local leaders will continue to work together to identify areas where a focused and coordinated approach can achieve decreases in water pollution. The Budget builds upon the collaborative process already underway among Federal partners to demonstrate substantial improvements in water quality from conservation programs by coordinating efforts between the Department of Agriculture (USDA) and EPA programs, such as EPA's Nonpoint Source Grants and Water Pollution Control Grants and USDA's Farm Bill conservation programs. This coordination will allow for more effective, targeted investments at the Federal and State level during a time of constrained budgets, and will ensure continued improvements in water quality.

Leverages Cost Effective Tools. Through the Urban Waters Federal partnership, Federal agencies, including EPA, are working together to help communities restore waterways and realize the economic, environmental, and social benefits of clean water. In many cities, stormwater has become a growing challenge to protecting and improving water quality. However, green infrastructure, such as green roofs, rain gardens, wetlands, and forest buffers, can be a cost-effective way to manage stormwater and meet Clean Water Act goals. In 2014, the Urban Waters Federal Partnership will partner with at least two communities to help incorporate green infrastructure into their stormwater management plans, eventually providing models for others also facing the same challenges.

Makes Focused Cuts

Reduces Funding for State Revolving Funds (SRFs). The Budget proposes a combined $1.9 billion for Federal capitalization of the SRFs, representing a reduction of $472 million from the 2012 enacted level. The Budget also proposes a gradual reduction to focus on communities most in need of assistance, but will still allow the SRFs to finance approximately $6 billion in wastewater and drinking water infrastructure projects annually. The Administration has strongly supported the SRFs, having received and/or requested a total of approximately $20 billion in funds for the SRFs since 2009. Since their inception, the SRFs have been provided with approximately $53 billion. Going forward, EPA will work to target SRF assistance to small and underserved communities with limited ability to repay loans. The Administration strongly supports efforts to expand the use of green infrastructure to meet Clean Water Act goals. To further these efforts, the Budget will target the funding intended for green infrastructure approaches to storm and wastewater, which will help communities improve water quality while creating green space, mitigating flooding, and enhancing air quality.

Provides Targeted Decreases to Hazardous Substance Superfund Account. The Budget reduces funding for the Hazardous Substance Superfund account by $33 million from the 2012 enacted level. These reductions will be targeted largely to new project phases of long-term remediation construction. The Budget maintains a funding level necessary for EPA to be prepared to respond to emergency releases of hazardous substances and circumstances that place the public at imminent risk of exposure and harm. The Administration has also put in place a more robust process for tracking and using special account (i.e., settlement) funds, in an effort to preserve Federal dollars for those sites where no viable, responsible party has been identified.

Eliminates Outdated, Underperforming, and Overlapping Programs. The Budget terminates $54 million in outdated, underperforming, or duplicative EPA programs. This reduction is part of the Administration's Government-wide effort to focus resources on programs that have the greatest impact and in areas that benefit most from Federal support, while eliminating those programs that are underperforming, or can be implemented through other Federal or State efforts (e.g., the Radon and Beaches grant programs).

NATIONAL AERONAUTICS AND SPACE ADMINISTRATION

Funding Highlights:

- Provides $17.7 billion in discretionary funding for the National Aeronautics and Space Administration (NASA), a decrease of 0.3 percent, or about $50 million, below the 2012 enacted level. While making tough choices, the Budget reinforces the agency's current balanced portfolio of aeronautics and space technology development, Earth and space science, the development of rockets and capsules to carry explorers deeper into space, and the use of innovative commercial partnerships for crew and cargo transport to the International Space Station.

- Includes funding needed to develop a Commercial Crew capability, with the intent of supporting a new industry that regains the capability to send American astronauts into space from U.S. soil and ends the need to pay foreign providers to transport American astronauts to the International Space Station.

- Increases investment in space technologies, such as advanced in-space propulsion and space propellant storage, which are necessary to increase America's capabilities in space, bring the cost of space exploration down, and pave the way for other Federal Government and commercial space activities.

- Fully funds the Space Launch System heavy-lift rocket and Orion Multi-Purpose Crew Vehicle, two key elements for pushing the boundaries of human space exploration. This funding level will enable a flight test of Orion in 2014 and the Space Launch System in 2017.

- Keeps development of the James Webb Space Telescope, the more powerful successor to the Hubble Space Telescope, on track for a 2018 launch.

- Provides over $1.8 billion for Earth Science to revamp the Landsat program, develop climate sensors for the Joint Polar Satellite System, and conduct numerous other satellite and research efforts.

- Begins work on a mission to rendezvous with—and then move—a small asteroid. Astronauts would later visit the asteroid and return samples to Earth, achieving one of the agency's major goals in a more cost-effective manner.

- Continues the agency's important role in the Nation's aeronautics research and development portfolio, including a new initiative to make lighter composite materials more easily useable in aviation.

155

- Funds research on the International Space Station, while identifying efficiencies in operations and space flight support.

- Consolidates $47.5 million of small science, technology, engineering, and mathematics (STEM) education programs from across NASA into larger programs at other agencies to achieve the best return on investment, while attaining tangible Government-wide STEM education goals. The Budget preserves $67.5 million for the Space Grant and Global Learning and Observations to Benefit the Environment programs at NASA, as well as key minority-serving education programs, and refocuses an additional $26.8 million from other NASA education and outreach programs to facilitate the wider application of its best education assets in close coordination with the National Science Foundation, the Department of Education, and the Smithsonian Institution.

The National Aeronautics and Space Administration (NASA) develops aeronautics and space technologies, studies the Earth from space, and pioneers the exploration of space. The Budget provides $17.7 billion for NASA to support investments that will ensure continued U.S. leadership in space, while helping to create new industries and capabilities. It supports research and development to drive advances in our space capabilities and strengthens NASA's ability to answer increasingly important scientific questions about the Earth.

Leads the World in Space Exploration

Invests in American Private Aerospace Enterprises. In order to reduce our reliance on foreign providers for transporting our astronauts to and from the International Space Station, the Budget invests in the innovative energies of U.S. industry to create transport capabilities at a lower cost than previous systems. Building on a successful commercial cargo program, the Commercial Crew Program is a uniquely American partnership aimed at introducing new efficiencies in space exploration that will strengthen U.S. leadership in space, help produce a more globally-competitive U.S. space industry, and enable the Nation to more fully benefit from the International Space Station's research capabilities.

Sustains Investment in Space Technologies. Advanced technology investments will increase the affordability, safety, and feasibility of NASA and other Federal Government and commercial space activities to ultimately enable travel to and exploration of destinations never before visited. From laboratory experiments to technology demonstrations onboard the International Space Station to future in-space missions, the Budget funds the testing and development of technologies that will be crucial to NASA's missions and will help to further develop a competitive U.S. aerospace sector.

Advances Human Exploration of the Solar System. The Budget fully funds the continued development of new systems that will support crewed missions to deep space. The Space Launch System heavy-lift rocket will eventually be the world's largest rocket since the Apollo-era Saturn V, and remains on track for its first test flight in 2017. The Orion Multi-Purpose Crew Vehicle will carry crews past the Moon and is scheduled for its first uncrewed flight test next year. Both programs leverage NASA's skilled workforce and contractor teams and builds upon existing capabilities to push the reach of humans farther into the solar system, with an initial goal of visiting an asteroid in the next decade, followed eventually by a human mission to Mars.

Unlocks Mysteries of the Universe. The Budget fully funds the James Webb Space Telescope, a 100-times more capable successor to the Hubble Telescope, to keep it on track for launch in 2018. Within the current constrained funding environment, the Budget funds high-priority planetary science missions, including a robotic sample return mission from an asteroid, and multiple missions focused on Mars exploration, including a new large rover to be launched in 2020.

Pursues Innovative Approach to Visiting an Asteroid. The Budget includes $78 million for NASA to develop needed technologies and study alternative approaches for a robotic mission to rendezvous with a small asteroid—one that would be harmless to Earth—and move it to a stable location outside the Moon's orbit. This mission would develop the technologies and capabilities required if in the future there is a need to move a hazardous asteroid. Eventually, astronauts would visit the retrieved asteroid using rockets and capsules NASA is already developing, fulfilling the President's goal of sending humans to an asteroid by 2025 in a more cost-effective manner and allowing the recovery and return to Earth samples of the asteroid's rocks. In addition, NASA will accelerate its efforts to detect and characterize potentially hazardous Earth asteroids, to both address the threat and clarify the opportunities these objects represent.

Discovers More About Our Home Planet

Supports a Robust Fleet of Earth Monitoring Spacecraft. NASA has unique expertise in satellite and sensor development, and the Budget makes best use of that expertise, providing over $1.8 billion to the Earth Science program, including funds to revamp the Landsat program. To minimize the risk of a gap in our Nation's climate monitoring data, NASA will develop climate sensors for the Joint Polar Satellite System program, as well as support other earth science and climate change research and development efforts.

Maximizes Resources

Consolidates STEM Education Programs. The President places a high priority on STEM education and has set ambitious goals of generating 100,000 new effective STEM teachers and one million more STEM graduates. In order to improve STEM education outcomes and achieve these goals, the Budget includes a bold reorganization of Federal STEM programs that uses existing resources more effectively and in a more streamlined, consolidated way. The Budget redirects $47.5 million of funding from small NASA education programs throughout the agency to other agencies where these funds will be consolidated with similar resources from across the Federal Government. NASA retains $67.5 million for high-performing existing programs, and an additional $26.8 million from other education and outreach programs previously distributed throughout the agency's mission directorates. NASA's assets will be used more effectively through coordination with the National Science Foundation, the Department of Education, and the Smithsonian Institution to achieve the Administration's wider STEM education goals.

Boosts Sustainability and Energy Efficiency of NASA Facilities. The Budget supports a number of initiatives to help NASA facilities operate in a more efficient and sustainable manner. Today, over 80 percent of NASA buildings are beyond their design life. The Budget continues to enable NASA to replace or modernize inefficient buildings, providing jobs to local communities and leading to increasingly efficient use of taxpayer dollars. For example, the Budget supports a building renovation at Langley Research Center in Virginia and a number of cost-savings investments across NASA that will reduce the footprint, co-locate personnel, consolidate data centers, increase energy efficiency, and improve sustainability.

NATIONAL SCIENCE FOUNDATION

Funding Highlights:

- Provides $7.6 billion for the National Science Foundation, an increase of $593 million above the 2012 enacted level, to expand the frontiers of knowledge, lay the foundation for economic growth and job creation, and educate a globally competitive workforce.

- Maintains the President's commitment to increase funding for key basic research agencies, including a robust 8.4 percent increase over the 2012 enacted level for the National Science Foundation.

- Builds an innovation economy through investments in a broad portfolio of foundational research, as well as investments in strategic areas, such as cyberinfrastructure, advanced manufacturing, and clean energy.

- Transforms science, technology, engineering, and mathematics education by empowering the National Science Foundation to lead undergraduate and graduate education reform, as part of a bold plan to strengthen education investments across the Federal Government.

- Increases agency efficiency by constraining administrative costs and making operations in Antarctica more cost-effective.

- Invests $6 million to strengthen the agency's capacity to evaluate the outcomes of its programs.

The National Science Foundation (NSF) is the key Federal grant-making agency responsible for supporting the full breadth of non-biomedical science and engineering research at the Nation's universities and colleges. NSF's research and high-tech workforce development programs help lay the foundation for economic growth by building an innovation economy and educating globally competitive American workers. To support this important mission, the President's 2014 Budget provides $7.6 billion for NSF, 8.4 percent above the 2012 enacted level, including strong support for cross-cutting research priorities such as advanced manufacturing and clean energy. The Budget also supports efforts to improve agency operations, for example, by strengthening the agency's ability to evaluate the effectiveness of its programs and by increasing the efficiency of Antarctic operations.

159

Builds an Innovation Economy

Supports the Fundamental Research That Underpins Progress in Science, Technology, and Innovation. The Budget proposes $6.2 billion for research and related activities at NSF and includes $63 million to continue an interdisciplinary research and education initiative that is changing the way the agency solicits and funds innovative cross-disciplinary proposals.

Lays the Groundwork for the Industries and Jobs of the Future. NSF links the results of fundamental research to societal needs, including building human capacity through educating tomorrow's technical workforce. To encourage interdisciplinary research for a future bio-economy, the Budget provides $51 million for innovative proposals at the interface of biology, mathematics, the physical sciences, and engineering. The Budget proposes $155 million, double the 2012 enacted level, for a cyberinfrastructure initiative that will accelerate the pace of discovery in all research disciplines by advancing high performance computing—increasingly essential to developments in fields such as climate science and clean energy—by creating new research networks and data repositories, and by developing new systems to visualize data.

Invests in the Long-Term Competitiveness of American Manufacturing. The Budget proposes $160 million, an increase of $49 million above the 2012 enacted level, for fundamental research on revolutionary new manufacturing technologies in partnership with other Federal agencies and the private sector. This advanced manufacturing research is part of a larger $300 million NSF research initiative aimed at transforming static systems, processes, and infrastructure into adaptive, pervasive "smart" systems with embedded computational intelligence that can sense, adapt, and react. This larger research effort also provides $32 million for NSF's contribution to the National Robotics Initiative, which will accelerate the development and use of robots in the United States. It also provides $42 million for NSF's contribution to the Materials Genome Initiative, which is designed to discover, manufacture, and deploy advanced materials twice as fast as the current state of the art, at a fraction of the cost.

Supports the Long-Term Development of a Clean Energy Economy. The Budget proposes $372 million for fundamental research that is directly relevant to future clean energy technologies such as solar power generation and energy efficiency. In coordination with other Federal agencies, this clean energy research is a key component of an integrated approach to increasing U.S. energy independence, enhancing environmental stewardship, reducing energy and carbon intensity, and generating sustainable economic growth.

Accelerates Innovations from the Laboratory to the Market. While the knowledge gained from NSF-supported fundamental research frequently advances a particular field of science or engineering, some results also show immediate potential for broader applicability and impact in the business world. The Budget proposes $25 million, an increase of $17 million above the 2012 enacted level, for the public-private "Innovation Corps" program at NSF aimed at bringing together the technological, entrepreneurial, and business know-how necessary to bring discoveries ripe for innovation out of the university lab.

Educates a Globally-Competitive American Workforce

Focuses Investments in Undergraduate Education to Increase Their Impact. In line with the Administration's bold reorganization of science, technology, engineering, and mathematics (STEM) education programs to improve effectiveness of Federal investments, the Budget proposes consolidating disparate STEM undergraduate education activities across the Government into a new consolidated program at NSF. This reform will increase the efficiency and effectiveness of these streamlined investments by implementing evidence-based instructional practices and supporting an expanded evidence base.

It includes research on how new technologies can facilitate adoption and use of new approaches to instruction. The Budget provides $123 million for this new program.

Expands Research Opportunities for Early College Students. The Administration has committed to increasing the number of college graduates with degrees in technical fields. Solving real-world research problems can help inspire students to pursue such degrees. The Budget proposes $79 million, an increase of $13 million above the 2012 enacted level, for NSF's Research Experiences for Undergraduates. Since early opportunities to conduct research can be especially influential in maintaining a student's interest in science, engineering, and mathematics, the program will increase its investment in research experiences for those in their first or second year of college.

Consolidates an Array of Graduate Education Programs. As part of the plan to reform STEM education, the Budget proposes consolidating an array of graduate fellowship programs, streamlining the application and award process, and reducing administrative costs. This consolidation will pave the way for a broad strategy to prepare young scientists and engineers for the high-tech jobs of the future, and will enable programmatic innovation and experimentation in ways previously not possible. The Budget proposes $325 million for the consolidated graduate research fellowship program.

Improves Efficiency and Increases Use of Evidence

Increases Efficiency of Agency Operations. NSF will improve the efficiency of its operations through an array of administrative savings initiatives, such as strategic sourcing of administrative support contracts and lowered printing costs. The agency will also increase the operational efficiency of U.S. activities in the Antarctic by implementing the highest-payoff recommendations of a blue ribbon panel of outside experts.

Strengthens the Agency's Capacity to Evaluate Its Programs. NSF must have the capacity to gauge the outcomes of its investments in both research and education in order to ensure that its investments have the desired near and long-term impacts and to enable the agency to operate from a basis of evidence in its policy decisions. To enable this strategic management, NSF will expand and coordinate program evaluation and the collection and use of programmatic data through new agency-wide mechanisms.

SMALL BUSINESS ADMINISTRATION

Funding Highlights:

- Provides $810 million for the Small Business Administration, a decrease of $109 million from the 2012 enacted level, due primarily to the decreased estimated subsidy cost of its 7(a) Business Loan Guarantee Program. This funding supports technical assistance programs and initiatives that will create jobs in America's small businesses.

- Supports more than $27 billion in loan guarantees to enable entrepreneurs to start up and expand small businesses and create jobs.

- Supports equity investments in underserved markets and helps innovative small businesses obtain early-stage financing, including increasing the total amount of financing available for Small Business Investment Companies.

- Waives fees on 7(a) loans that are less than $150,000, where analysis suggests the largest credit gap exists and because small loans are important for underserved communities.

- Expands refinancing opportunities for small businesses, similar to the President's plan to help responsible homeowners refinance their mortgages, so that small businesses can lock in lower interest rates for their commercial mortgage debt and get cash out to invest in their businesses.

- Creates a single, streamlined application for all Small Business Administration 7(a) loan products, which will reduce the time and cost for lenders to process loans and encourage lenders to make more loans.

- Supports over $1 billion in direct disaster assistance loans for homeowners, renters, and businesses of all sizes, ensuring that the agency can continue to fulfill its critical role in the Federal Government's disaster response efforts.

- Significantly expands entrepreneurship training opportunities for underserved communities through a re-launch of the Emerging Leaders program, which seeks to train and develop existing small business owners with the potential to grow. In addition, the Budget expands entrepreneurship education for veterans transitioning to civilian life as part of the Administration's Boots to Business initiative.

- Funds the agency's role in BusinessUSA, a one-stop shop for firms looking to do business with the Federal Government and gain access to resources to create and grow their businesses.

- Supports the use of evidence and the evaluation of programs to measure their impact and improve performance.

Small businesses play a vital role in supporting job creation, U.S. global competitiveness, and economic growth. The Small Business Administration's (SBA) mission is to help Americans start, build, and grow businesses. To achieve this mission, the President's 2014 Budget provides $810 million through regular appropriations and an additional $159 million in disaster funding. Small business loan guarantees are funded at levels above historical demand, but at a greatly reduced subsidy cost from the 2012 enacted level and the 2013 Budget level, largely due to the improving economic forecast and lower estimated loan defaults. The savings realized through the reduced need for credit subsidy funding allow greater investments to be made in SBA's technical assistance programs and other initiatives aimed at growing America's small businesses.

Provides Small Businesses with Access to Capital and Disaster Assistance

Spurs Job Creation by Providing Access to Capital. To encourage economic growth and job creation, the Budget provides $112 million in subsidy for SBA's business loan programs. This funding supports $17.5 billion in 7(a) loan guarantees (including $1.8 billion in revolving lines of credit that support $65 billion in total economic activity), which help small businesses operate and grow their businesses, as well as $6.3 billion in guaranteed lending under the 504 Certified Development Company (CDC) program to finance small businesses' commercial real estate development and heavy machinery purchases. In addition, the Budget proposes to increase guarantees for the Small Business Investment Company (SBIC) program from $3 billion to $4 billion at no expected subsidy cost to the taxpayer, to enable SBICs to invest in more high-growth

and impact-oriented small businesses that create jobs and strengthen communities.

Waives Fees for Small Dollar Loans. The Budget waives fees on loans less than $150,000 in SBA's 7(a) loan program to promote lending to small businesses that face the most constraints on credit access.

Expands Refinancing Opportunities for Small Businesses. Consistent with the President's plan to help responsible homeowners refinance their mortgages, the Budget proposes to reauthorize the 504 Loan Refinancing program through September 30, 2014. The program, originally established in the Small Business Jobs Act of 2010, will help small businesses lock in low, long-term interest rates on commercial mortgage and equipment debts and free up resources that can be re-invested in their businesses.

Streamlines Loan Applications for SBA Lenders. The Budget provides $7 million for SBA ONE, a revamped lending platform that will use one set of forms for all 7(a) loans; serve as a one-stop shop for all steps of the loan process, from determining eligibility through closing out the loan; and provide one data management system to measure and evaluate loan trends and performance. SBA ONE will simplify the lending process, which is expected to increase the total number of lenders offering SBA financing and therefore expand access to capital for small business owners and entrepreneurs.

Fully Funds Disaster Assistance Loans. The Budget supports $1.1 billion in direct disaster assistance loans, the normalized 10-year average. In the wake of Hurricane Sandy, the Budget provides $192 million for loan administrative expenses to operate the Disaster Loans Program. Of this total, $159 million will be designated as qualifying disaster funding under the Budget Control Act's cap adjustment. SBA's Disaster Loans Program provides low-interest disaster loans to homeowners, renters, and businesses of all sizes whose property is damaged or destroyed in a disaster.

Fosters Entrepreneurship and Expands Opportunities for Small Business Growth

Invests in Small Business Leadership Program. The Budget includes $40 million for Emerging Leaders, an entrepreneurial education initiative that SBA initially launched in 2008 to educate existing small businesses with the potential to grow their business. The revamped program will become a public-private partnership, funded with SBA and private matching dollars, to support a small business leadership model built on the best practices of other working private sector and non-profit models.

Invests in Entrepreneurship Training for America's Transitioning Veterans. The Budget provides $7 million to support SBA's Boots to Business initiative, which will build upon SBA's successful pilot programs that provide veterans transitioning to civilian life with the training and tools they need to start their own businesses. The Boots to Business initiative will reach veterans of all military branches nationwide by offering informational videos, 90-minute introduction to entrepreneurship sessions, a two-day entrepreneurship classroom course, and an eight-week online entrepreneurship course as part of the Department of Defense's enhanced Transition Assistance Program.

Supports Entrepreneurship Counseling and Regional Economic Development. The Budget includes $210 million for SBA's non-credit technical assistance programs, including $104 million for Small Business Development Centers and $20 million in technical assistance for microloan programs, to help businesses get started. The Budget also includes $5 million each for SBA's growth accelerators program and Regional Innovation Clusters program, which

help connect small businesses with universities, venture capitalists, and regional industry leaders to leverage a region's unique assets to turn entrepreneurial ideas into sustainable high-growth small businesses.

Provides Small Businesses with Increased Federal Contracting and Exporting Resources. The Budget provides $4 million for SBA to hire 32 new Procurement Center Representatives, who will be strategically embedded across the Federal Government to increase the small business share of Federal procurement awards through such actions as reserving procurements for competition among small business firms and providing small business sources to Federal buying agents. In addition, the Budget provides $2 million to support the work of the President's Export Promotion Cabinet, helping small businesses to expand their exporting capabilities and thereby increase their revenue.

Provides a One-Stop Shop for Federal Business Assistance Resources. The Budget provides $6 million for SBA to fund its contribution to BusinessUSA, an interagency Administrative initiative to streamline and integrate customer service and program information across Federal programs that support small businesses and exporters. BusinessUSA will provide a one-stop shop for businesses looking for assistance from the Federal Government or looking to do business with the Federal Government, rather than making businesses search for and solicit a number of separate websites and points of contact. This consolidation of resources enables entrepreneurs and small businesses to find and use Government services more efficiently.

Supports Evidence-based Decision Making and Increases Oversight

Enhances Evaluation of Technical Assistance Programs. SBA, along with the Departments of Commerce and Agriculture, will continue to participate in an interagency group designed to evaluate the impact of Federal business technical assistance programs. SBA will evaluate its programs, such as Small Business

Development Centers, with the goal of developing a standard methodology for measuring the impact of these types of technical assistance programs across the Federal Government. The Budget provides $3 million to support evidence-based and evaluation activities at SBA.

Enhances Oversight Activities of Taxpayer Dollars. The Budget provides $20 million for SBA's Office of the Inspector General, a $3 million increase over the 2012 enacted level. This funding will support the Inspector General's efforts to detect and prevent waste, fraud, and abuse across SBA's programs, including the Business and Disaster Loans Programs.

SOCIAL SECURITY ADMINISTRATION

Funding Highlights:

- Provides $12.3 billion in funding for the operations of the Social Security Administration, a seven percent increase over the 2012 enacted level, with the increased funding directed at expanding program integrity investments.

- Establishes a dependable source of funding for Continuing Disability Reviews and Supplemental Security Income Redeterminations, which ensure that only those eligible for benefits receive them and generate significant deficit reduction.

- Proposes reforms to improve Disability Insurance and Supplemental Security Income program integrity and give the agency the authority to test new ways of encouraging and supporting employment for people with disabilities.

The Social Security Administration (SSA) administers the Old Age, Survivors, and Disability Insurance program and the Supplemental Security Income (SSI) program. The President believes that Social Security is critical to ensuring that all Americans have the opportunity to retire with dignity and that Americans with disabilities do not have to experience economic hardship. To fund this commitment, the 2014 Budget includes $12.3 billion for SSA operations, a seven percent increase over the 2012 enacted level. It supports pilot programs to improve education and employment outcomes for people with disabilities and enhancements to program integrity to cut down on waste, fraud, and abuse.

Protects Social Security for Future Generations

The President recognizes that Social Security is indispensable to workers, retirees, survivors, and people with disabilities and that it is one of the most important and successful programs ever established in the United States. Although current forecasts indicate that Social Security can pay full benefits until 2033, the President is committed to making sure that it is solvent and viable for the American people, now and in the future. He is strongly opposed to privatizing Social Security and looks forward to working in a bipartisan way to preserve it for future generations.

Enhances Program Integrity in Disability Programs and Pilots Pro-Work Interventions

Locks in Savings by Providing Reliable Funding for Program Integrity Work. The Budget proposes to establish a dependable source of mandatory funding for Continuing Disability Reviews (CDRs) and SSI Redeterminations, which ensure that only those eligible for benefits continue to receive them. To date, the annual appropriations process has failed to provide SSA with the resources necessary to conduct scheduled CDRs and Redeterminations. SSA estimates that each additional $1 spent on CDRs would save the Federal Government $9, yet SSA has a backlog of 1.3 million overdue CDRs. Compared to continued shortfalls in program integrity funding, this proposal would save $38 billion over 10 years.

Tests New Ways to Boost Employment. The Budget calls for providing SSA and partner agencies with authority to test innovative techniques to help people with disabilities remain in the workforce. These measures have the potential to achieve long-term improvements in the employment and the quality of life of people with disabilities, while reducing Government expenditures on income support. In addition to providing new authority to test early interventions, the Budget also proposes reauthorization of SSA's demonstration authority for the Disability Insurance (DI) program, allowing SSA to continue to test effective ways to boost employment and support current DI and SSI beneficiaries who are seeking to return to work.

Improves Services for Children with Disabilities. The Budget supports the continued implementation of the interagency Promoting Readiness of Minors in SSI (PROMISE) pilot, initiated in 2012. The Department of Education and SSA, in consultation with the Department of Labor and the Department of Health and Human Services, will provide competitive grants to test and evaluate interventions that successfully improve child and family outcomes and reduce the need for children to remain in the SSI program.

Improves Tax Administration by Restructuring the Federal Wage Reporting Process. The Budget proposes to restructure the Federal wage reporting process by moving from an annual reporting process to quarterly wage reporting. Increasing the timeliness of wage reporting will enhance tax administration and improve program integrity for a range of programs. The Administration will work with States to ensure that the overall reporting burden on employers is not increased. The Budget also proposes to lower the Electronic Wage Reporting Threshold for W-2/3s from 250 employees to 50. The vast majority of employers with between 50 and 250 employees already choose to report electronically.

Maintains Services to the Public. The Budget maintains services to the public, which SSA provides through multiple avenues, including through the Internet, over the phone, and in-person at hundreds of local offices. SSA will continue to handle high volumes of work and focus on providing quality services, while significantly increasing program integrity efforts. The Budget also allows SSA to maintain and improve its information technology systems, which will help SSA be as efficient as possible, saving time not only for the agency, but also for the public.

CORPORATION FOR NATIONAL AND COMMUNITY SERVICE

Funding Highlights:

- Provides $1.06 billion for the Corporation for National and Community Service, roughly even with the 2012 enacted level, to support efforts to address national and local challenges through service.

- Supports the service of approximately 82,000 AmeriCorps members across the United States.

- Invests in promising new approaches to major community challenges through a $49 million investment in the Social Innovation Fund, including $4 million to improve nonprofit evaluation capacity by facilitating access to State and Federal administrative data.

- Strengthens the Senior Corps by using competition to improve the way Federal dollars are spent and establishing a renewed focus on outcomes and impact.

- Creates the George H.W. Bush Volunteer Generation Fund, a $10 million program focused on improving the capacity of nonprofits working with volunteers.

Through national service, volunteering, and other forms of civic participation, millions of Americans each year help to address our Nation's greatest challenges and speed our economic recovery. The Corporation for National and Community Service (CNCS) provides an on-ramp for Americans of all ages to serve their community and country in sustained and effective ways, from tutoring at-risk youth to responding to natural disasters to building homes for low-income families. Many of the most creative solutions to America's challenges have been developed not in Washington, but in communities across the country where citizens work hand in hand to make a difference. The 2014 Budget proposes $1.06 billion for CNCS, which reflects the Administration's continuing commitment to providing opportunities for Americans to address local challenges through service.

Invests in Community Solutions

Supports National Service. The Budget funds approximately 82,000 AmeriCorps members, enabling them to serve and support the efforts of nonprofit organizations to address a wide range of critical community challenges, from hurricanes to homelessness to failing schools. It focuses national service resources in those areas where service can achieve the greatest results for communities.

169

Invests in Innovative Nonprofits. Innovative solutions developed in the nonprofit sector for addressing critical national challenges cannot be carried out unless capital is available to develop, evaluate, and replicate successful approaches. The Budget invests $49 million in the Social Innovation Fund to test promising new approaches to major challenges, leverage private and philanthropic capital to meet these needs, and grow evidence-based programs that demonstrate measurable outcomes. This funding level includes $4 million for a pilot to improve grantee access to State and Federal administrative data. This investment has the potential to reduce the cost and improve the quality of evaluations and performance reporting, and could help break down barriers for all nonprofit organizations looking to demonstrate measurable impact in communities.

Strengthens Programs That Engage Seniors. Many older Americans are eager to serve our Nation and have a wide range of skills and knowledge to give back to their communities. For decades, the Senior Corps program has been an important conduit for connecting seniors to local volunteer opportunities. The Budget proposes to reinvigorate the program by using competition to allocate funds to those organizations that have the biggest impact in their communities.

Increases Capacity of Nonprofits to Support Volunteers. With the number of Americans engaged in volunteering having reached its highest point in five years, many nonprofits could benefit from management practices to handle this influx of talent. The Budget proposes to reactivate the Volunteer Generation Fund with a focus on strengthening nonprofits' ability to recruit, retain, and manage volunteers, and using volunteers to tackle national priorities such as integrating returning veterans and supporting military families. By reactivating the program as the George H.W. Bush Volunteer Generation Fund, we also honor the legacy of service of the 41st President of the United States, who has pioneered important work in the field of volunteering both during and after his time in office.

CUTS, CONSOLIDATIONS, AND SAVINGS

Whether the Budget is in surplus or deficit, wasting taxpayer dollars on programs that are outdated, ineffective, or duplicative is wrong. Given the current fiscal environment, it is critical that we redouble our efforts to scour the Budget for waste and make tough decisions about reducing funding for or ending programs that are laudable, but not essential. This exercise is difficult but necessary, and it builds on efforts the Administration has undertaken since the President first took office.

The Administration has already made significant progress in cutting waste in areas across the Government. We have successfully targeted a series of programs for elimination, reduction, or consolidation. For example, at the Department of Defense, we eliminated the F-22 fighter aircraft that were no longer needed as part of the new defense strategy developed by our military leadership, and the Expeditionary Fighting Vehicle, which was performing poorly. These and other program terminations at the Pentagon will save over $20 billion. At the Department of Agriculture (USDA), we closed or consolidated 260 USDA field offices, saving $58 million. At the Department of Health and Human Services, we ended three duplicative health programs, saving taxpayers over $380 million.

As part of the President's Campaign to Cut Waste, we have cut unnecessary travel and conference spending by billions of dollars, and overall administrative spending in areas such as printing, fleet management, and advisory service contracts by billions more. In aggregate, agencies have targeted $8.8 billion in annual administrative savings by the end of 2013 as detailed in this section. The Administra-

tion has already announced significant progress made toward this goal and will provide periodic updates on savings achieved during the year. We are selling off excess Federal real estate. We are also leveraging the buying power of the Federal Government to save money on the purchase of commodity goods such as office supplies and shipping services.

The President has also engaged the Federal workforce and the public in cutting waste through his SAVE Award program, tapping the knowledge and expertise of frontline employees. Over the last three years, 66 SAVE Award ideas have been included in the President's Budget, ranging from ending the mailing of the Federal Register to Government offices to automatically powering off computers at the Department of Labor.

In each of the President's first three Budgets, he identified, on average, more than 150 terminations, reductions, and savings proposals, totaling nearly $25 billion each year. In last year's Budget, the Administration detailed 210 cuts, consolidations, and savings proposals, totaling more than $24 billion in 2013. This year, the Budget includes a total of 215 cuts, consolidations, and savings proposals, which are projected to save more than $25 billion in 2014, and $539 billion through 2023.

Discretionary and mandatory cuts, consolidations, and savings proposals are detailed on the following tables, as well as savings activities agencies are undertaking that require no further action by the Congress, many of which were suggested through the President's SAVE Award: Savings from program integrity proposals, totaling $98 billion through 2023, are detailed in the Budget Process chapter of the Analytical Perspectives volume.

As these tables show, the Budget includes a robust package of proposals that modify Medicare provider payments totaling $306 billion over the next 10 years. These include a number of measures detailed in Table S–9 (see Summary Tables section of this volume), including a proposal to align Medicare drug payment policies with Medicaid rebate policies for low-income beneficiaries, allowing Medicare to benefit from lower drug prices. This change alone will save $123 billion over the next 10 years. The Budget takes other critical steps to save money, such as closing the loophole in current law that allows people to collect both full disability benefits and unemployment benefits that cover the same period of time. Shutting this loophole will save $1 billion over 10 years. The single biggest consolidation proposed this year is in the area of science, technology, engineering, and mathematics (STEM) education, where the Administration is proposing a bold restructuring of STEM education programs—consolidating 90 programs and realigning ongoing STEM education activities to improve the delivery, impact, and visibility of these efforts.

DISCRETIONARY CUTS, CONSOLIDATIONS, AND SAVINGS
(Budget authority in millions of dollars)

	2012	2014	2014 Change from 2012
Cuts			
Agricultural Marketing Service - Microbiological Data Program, Department of Agriculture[1]	5	....	−5
Agricultural Marketing Service - Pesticide Recordkeeping Program, Department of Agriculture[1]	2	....	−2
Alaska Conveyance Program, Department of the Interior	29	17	−12
Area Health Education Centers, Department of Health and Human Services	27	....	−27
Assistance for Europe, Eurasia, and Central Asia, Department of State and Other International Programs	627	497	−130
Beach Grants, Environmental Protection Agency	10	....	−10
Brownfields Projects, Environmental Protection Agency	95	85	−10
Bureau of Indian Affairs Construction, Department of the Interior	124	107	−17
Bureau of Indian Affairs Housing Improvement Program, Department of the Interior[1]	13	....	−13
Bureau of Labor Statistics' Green Jobs Program, Department of Labor	8	....	−8
Bureau of Labor Statistics' Mass Layoff Statistics Program, Department of Labor[1]	2	....	−2
C–130 Avionics Modernization, Department of Defense	208	....	−208
C–27 Joint Cargo Aircraft, Department of Defense	480	....	−480
Capacity Building (Section 4 and Rural Housing), Department of Housing and Urban Development	40	20	−20
Centers for Disease Control and Prevention Direct Healthcare Screenings, Department of Health and Human Services	257	225	−32
Chemical Risk Management Fibers Program, Environmental Protection Agency	2	....	−2
Children's Hospital Graduate Medical Education Payment Program, Department of Health and Human Services	265	88	−177
Christopher Columbus Fellowship Foundation	....	....	....
Clean Automotive Technologies, Environmental Protection Agency	16	....	−16
Clean Water and Drinking Water State Revolving Funds, Environmental Protection Agency	2,384	1,912	−472
CMRR Facility, Department of Energy	200	35	−165
Community Services Block Grant, Department of Health and Human Services	679	350	−329
Computer and Information Science and Engineering Research Programs, National Science Foundation:			
Interface Between Computer Science and Economics and Social Sciences	7	....	−7
Network Science and Engineering	3	....	−3
Social-Computational Systems	7	....	−7
Virtual Organizations	5	....	−5
Cruiser Modernization Program, Department of Defense	573	11	−562
Cyber-Enabled Discovery and Innovation Program, National Science Foundation	29	....	−29
Diesel Emissions Reduction Grant Program, Environmental Protection Agency	30	6	−24
Drawdown of Military End Strength, Department of Defense	....	−1,384	−1,384
Economic Impact Grants, Department of Agriculture[1]	6	....	−6
Education Research Centers and Agricultural Research, Department of Health and Human Services:			
Agricultural, Forestry, and Fishing Program[1]	26	....	−26
Education Research Centers[1]	29	....	−29
Electric Guaranteed Underwriting Loan Program, Department of Agriculture[1]	1	....	−1
Elimination of Overlapping Programs, Department of Labor:			
Veterans Workforce Investment Program[1]	15	....	−15
Women in Apprenticeship in Non-Traditional Occupations[1]	1	....	−1
Environmental Education, Environmental Protection Agency	10	....	−10
Farm Service Agency Discretionary Conservation Programs, Department of Agriculture[1]	5	....	−5
Federal Flight Deck Officer Program, Department of Homeland Security	25	....	−25
Fissile Materials Disposition, Department of Energy	685	503	−182
Fossil Energy Research and Development, Department of Energy	534	421	−113
Geographic Programs, Environmental Protection Agency	30	17	−13
Global Hawk Unmanned Aerial Vehicle, Department of Defense	324	....	−324
Grants for Abstinence-Only Programs, Department of Health and Human Services	5	....	−5
Grants-in-Aid for Airports, Department of Transportation[1]	3,350	2,900	−450
Harry S. Truman Scholarship Foundation	1	....	−1
Health Care Services Grant Program, Department of Agriculture[1]	3	....	−3
Health Careers Opportunity Program, Department of Health and Human Services	15	....	−15
High Energy Cost Grants, Department of Agriculture[1]	10	....	−10

DISCRETIONARY CUTS, CONSOLIDATIONS, AND SAVINGS—Continued
(Budget authority in millions of dollars)

	2012	2014	2014 Change from 2012
High Intensity Drug Trafficking Areas, Office of National Drug Control Policy	239	193	−46
High Mobility Multipurpose Wheeled Vehicle Modernized Expanded Capacity Vehicle Recapitalization, Department of Defense	4	....	−4
HOME Investment Partnerships Program, Department of Housing and Urban Development	1,000	950	−50
Hospital Preparedness Program, Department of Health and Human Services	380	255	−125
Housing for Persons with Disabilities, Department of Housing and Urban Development	165	126	−39
Hypersonics, National Aeronautics and Space Administration[1]	25	4	−21
Impact Aid - Payments for Federal Property, Department of Education[1]	1,291	1,224	−67
International Forestry, Department of Agriculture[1]	8	4	−4
Investigator-Initiated Research Grants, Department of Health and Human Services	43	29	−14
Joint Air-to-Ground Missile Program, Department of Defense	235	21	−214
Joint High Speed Vessel, Department of Defense	372	3	−369
Light Attack and Armed Reconnaissance Aircraft, Department of Defense	115	....	−115
Low Income Home Energy Assistance Program, Department of Health and Human Services	3,472	3,020	−452
Low-Priority Studies and Construction, Corps of Engineers[1]	1,819	1,440	−379
Mathematics and Physical Sciences Research Programs, National Science Foundation:			
Cerro Chajnator Atacama Telescope Design and Development	2	....	−2
Cultural Heritage Science	4	....	−4
Grid Computing	2	....	−2
International Materials Institutes[1]	2	....	−2
Mathematical Physics	2	....	−2
Solar Energy Initiative (SOLAR)	2	....	−2
University Radio Observatories	8	6	−2
Mine Safety and Health Administration State Grants Program, Department of Labor	8	....	−8
Nanoscale Science and Engineering Centers, National Science Foundation	31	12	−19
National Drug Intelligence Center, Department of Justice[1]	20	....	−20
National Heritage Areas, Department of the Interior[1]	17	9	−8
National Pre-Disaster Mitigation Fund, Department of Homeland Security	36	....	−36
National Undersea Research Program, Department of Commerce[1]	4	....	−4
National Wildlife Refuge Fund, Department of the Interior[1]	14	....	−14
Office of Assistant Secretary Grant Programs, Department of Health and Human Services	89	67	−22
Office of the Special Trustee for American Indians, Department of the Interior	152	140	−12
Patient-Centered Health Research, Department of Health and Human Services[1]	17	....	−17
Pest and Disease Programs, Department of Agriculture[1]	817	798	−19
Precision Tracking and Space System, Department of Defense	81	....	−81
Presidio Trust	12	....	−12
Preventive Health and Health Services Block Grant, Department of Health and Human Services[1]	80	....	−80
PRIME Technical Assistance, Small Business Administration[1]	4	....	−4
Promoting Greener Economies, Environmental Protection Agency	3	....	−3
Public Broadcasting Grants, Department of Agriculture[1]	3	....	−3
Public Outreach Programs, National Science Foundation:			
Communicating Science Broadly[1]	2	....	−2
Connecting Researchers with Public Audiences[1]	4	....	−4
REACH, Department of Health and Human Services	14	....	−14
Rehabilitation Act Programs, Department of Education[1]	36	....	−36
Research, Education, and Extension Grants, Department of Agriculture:			
Animal Health (Sec. 1433)[1]	4	....	−4
Capacity Building: Non-Land Grant Colleges[1]	4	....	−4
Competitive Grants for Policy Research[1]	4	....	−4
Critical Agricultural Materials[1]	1	....	−1
Farm Business Management and Benchmarking[1]	1	....	−1
Food Animal Residue Avoid Database[1]	1	....	−1
Forest Products Research[1]	1	....	−1
Methyl Bromide Transition Program[1]	2	....	−2

DISCRETIONARY CUTS, CONSOLIDATIONS, AND SAVINGS—Continued

(Budget authority in millions of dollars)

	2012	2014	2014 Change from 2012
Potato Breeding Research (Competitive)[1]	1	....	−1
Rangeland Restoration[1]	1	....	−1
Rural Health and Safety[1]	2	....	−2
Sungrants[1]	2	....	−2
Supplemental and Alternative Crops[1]	1	....	−1
Water Quality[1]	5	....	−5
Youth Organizations[1]	1	....	−1
Rural Access to Emergency Devices, Department of Health and Human Services[1]	1	....	−1
Rural Community Facilities, Department of Health and Human Services[1]	5	....	−5
Rural Hospital Flexibility Grant Programs, Department of Health and Human Services	41	26	−15
Rural Multifamily Housing Preservation Grants, Department of Agriculture[1]	4	....	−4
Rural Single Family Housing Grant Programs, Department of Agriculture	60	35	−25
Sea-Based X-Band Radar, Department of Defense	177	45	−132
Second Line of Defense, Department of Energy[1]	262	140	−122
Sensors and Sensing Systems, Engineering Research Programs, National Science Foundation[1]	5	2	−3
Single Family Housing Direct Loans, Department of Agriculture[1]	43	10	−33
Standard Missile–3 Block IIB, Department of Defense	13	....	−13
State and Volunteer Fire Assistance Grants, Department of Agriculture[1]	99	81	−18
State Criminal Alien Assistance Program, Department of Justice	240	....	−240
State Indoor Radon Grant Program, Environmental Protection Agency	8	....	−8
Streamline Federal Air Marshals Service, Department of Homeland Security	966	827	−139
Sunwise, Environmental Protection Agency	1	....	−1
Superfund Remedial, Environmental Protection Agency	565	539	−26
Superfund Support to Other Federal Agencies, Environmental Protection Agency	6	....	−6
T-AGOS Ocean Surveillance Ship, Department of Defense	10	....	−10
Transfer Exit Lane Staffing Responsibilities to Airports, Department of Homeland Security	88	....	−88
Valles Caldera, Department of Agriculture[1]	3	....	−3
Water and Wastewater and Community Facilities Loan Guarantees, Department of Agriculture[1]	6	....	−6
Water and Wastewater Grants and Loans, Department of Agriculture	504	304	−200
Watershed Rehabilitation Program, Department of Agriculture[1]	15	....	−15
Wildland Fire Program/Hazardous Fuels Reduction, Department of the Interior	183	96	−87
Total, Discretionary Cuts	**25,172**	**16,216**	**−8,956**
Consolidations			
Central Utah Project, Department of the Interior	29	4	−25
Community Economic Development Program, Department of Health and Human Services	30	....	−30
Data Centers Closures, Department of Defense	....	−575	−575
Elementary and Secondary Education Act, Department of Education	....	....	....
Family Self-Sufficiency, Department of Housing and Urban Development	75	75	....
Food Aid Reform, Multi-Agency:	1,766	1,766	....
U.S. Agency for International Development	*300*	*1,741*	*1,441*
Department of Agriculture	*1,466*		*−1,466*
Maritime Administration, Department of Transportation		*25*	*25*
Forest Service Integrated Resource Restoration, Department of Agriculture	805	757	−48
Higher Education Programs, Department of Education	....	....	....
International Trade Administration Business Units, Department of Commerce	....	−8	−8
NASA Education, National Aeronautics and Space Administration	....	....	....
Rural Business & Cooperative Grants, Department of Agriculture	....	....	....
Science, Technology, Engineering, and Mathematics (STEM) Consolidation, Multi-Agency:	....	....	....
Eliminated and Reorganized Programs Total - 90 Programs:			
Eliminated Programs and Redirected Funding - 78 Programs:			
Department of Agriculture - 6 Programs	*[11]*		
Department of Commerce - 6 Programs	*[13]*		
Department of Defense - 6 Programs	*[49]*		

DISCRETIONARY CUTS, CONSOLIDATIONS, AND SAVINGS—Continued
(Budget authority in millions of dollars)

	2012	2014	2014 Change from 2012
Department of Energy - 8 Programs	*[11]*		
Department of Health and Human Services - 10 Programs	*[28]*		
Department of Homeland Security - 1 Program	*[1]*		
Environmental Protection Agency - 2 Programs	*[16]*		
National Aeronautics and Space Administration - 38 Programs	*[48]*		
Nuclear Regulatory Commission - 1 Program	*[0]*		
Reorganized Programs Within the Agency - 12 Programs:			
National Science Foundation - 11 Programs	*[118]*		
National Aeronautics and Space Administration - 1 Program	*[2]*		
Self-Help and Assisted Homeownership Opportunity Program, Department of Housing and Urban Development	14	10	–4
State and Local Grants Reform, Department of Homeland Security	....	....	....
United States Visitor and Immigrant Status Indicator Technology, Department of Homeland Security	....	....	....
Total, Discretionary Consolidations	**2,719**	**2,029**	**–690**
Savings			
Agency-Wide Efficiency Savings, Department of Justice	....	–237	–237
B–83 Reserve Status, Department of Energy	....	–3	–3
Increased Flexibility for the U.S. Mint in Coinage, Department of the Treasury	....	....	....
Internal Revenue Service Business Systems Modernization, Department of the Treasury	330	301	–29
Joint Polar Satellite System Savings, Department of Commerce	924	886	–38
Law Enforcement-Wide Administrative Efficiencies, Department of Justice	....	–93	–93
Pit Disassembly and Conversion Savings, Department of Energy	26	....	–26
Senate Campaign Finance Reports Electronic Submission, Federal Election Commission	....	....	....
Streamline Farm Service Agency Operations, Department of Agriculture	1,199	1,176	–23
Technology Infrastructure Modernization, Environmental Protection Agency	186	179	–7
W 78/88 Life Extension Program, Department of Energy	....	–72	–72
Total, Discretionary Savings	**2,665**	**2,137**	**–528**
Total, Discretionary Cuts, Consolidations, and Savings	**30,556**	**20,382**	**–10,174**

[1] This cut has been identified as a lower-priority program activity for purposes of the GPRA Modernization Act, at 31 U.S.C. 1115(b)(10). Additional information regarding this proposed cut is included in the respective agency's Congressional Justification submission.

MANDATORY CUTS AND SAVINGS
(Outlays and receipts in millions of dollars)

	2014	2015	2016	2017	2018	2014–2018	2014–2023
Cuts							
Coal Tax Preferences, Department of Energy:							
Domestic Manufacturing Deduction for Hard Mineral Fossil Fuels[1]	−33	−34	−36	−39	−40	−182	−409
Expensing of Exploration and Development Costs[1]	−25	−43	−45	−47	−49	−209	−432
Percent Depletion for Hard Mineral Fossil Fuels[1]	−113	−193	−196	−198	−201	−901	−1,982
Royalty Taxation[1]	−14	−31	−37	−42	−45	−169	−432
Eliminate Direct Payments, Department of Agriculture	....	−3,300	−3,300	−3,300	−3,300	−13,200	−29,700
Conservation Reserve Program, Department of Agriculture	15	15	−200	−220	−315	−705	−2,915
Conservation Stewardship Program, Department of Agriculture	−5	−50	−90	−130	−170	−445	−1,964
Crop Insurance Program, Department of Agriculture	−513	−1,005	−1,238	−1,244	−1,256	−5,256	−11,716
Geothermal Payments to Counties, Department of the Interior[2]	−4	−4	−5	−5	−5	−23	−48
Oil and Gas Company Tax Preferences, Department of Energy:							
Increase Geological and Geophysical Amortization Period for Independent Producers to Seven Years[1]	−60	−220	−333	−304	−221	−1,138	−1,363
Repeal Credit for Oil and Gas Produced from Marginal Wells[1]	....	....	....	....	....	....	....
Repeal Deduction for Tertiary Injectants[1]	−8	−12	−12	−11	−11	−54	−107
Repeal Domestic Manufacturing Tax Deduction for Oil and Natural Gas Companies[1]	−1,119	−1,926	−1,951	−1,944	−1,884	−8,824	−17,447
Repeal Enhanced Oil Recovery Credit[1]	....	....	....	....	....	....	....
Repeal Exception to Passive Loss Limitations for Working Interests in Oil and Natural Gas Properties[1]	−7	−10	−9	−8	−8	−42	−74
Repeal Expensing of Intangible Drilling Costs[1]	−1,663	−2,460	−2,125	−1,639	−1,099	−8,986	−10,993
Repeal Percentage Depletion for Oil and Natural Gas Wells[1]	−1,039	−1,044	−1,042	−1,041	−1,045	−5,211	−10,723
Offset Disability Benefits for Period of Concurrent Unemployment Insurance Receipt	−100	−100	−100	−100	−100	−500	−1,000
Ultradeep Oil and Gas Research and Development Program, Department of Energy[2]	−20	−20	−10	....	....	−50	−50
Payments to Guarantee Agencies - Federal Family Education Loan Program	−3,657	....	....	....	....	−3,657	−3,657
Unrestricted Abandoned Mine Lands Payments, Department of the Interior[2]	−32	−33	−27	−31	−40	−163	−327
Total, Mandatory Cuts	**−8,397**	**−10,470**	**−10,756**	**−10,303**	**−9,789**	**−49,715**	**−95,339**
Savings							
FECA Reform, Department of Labor	−9	−10	−19	−29	−39	−106	−462
Federal Employee Health Benefits Program Reforms, Office of Personnel Management	....	−422	−665	−725	−794	−2,606	−8,367
Health Care (Medicaid Proposals), Department of Health and Human Services	−301	−1,051	−1,401	−1,397	−1,316	−5,466	−16,914
Health Care (Pharmaceuticals), Department of Health and Human Services[3]	−740	−870	−1,000	−1,150	−1,330	−5,090	−14,280
Medicare Provider Payment Modifications, Department of Health and Human Services[3,4]	−5,630	−13,460	−17,560	−22,000	−26,810	−85,460	−306,230
Total, Mandatory Savings	**−6,680**	**−15,813**	**−20,645**	**−25,301**	**−30,289**	**−98,728**	**−346,253**
Total, Mandatory Cuts and Savings	**−15,077**	**−26,283**	**−31,401**	**−35,604**	**−40,078**	**−148,443**	**−441,592**

[1] This cut has been identified as a lower-priority program activity for purposes of the GPRA Modernization Act, at 31 U.S.C. 1115(b)(10). Additional information regarding this proposed cut is included in the Governmental Receipts chapter of the Analytical Perspectives volume.

[2] This cut has been identified as a lower-priority program activity for purposes of the GPRA Modernization Act, at 31 U.S.C. 1115(b)(10). Additional information regarding this proposed cut is included in the respective agency's Congressional Justification submission.

[3] Medicare savings estimates do not include interactions.

[4] In addition to the savings reported on this table, the Budget includes an additional $67.8 billion in 10-year savings for Medicare Structural Reforms, as detailed on table S-9.

The SAVE Award logo denotes a proposal that was suggested by a Federal employee through the SAVE Award program.

ADMINISTRATIVELY IMPLEMENTED CONSOLIDATIONS AND SAVINGS
(In millions of dollars)

	2013	2014	2013–2017
Department of Education			
Workspace Redesign and Consolidation	0.00	0.00	−3.00
Department of Health and Human Services			
FreeStuff	−0.25	−0.38	−1.50
Department of Homeland Security			
Post Customs Inspection Information Online	*	*	*
Department of the Interior			
Leverage Digital Recording Technology Instead of Court Reporters	0.00	−0.13	−1.63
Standardize Relocation Policies and Processes by Implementing Shared Services	0.00	−0.11	−1.49
Department of Justice			
Encourage Use of Non-Contract Airfares	−2.50	−2.50	−12.50
Reduce Unnecessary Publications Acquisitions	−0.19	−0.19	−0.95
Reexamine Contract Structure	0.00	−0.73	−27.13
Department of Labor			
Bureau of Labor Statistics' International Labor Comparisons Program	−2.00	−2.00	−10.00
Regional Office Consolidations	0.00	−3.80	−15.89
Wage and Hour Division Questionnaire Postage	−0.07	−0.16	−0.78
Department of State and Other International Programs			
Change Printer Default Settings to Copier/Scanners	−0.60	−0.10	−0.80
Increase Tech Literacy to Eliminate Physical Assets & Operating Expenditures	−0.60	−0.60	−5.70
Use of Online Federal Acquisition Regulation	−0.20	0.00	−0.80
Department of the Treasury			
Order Electronic Transcripts Online	0.00	0.00	−14.25
Replace Lighting with LED Technology	−0.01	−0.09	−0.62
Savings from IRS Space Optimization	0.00	−76.70	−76.70
National Aeronautics and Space Administration			
Eliminate Cell Phones and Offer Allowance	*	*	*
National Science Foundation			
Consolidation of Mobile Devices	0.00	−0.05	−0.18
Increased Use of Virtual Meetings	−1.78	−1.78	−8.92
Consumer Product Safety Commission			
Use Electronic Travel System	−0.10	−0.10	−0.40
Multi-Agency			
Reduce Employee Shuttle Buses	*	*	*
Senior Transit Savings	0.00	−3.00	−12.00

Note: Amounts in this table include estimated savings from actions agencies are implementing to reduce costs that require no further action by the Congress.

* Savings estimates under development.

    The SAVE Award logo denotes this savings action was suggested by a Federal employee through the SAVE Award program.

ADMINISTRATIVE SAVINGS
(In millions of dollars)

	2013 Savings Target
Department of Agriculture	−196
Department of Commerce	−184
Department of Defense	−4,731
Department of Education	−11
Department of Energy	−223
Department of Health and Human Services	−881
Department of Homeland Security	−866
Department of Housing and Urban Development	−12
Department of the Interior	−205
Department of Justice	−160
Department of Labor	−61
Department of State	−182
Agency for International Development	−15
Department of Transportation	−156
Department of the Treasury	−241
Department of Veterans Affairs	−175
Corps of Engineers -- Civil Works	−77
Environmental Protection Agency	−72
General Services Administration	−56
National Aeronautics and Space Administration	−202
National Science Foundation	−19
Office of Personnel Management	−4
Small Business Administration	−3
Social Security Administration	−81
Total	**−8,812**

SUMMARY TABLES

Table S–1. Budget Totals
(In billions of dollars and as a percent of GDP)

	2012	2013	2014	2015	2016	2017	2018	2019	2020	2021	2022	2023	Totals 2014–2018	Totals 2014–2023
Budget Totals in Billions of Dollars:														
Receipts	2,450	2,712	3,034	3,332	3,561	3,761	3,974	4,226	4,464	4,709	4,951	5,220	17,661	41,231
Outlays	3,537	3,685	3,778	3,908	4,090	4,247	4,449	4,724	4,967	5,209	5,470	5,660	20,472	46,502
Deficit	1,087	973	744	576	528	487	475	498	503	501	519	439	2,811	5,271
Debt held by the public	11,281	12,404	13,296	14,032	14,714	15,344	15,954	16,583	17,212	17,836	18,473	19,030		
Debt net of financial assets	10,282	11,255	11,999	12,575	13,103	13,590	14,065	14,563	15,066	15,567	16,085	16,524		
Gross domestic product (GDP)	15,547	16,203	17,011	17,936	18,934	19,980	21,025	22,009	22,974	23,964	24,990	26,057		
Budget Totals as a Percent of GDP:														
Receipts	15.8%	16.7%	17.8%	18.6%	18.8%	18.8%	18.9%	19.2%	19.4%	19.6%	19.8%	20.0%	18.6%	19.1%
Outlays	22.8%	22.7%	22.2%	21.8%	21.6%	21.3%	21.2%	21.5%	21.6%	21.7%	21.9%	21.7%	21.6%	21.6%
Deficit	7.0%	6.0%	4.4%	3.2%	2.8%	2.4%	2.3%	2.3%	2.2%	2.1%	2.1%	1.7%	3.0%	2.5%
Debt held by the public	72.6%	76.6%	78.2%	78.2%	77.7%	76.8%	75.9%	75.3%	74.9%	74.4%	73.9%	73.0%		
Debt net of financial assets	66.1%	69.5%	70.5%	70.1%	69.2%	68.0%	66.9%	66.2%	65.6%	65.0%	64.4%	63.4%		

Table S–2. Effect of Budget Proposals on Projected Deficits

(Deficit increases (+) or decreases (–) in billions of dollars)

	2013	2014	2015	2016	2017	2018	2019	2020	2021	2022	2023	Totals 2014–2018	Totals 2014–2023
Projected deficits in the adjusted baseline [1]	919	627	536	547	556	571	637	678	723	889	913	2,837	6,678
Percent of GDP	5.7%	3.7%	3.0%	2.9%	2.8%	2.7%	2.9%	3.0%	3.0%	3.6%	3.5%	3.0%	3.1%
Proposals in the 2014 Budget: [2]													
Proposals contained in the December Compromise Deficit Reduction Package:													
Discretionary program reductions	.....	.....	.....	.....	–5	–12	–19	–27	–35	–46	–58	–16	–202
Health savings	.....	–6	–16	–21	–29	–35	–40	–49	–57	–68	–81	–107	–401
Other mandatory savings	*	–1	–12	–16	–19	–21	–23	–25	–26	–29	–28	–69	–201
Revenue proposals	.....	–30	–42	–46	–52	–57	–62	–66	–71	–76	–81	–228	–583
Immediate investments in infrastructure	.....	6	18	12	6	4	2	2	1	*	*	45	50
Programmatic effects of moving to the chained CPI	.....	.....	–3	–8	–14	–19	–24	–31	–37	–44	–50	–44	–230
Discretionary effects of program integrity cap adjustments	.....	*	1	*	1	1	1	1	1	1	1	3	9
Debt service and accrual effects	*	1	1	–*	–3	–10	–18	–27	–37	–48	–61	–12	–202
Total, December Package proposals	*	–31	–53	–79	–117	–148	–183	–222	–261	–308	–357	–428	–1,760
Policy initiatives:													
Surface transportation initiatives	.....	*	2	5	10	14	18	22	18	9	5	31	104
Job creation initiatives	2	31	11	9	4	1	1	1	1	1	1	55	62
Reductions in overseas contingency operations reserved for surface transportation and job creation	–1	–3	–19	–29	–32	–43	–41	.....	.....	.....	.....	–126	–167
Early childhood investments	.....	*	1	3	6	8	10	11	12	12	12	19	77
Tobacco tax financing	.....	–8	–10	–9	–9	–8	–8	–7	–7	–6	–6	–44	–78
Other mandatory proposals	9	25	20	12	1	–1	–5	–9	–11	–18	–17	57	–3
Reserve for revenue-neutral business tax reform	.....	.....	.....	.....	1	1	–*	–*	–*	–*	–*	.....	.....
Debt service	*	*	*	1	1	1	–*	–*	*	*	*	2	2
Total, policy initiatives	10	46	6	–9	–19	–28	–25	18	15	–*	–5	–5	–2
Additional changes to deficits:													
Remaining reductions in overseas contingency operations including amounts reserved for additional surface transportation transfers	.....	–1	–19	–30	–34	–26	–30	–74	–77	–101	–115	–111	–508
Revenue proposals available to pay for extension of baseline tax items	*	5	3	–7	–9	–10	–23	–25	–26	–28	–29	–18	–149
Proposed BCA disaster relief cap adjustment	–*	2	2	1	–*	–*	–*	–*	*	–*	–*	5	5
Outlay effects of discretionary policy	–5	9	2	–2	–4	–4	–3	–1	–4	–4	–3	2	–13
Debt service and indirect interest effects	*	*	1	*	–1	–3	–6	–9	–14	–19	–25	–4	–76
Total, additional deficit reduction	–4	15	–12	–38	–48	–43	–63	–110	–121	–151	–171	–125	–741
Total proposals in the 2014 Budget	5	30	–59	–126	–184	–220	–271	–314	–367	–460	–533	–558	–2,503

Table S–2. Effect of Budget Proposals on Projected Deficits—Continued

(Deficit increases (+) or decreases (–) in billions of dollars)

	2013	2014	2015	2016	2017	2018	2019	2020	2021	2022	2023	Totals 2014–2018	Totals 2014–2023
Effect of replacing Joint Committee enforcement with 2014 Budget deficit reduction proposals:													
Programmatic effects	48	87	99	104	107	108	108	108	109	48	15	505	893
Debt service	*	*	1	3	8	16	24	30	36	41	44	27	203
Total effect of replacing Joint Committee enforcement	48	87	100	107	115	124	132	139	145	89	59	532	1,096
Resulting deficits in 2014 Budget	**973**	**744**	**576**	**528**	**487**	**475**	**498**	**503**	**501**	**519**	**439**	**2,811**	**5,271**
Percent of GDP	6.0%	4.4%	3.2%	2.8%	2.4%	2.3%	2.3%	2.2%	2.1%	2.1%	1.7%	3.0%	2.5%

* $500 million or less.

[1] See Tables S–4 and S–8 for information on the adjusted baseline.

[2] For total deficit reduction since January 2011, see Table S–3.

Table S–3. Cumulative Deficit Reduction

(Deficit reduction (–) or increase (+) in billions of dollars)

	2014–2023
Deficit reduction achieved through January 2013:	
Discretionary savings [1]	–1,444
Upper-income tax revenues	–660
Debt service	–480
Total, achieved deficit reduction	–2,585
December Compromise Deficit Reduction Package:	
Discretionary program reductions	–202
Health savings	–401
Other mandatory savings	–201
Revenue proposals	–583
Immediate investments in infrastructure	50
Programmatic effects of moving to the chained CPI	–230
Discretionary effects of program integrity cap adjustments	9
Debt service and accrual effects	–202
Total, December Package	–1,760
Total deficit reduction	–4,344
Policy initiatives:	
Surface transportation and job creation initiatives	166
Savings in Overseas Contingency Operations reserved for initiatives	–167
Early childhood investments	77
Tobacco tax financing	–78
Other mandatory proposals	–3
Reserve for revenue-neutral business tax reform	—
Debt service	2
Total, policy initiatives	–2
Overseas contingency operations (OCO) and additional changes to deficits:	
Enacted reduction in OCO funding	–1,288
Remaining reductions in overseas contingency operations	–508
Other proposals	–157
Debt service	–339
Total, OCO and additional changes to deficits	–2,293
Total, deficit reduction including policy initiatives, OCO, and additional changes to deficits	–6,639
Memorandum: revenue and outlay effects of enacted deficit reduction and the President's December Compromise Deficit Reduction Package:	
Enacted outlay reductions and 2014 Budget spending proposals	–3,001
Enacted receipt increases and 2014 Budget revenue proposals	–1,343

[1] Excludes savings from reductions in OCO.

Table S–4. Adjusted Baseline by Category¹

(In billions of dollars)

	2012	2013	2014	2015	2016	2017	2018	2019	2020	2021	2022	2023	Totals 2014–2018	Totals 2014–2023
Outlays:														
Appropriated ("discretionary") programs:²														
Defense	671	652	615	657	666	677	688	699	717	733	751	768	3,302	6,971
Non-defense	614	611	620	610	611	615	620	630	642	655	669	684	3,076	6,357
Subtotal, appropriated programs	1,285	1,264	1,235	1,266	1,277	1,292	1,308	1,329	1,359	1,388	1,420	1,452	6,378	13,327
Mandatory programs:														
Social Security	768	812	860	911	965	1,022	1,081	1,144	1,210	1,277	1,350	1,427	4,840	11,247
Medicare²	466	504	530	551	597	614	639	702	756	813	902	941	2,932	7,046
Medicaid	251	267	304	329	352	373	392	416	441	467	495	529	1,750	4,098
Other mandatory programs²	548	610	559	595	630	642	655	696	719	757	805	809	3,082	6,868
Subtotal, mandatory programs	2,032	2,193	2,253	2,386	2,545	2,651	2,768	2,958	3,126	3,315	3,552	3,706	12,603	29,260
Net interest	220	222	222	252	298	370	459	544	616	677	741	804	1,601	4,984
Adjustments for disaster costs³	....	1	5	7	8	9	9	10	10	10	10	10	38	88
Joint Committee enforcement	....	–48	–87	–99	–104	–107	–108	–108	–108	–109	–48	–15	–505	–893
Total outlays	3,537	3,632	3,627	3,812	4,023	4,216	4,437	4,733	5,003	5,282	5,674	5,959	20,116	46,767
Receipts:														
Individual income taxes	1,132	1,234	1,358	1,512	1,645	1,776	1,900	2,017	2,144	2,274	2,402	2,559	8,190	19,587
Corporation income taxes	242	288	335	376	399	427	446	465	475	487	504	523	1,983	4,438
Social insurance and retirement receipts:														
Social Security payroll taxes	570	673	740	779	828	871	919	967	1,009	1,065	1,116	1,163	4,136	9,455
Medicare payroll taxes	201	208	224	237	253	267	283	298	311	329	345	360	1,264	2,906
Unemployment insurance	67	61	60	60	59	56	55	54	56	58	54	56	289	567
Other retirement	8	9	9	9	9	10	10	10	11	12	12	13	47	105
Excise taxes	79	85	93	99	100	104	112	125	130	137	145	155	509	1,201
Estate and gift taxes	14	13	13	14	15	16	18	19	20	21	22	23	76	182
Customs duties	30	34	39	43	46	49	53	55	58	61	65	68	230	538
Deposits of earnings, Federal Reserve System	82	83	92	79	51	12	....	10	30	33	37	39	234	383
Other miscellaneous receipts	25	24	38	70	72	72	70	75	80	81	83	85	321	727
Total receipts	2,450	2,712	3,000	3,277	3,476	3,660	3,865	4,097	4,325	4,559	4,785	5,045	17,279	40,089
Deficit	**1,087**	**919**	**627**	**536**	**547**	**556**	**571**	**637**	**678**	**723**	**889**	**913**	**2,837**	**6,678**
Net interest	220	222	222	252	298	370	459	544	616	677	741	804	1,601	4,984
Primary deficit	867	697	405	283	250	186	112	92	62	46	148	109	1,236	1,694
On-budget deficit	1,149	953	646	543	550	548	556	612	632	672	819	817	2,843	6,394
Off-budget deficit / surplus (–)	–62	–33	–19	–7	–3	8	16	25	46	52	70	96	–5	284

Table S–4. Adjusted Baseline by Category[1]—Continued

(In billions of dollars)

													Totals	
	2012	2013	2014	2015	2016	2017	2018	2019	2020	2021	2022	2023	2014–2018	2014–2023
Memorandum, budget authority for appropriated programs: [2]														
Defense	670	641	642	658	671	685	700	715	731	747	765	784	3,356	7,097
Non-defense	527	553	516	530	541	552	564	577	590	602	617	633	2,703	5,722
Total, appropriated funding	1,196	1,194	1,158	1,188	1,211	1,237	1,264	1,292	1,320	1,349	1,382	1,416	6,058	12,818

[1] See Table S–8 for information on adjustments to the Balanced Budget and Emergency Deficit Control Act (BBEDCA) baseline.
[2] Does not include effects of Joint Committee enforcement.
[3] These amounts represent a placeholder for major disasters requiring Federal assistance for relief and reconstruction. Such assistance might be provided in the form of discretionary or mandatory outlays or tax relief. These amounts are included as outlays for convenience.

Table S–5. Proposed Budget by Category

(In billions of dollars)

	2012	2013	2014	2015	2016	2017	2018	2019	2020	2021	2022	2023	Totals 2014–2018	Totals 2014–2023
Outlays:														
Appropriated ("discretionary") programs:[1]														
Defense	671	651	618	604	581	581	583	589	601	612	622	631	2,967	6,021
Non-defense	614	606	624	628	637	638	641	647	657	662	648	647	3,168	6,429
Subtotal, appropriated programs	1,285	1,258	1,242	1,232	1,218	1,219	1,224	1,236	1,258	1,274	1,270	1,278	6,135	12,451
Mandatory programs:														
Social Security	768	813	860	911	965	1,021	1,080	1,142	1,208	1,275	1,347	1,424	4,837	11,234
Medicare	466	504	524	537	578	587	607	665	709	758	837	867	2,832	6,668
Medicaid	251	267	304	328	351	371	391	414	438	465	493	523	1,743	4,076
Allowance for moving to the chained CPI	......	......	......	–2	–5	–8	–11	–14	–18	–21	–24	–27	–26	–130
Other mandatory programs	548	620	621	642	676	675	688	728	753	786	821	822	3,301	7,211
Subtotal, mandatory programs	2,032	2,203	2,308	2,415	2,564	2,646	2,754	2,934	3,090	3,263	3,475	3,609	12,688	29,059
Net interest	220	223	223	254	300	373	461	543	609	663	715	763	1,611	4,905
Adjustments for disaster costs[2]	......	1	5	7	8	9	9	10	10	10	10	10	38	88
Total outlays	3,537	3,685	3,778	3,908	4,090	4,247	4,449	4,724	4,967	5,209	5,470	5,660	20,472	46,502
Receipts:														
Individual income taxes	1,132	1,234	1,383	1,552	1,700	1,844	1,977	2,105	2,241	2,380	2,517	2,684	8,456	20,382
Corporation income taxes	242	288	333	376	401	430	450	470	481	494	511	531	1,991	4,478
Social insurance and retirement receipts:														
Social Security payroll taxes	570	673	739	778	826	869	917	965	1,008	1,063	1,114	1,161	4,129	9,440
Medicare payroll taxes	201	208	224	238	254	268	284	299	313	330	347	362	1,268	2,919
Unemployment insurance	67	61	58	58	69	69	66	64	64	66	68	68	320	651
Other retirement	8	9	10	11	12	12	12	13	13	14	14	15	56	125
Excise taxes	79	85	105	114	115	118	125	138	142	149	156	166	577	1,327
Estate and gift taxes	14	13	13	14	15	17	18	31	33	36	38	41	78	257
Customs duties	30	34	39	42	46	49	53	55	58	61	65	68	228	537
Deposits of earnings, Federal Reserve System	82	83	92	79	51	12	......	10	30	33	37	39	234	383
Other miscellaneous receipts	25	24	38	70	73	72	70	76	81	82	84	86	324	733
Total receipts	2,450	2,712	3,034	3,332	3,561	3,761	3,974	4,226	4,464	4,709	4,951	5,220	17,661	41,231
Deficit	1,087	973	744	576	528	487	475	498	503	501	519	439	2,811	5,271
Net interest	220	223	223	254	300	373	461	543	609	663	715	763	1,611	4,905
Primary deficit / surplus (–)	867	750	521	323	228	113	14	–45	–106	–162	–197	–323	1,200	366
On-budget deficit	1,149	1,006	768	584	525	478	460	474	459	451	450	345	2,814	4,993
Off-budget deficit / surplus (–)	–62	–33	–24	–7	4	9	16	24	44	50	69	94	–3	278

Table S–5.　Proposed Budget by Category—Continued
(In billions of dollars)

	2012	2013	2014	2015	2016	2017	2018	2019	2020	2021	2022	2023	Totals 2014–2018	Totals 2014–2023
Memorandum, budget authority for appropriated programs: [1]														
Defense	670	639	640	566	577	586	595	604	614	624	634	644	2,964	6,084
Non-defense	527	551	515	556	566	574	582	591	599	607	578	587	2,792	5,753
Total, appropriated funding	1,196	1,190	1,155	1,122	1,143	1,160	1,177	1,195	1,213	1,231	1,212	1,231	5,757	11,837

[1] The 2014 Budget proposes changes to the current law caps in the BBEDCA, for the reclassification of certain transportation programs and further reductions as part of the Administration's policy to achieve additional deficit reduction.

[2] These amounts represent a placeholder for major disasters requiring Federal assistance for relief and reconstruction. Such assistance might be provided in the form of discretionary or mandatory outlays or tax relief. These amounts are included as outlays for convenience.

Table S–6. Proposed Budget by Category as a Percent of GDP

(As a percent of GDP)

	2012	2013	2014	2015	2016	2017	2018	2019	2020	2021	2022	2023	Averages 2014-2018	Averages 2014-2023
Outlays:														
Appropriated ("discretionary") programs:[1]														
Defense	4.3	4.0	3.6	3.4	3.1	2.9	2.8	2.7	2.6	2.6	2.5	2.4	3.1	2.9
Non-defense	4.0	3.7	3.7	3.5	3.4	3.2	3.0	2.9	2.9	2.8	2.6	2.5	3.4	3.0
Subtotal, appropriated programs	8.3	7.8	7.3	6.9	6.4	6.1	5.8	5.6	5.5	5.3	5.1	4.9	6.5	5.9
Mandatory programs:														
Social Security	4.9	5.0	5.1	5.1	5.1	5.1	5.1	5.2	5.3	5.3	5.4	5.5	5.1	5.2
Medicare	3.0	3.1	3.1	3.0	3.1	2.9	2.9	3.0	3.1	3.2	3.3	3.3	3.0	3.1
Medicaid	1.6	1.6	1.8	1.8	1.9	1.9	1.9	1.9	1.9	1.9	2.0	2.0	1.8	1.9
Allowance for moving to the chained CPI	.....	.....	–*	–*	–*	–*	-0.1	-0.1	-0.1	-0.1	-0.1	-0.1	–*	-0.1
Other mandatory programs	3.5	3.8	3.6	3.6	3.6	3.4	3.3	3.3	3.3	3.3	3.3	3.2	3.5	3.4
Subtotal, mandatory programs	13.1	13.6	13.6	13.5	13.5	13.2	13.1	13.3	13.5	13.6	13.9	13.9	13.4	13.5
Net interest	1.4	1.4	1.3	1.4	1.6	1.9	2.2	2.5	2.7	2.8	2.9	2.9	1.7	2.2
Adjustments for disaster costs[2]	.....	*	*	*	*	*	*	*	*	*	*	*	*	*
Total outlays	22.8	22.7	22.2	21.8	21.6	21.3	21.2	21.5	21.6	21.7	21.9	21.7	21.6	21.6
Receipts:														
Individual income taxes	7.3	7.6	8.1	8.7	9.0	9.2	9.4	9.6	9.8	9.9	10.1	10.3	8.9	9.4
Corporation income taxes	1.6	1.8	2.0	2.1	2.1	2.2	2.1	2.1	2.1	2.1	2.0	2.0	2.1	2.1
Social insurance and retirement receipts:														
Social Security payroll taxes	3.7	4.2	4.3	4.3	4.4	4.3	4.4	4.4	4.4	4.4	4.5	4.5	4.4	4.4
Medicare payroll taxes	1.3	1.3	1.3	1.3	1.3	1.3	1.4	1.4	1.4	1.4	1.4	1.4	1.3	1.4
Unemployment insurance	0.4	0.4	0.3	0.3	0.4	0.3	0.3	0.3	0.3	0.3	0.3	0.3	0.3	0.3
Other retirement	0.1	0.1	0.1	0.1	0.1	0.1	0.1	0.1	0.1	0.1	0.1	0.1	0.1	0.1
Excise taxes	0.5	0.5	0.6	0.6	0.6	0.6	0.6	0.6	0.6	0.6	0.6	0.6	0.6	0.6
Estate and gift taxes	0.1	0.1	0.1	0.1	0.1	0.1	0.1	0.1	0.1	0.2	0.2	0.2	0.1	0.1
Customs duties	0.2	0.2	0.2	0.2	0.2	0.2	0.2	0.3	0.3	0.3	0.3	0.3	0.2	0.2
Deposits of earnings, Federal Reserve System	0.5	0.5	0.5	0.4	0.3	0.1	....	*	0.1	0.1	0.1	0.2	0.3	0.2
Other miscellaneous receipts	0.2	0.2	0.2	0.4	0.4	0.4	0.3	0.3	0.4	0.3	0.3	0.3	0.3	0.3
Total receipts	15.8	16.7	17.8	18.6	18.8	18.8	18.9	19.2	19.4	19.6	19.8	20.0	18.6	19.1
Deficit	**7.0**	**6.0**	**4.4**	**3.2**	**2.8**	**2.4**	**2.3**	**2.3**	**2.2**	**2.1**	**2.1**	**1.7**	**3.0**	**2.5**
Net interest	1.4	1.4	1.3	1.4	1.6	1.9	2.2	2.5	2.7	2.8	2.9	2.9	1.7	2.2
Primary deficit / surplus (–)	5.6	4.6	3.1	1.8	1.2	0.6	0.1	-0.2	-0.5	-0.7	-0.8	-1.2	1.3	0.3
On-budget deficit	7.4	6.2	4.5	3.3	2.8	2.4	2.2	2.2	2.0	1.9	1.8	1.3	3.0	2.4
Off-budget deficit / surplus (–)	-0.4	-0.2	-0.1	–*	*	*	0.1	0.1	0.2	0.2	0.3	0.4	–*	0.1

Table S–6. Proposed Budget by Category as a Percent of GDP—Continued

(As a percent of GDP)

	2012	2013	2014	2015	2016	2017	2018	2019	2020	2021	2022	2023	Averages 2014-2018	Averages 2014-2023
Memorandum, budget authority for appropriated programs: [1]														
Defense	4.3	3.9	3.8	3.2	3.0	2.9	2.8	2.7	2.7	2.6	2.5	2.5	3.1	2.9
Non-defense	3.4	3.4	3.0	3.1	3.0	2.9	2.8	2.7	2.6	2.5	2.3	2.3	3.0	2.7
Total, appropriated funding	7.7	7.3	6.8	6.3	6.0	5.8	5.6	5.4	5.3	5.1	4.8	4.7	6.1	5.6

*0.05 percent of GDP or less.

[1] The 2014 Budget proposes changes to the current law caps in the BBEDCA, for the reclassification of certain transportation programs and further reductions as part of the Administration's policy to achieve additional deficit reduction.

[2] These amounts represent a placeholder for major disasters requiring Federal assistance for relief and reconstruction. Such assistance might be provided in the form of discretionary or mandatory outlays or tax relief. These amounts are included as outlays for convenience.

Table S–7. Proposed Budget in Population- and Inflation-Adjusted Dollars

(In billions of constant dollars, adjusted for population growth)

	2014	2015	2016	2017	2018	2019	2020	2021	2022	2023
Outlays:										
Appropriated ("discretionary") programs:[1]										
Defense	618	585	545	529	515	504	498	491	484	477
Non-defense	624	609	598	581	566	553	544	532	505	488
Subtotal, appropriated programs	1,242	1,194	1,144	1,110	1,080	1,057	1,042	1,023	989	965
Mandatory programs:										
Social Security	860	883	906	929	953	977	1,001	1,025	1,049	1,075
Medicare	524	520	543	534	535	569	588	609	652	654
Medicaid	304	317	329	338	345	354	363	373	384	395
Allowance for moving to the chained CPI	....	–2	–5	–7	–10	–12	–15	–17	–19	–20
Other mandatory programs	621	622	635	615	607	622	624	631	640	621
Subtotal, mandatory programs	2,308	2,341	2,408	2,409	2,430	2,509	2,561	2,621	2,706	2,725
Net interest	223	246	282	340	407	465	505	533	557	576
Adjustments for disaster costs[2]	5	7	8	8	8	8	8	8	8	8
Total outlays	3,778	3,787	3,841	3,866	3,925	4,039	4,117	4,185	4,260	4,273
Receipts:										
Individual income taxes	1,383	1,504	1,597	1,678	1,744	1,800	1,857	1,912	1,961	2,026
Corporation income taxes	333	364	377	392	397	402	399	397	398	401
Social insurance and retirement receipts										
Social Security payroll taxes	739	754	775	791	809	825	835	854	868	877
Medicare payroll taxes	224	230	239	244	251	256	259	265	270	273
Unemployment insurance	58	56	65	63	58	55	53	53	53	51
Other retirement	10	10	11	11	11	11	11	11	11	12
Excise taxes	105	110	108	108	110	118	118	120	122	125
Estate and gift taxes	13	14	15	15	16	27	28	29	30	31
Customs duties	39	41	43	45	46	47	48	49	50	52
Deposits of earnings, Federal Reserve System	92	77	48	11	....	9	25	27	28	30
Other miscellaneous receipts	38	68	68	66	62	65	67	66	65	65
Total receipts	3,034	3,229	3,345	3,423	3,506	3,613	3,700	3,783	3,856	3,942
Deficit	**744**	**559**	**496**	**443**	**419**	**426**	**417**	**402**	**404**	**332**
Net interest	223	246	282	340	407	465	505	533	557	576
Primary deficit / surplus (–)	521	313	214	103	12	–39	–88	–130	–153	–244
On-budget deficit	768	566	493	435	406	405	380	362	350	260
Off-budget deficit / surplus (–)	–24	–7	4	8	14	21	37	40	54	71

Table S–7. Proposed Budget in Population- and Inflation-Adjusted Dollars—Continued

(In billions of constant dollars, adjusted for population growth)

	2014	2015	2016	2017	2018	2019	2020	2021	2022	2023
Memorandum, budget authority for appropriated programs: [1]										
Defense	640	549	542	533	525	516	509	501	494	486
Non-defense	515	539	532	522	513	505	496	488	450	443
Subtotal, appropriated programs	1,155	1,087	1,074	1,056	1,038	1,022	1,005	989	944	929
Memorandum, index of population growth and inflation	1.00	1.03	1.06	1.10	1.13	1.17	1.21	1.24	1.28	1.32

[1] The 2014 Budget proposes changes to the current law caps in the BBEDCA, for the reclassification of certain transportation programs and further reductions as part of the Administration's policy to achieve additional deficit reduction.

[2] These amounts represent a placeholder for major disasters requiring Federal assistance for relief and reconstruction. Such assistance might be provided in the form of discretionary or mandatory outlays or tax relief. These amounts are included as outlays for convenience.

Table S–8. Bridge From Balanced Budget and Emergency Control Act (BBEDCA) Baseline to Adjusted Baseline

(Deficit increases (+) or decreases (–) in billions of dollars)

	2012	2013	2014	2015	2016	2017	2018	2019	2020	2021	2022	2023	Totals 2014–2018	Totals 2014–2023
BBEDCA baseline deficit	1,087	912	687	655	698	728	764	815	869	928	1,041	1,041	3,532	8,227
Adjustments for current policy:														
Continue tax benefits provided under the American Taxpayer Relief Act (ATRA) [1]	......	......	......	......	......	......	2	30	31	32	33	33	2	161
Prevent reduction in Medicare physician payments	......	......	15	21	22	23	22	25	27	29	32	32	103	249
Reflect incremental cost of funding existing Pell maximum grant award	......	......	–1	–1	5	5	3	3	3	3	3	3	12	28
Reflect Postal Service default on 2013 retiree health benefit payment	......	6	–*				–*	–*	–*	–*	–*	–*	–1	–3
Subtotal	......	6	14	20	28	27	26	58	61	64	68	68	115	436
Adjustments for provisions contained in the Budget Control Act:														
Set discretionary budget authority at cap levels	......	*	–20	–34	–43	–48	–53	–57	–62	–68	–71	–74	–198	–531
Reflect Joint Committee enforcement [2]	......	......	–50	–86	–101	–105	–107	–108	–108	–109	–48	–15	–450	–838
Subtotal	......	*	–70	–120	–145	–154	–160	–165	–171	–176	–120	–88	–648	–1,369
Adjustments for disaster costs:														
Remove non-recurring emergency costs	......	......	–9	–27	–40	–46	–50	–52	–55	–56	–58	–59	–171	–451
Add placeholder for future emergency costs [2]	......	1	5	7	8	9	9	10	10	10	10	10	38	88
Reclassify surface transportation outlays:														
Remove outlays from appropriated category	–1	–1	–1	–1	–2	–2	–2	–2	–2	–2	–2	–2	–8	–16
Add outlays to mandatory category	1	1	1	1	2	2	2	2	2	2	2	2	8	16
Subtotal	......	......	......	......	......	......	......	......	......	......	......	......	......	......
Total program adjustments	......	7	–60	–120	–148	–164	–174	–150	–154	–159	–99	–69	–666	–1,297
Debt service on adjustments	......	*	–*	–*	–2	–8	–18	–29	–37	–46	–53	–58	–29	–252
Total adjustments	......	7	–60	–120	–151	–172	–192	–179	–191	–204	–152	–127	–695	–1,549
Adjusted baseline deficit	1,087	919	627	536	547	556	571	637	678	723	889	913	2,837	6,678

*$500 million or less.

[1] The baseline permanently continues the tax benefits provided to individuals and families that were extended only through taxable year 2017 under ATRA.

[2] These amounts represent a placeholder for major disasters requiring Federal assistance for relief and reconstruction.

S–9. Mandatory and Receipt Proposals

(Deficit increases (+) or decreases (−) in millions of dollars)

	2013	2014	2015	2016	2017	2018	2019	2020	2021	2022	2023	Totals 2014–2018	2014–2023
Savings Consistent with the December Compromise Deficit Reduction Package:													
Health Savings:													
Health and Human Services (HHS):													
Medicare providers:													
Bad debts:													
Reduce Medicare coverage of bad debts	....	−200	−860	−1,930	−2,570	−2,800	−3,000	−3,190	−3,410	−3,640	−3,890	−8,360	−25,490
Graduate medical education:													
Better align graduate medical education payments with patient care costs	....	−780	−930	−960	−990	−1,050	−1,100	−1,170	−1,250	−1,330	−1,420	−4,710	−10,980
Better align payments to rural providers with the cost of care:													
Reduce Critical Access Hospital (CAH) payments from 101% of reasonable costs to 100% of reasonable costs	....	−90	−110	−120	−120	−130	−150	−160	−170	−190	−190	−570	−1,430
Prohibit CAH designation for facilities that are less than 10 miles from the nearest hospital	....	−40	−50	−60	−60	−70	−70	−80	−80	−90	−90	−280	−690
Cut waste, fraud, and improper payments in Medicare:													
Reduce fraud, waste, and abuse in Medicare	....	....	−20	−20	−30	−50	−50	−50	−60	−60	−60	−120	−400
Require prior authorization for advanced imaging	....	....	....	....	....	....	....	....	....	....	....	....	....
Drug rebates and additional Part D savings:													
Align Medicare drug payment policies with Medicaid policies for low-income beneficiaries	....	−3,140	−7,720	−8,450	−9,720	−11,260	−12,510	−14,310	−16,400	−18,220	−21,440	−40,290	−123,170
Accelerate manufacturer drug rebates to provide relief to Medicare beneficiaries in the coverage gap	....	....	−140	−230	−450	−760	−1,210	−1,780	−2,010	−2,320	−2,310	−1,580	−11,210
Encourage efficient post-acute care:													
Adjust payment updates for certain post-acute care providers	....	−830	−1,930	−3,220	−4,540	−6,020	−7,870	−9,880	−12,140	−14,980	−17,630	−16,540	−79,040
Equalize payments for certain conditions commonly treated in inpatient rehabilitation facilities and Skilled Nursing Facilities (SNFs)	....	−140	−160	−180	−180	−190	−200	−210	−220	−230	−240	−850	−1,950
Encourage appropriate use of inpatient rehabilitation hospitals	....	−190	−230	−240	−240	−240	−250	−260	−280	−290	−300	−1,140	−2,520

S–9. Mandatory and Receipt Proposals—Continued

(Deficit increases (+) or decreases (−) in millions of dollars)

	2013	2014	2015	2016	2017	2018	2019	2020	2021	2022	2023	Totals 2014–2018	Totals 2014–2023
Adjust SNF payments to reduce hospital readmissions	......	......	......	......	−230	−270	−290	−310	−340	−370	−400	−500	−2,210
Implement bundled post-acute care payment	......	......	......	......	......	−290	−820	−1,520	−1,720	−1,850	−1,960	−290	−8,160
Additional provider efficiencies:													
Exclude certain services from the in-office ancillary services exception ...	......	......	−350	−550	−600	−640	−680	−730	−780	−830	−890	−2,140	−6,050
Reduce overpayment of Part B drugs ...	......	−220	−380	−390	−410	−440	−460	−490	−530	−560	−600	−1,840	−4,480
Modernize payments for clinical laboratory services	......	......	......	−120	−350	−610	−900	−1,240	−1,620	−2,060	−2,560	−1,080	−9,460
Expand sharing Medicare data with qualified entities	......	......	......	......	......	......	......	......	......	......	......	......	......
Clarify the Medicare Fraction in the Medicare Disproportionate Share Hospital (DSH) statute	......	......	......	......	......	......	......	......	......	......	......	......	......
Improve payment accuracy for Medicare Advantage (MA):													
Increase the minimum MA coding intensity adjustment	......	......	−320	−750	−1,180	−1,660	−1,890	−2,070	−2,270	−2,490	−2,710	−3,910	−15,340
Align employer group waiver plan payments with average MA plan bids	......	......	−280	−360	−360	−380	−420	−480	−540	−590	−640	−1,380	−4,050
Total, Medicare providers	......	−5,630	−13,480	−17,580	−22,030	−26,860	−31,870	−37,930	−43,820	−50,100	−57,330	−85,580	−306,630
Medicare structural reforms:													
Increase income-related premium under Medicare Parts B and D	......	......	......	......	−3,000	−3,000	−4,000	−7,000	−9,000	−11,000	−13,000	−6,000	−50,000
Modify Part B deductible for new enrollees	......	......	......	......	−50	−60	−250	−350	−760	−890	−960	−110	−3,320
Introduce home health co-payments for new beneficiaries	......	......	......	......	−20	−40	−70	−100	−130	−170	−200	−60	−730
Introduce a Part B premium surcharge for new beneficiaries who purchase near first-dollar Medigap coverage	......	......	......	......	−70	−180	−290	−410	−540	−670	−750	−250	−2,910
Encourage the use of generic drugs by low-income beneficiaries	......	−350	−500	−540	−580	−630	−690	−750	−820	−900	−970	−2,600	−6,730
Strengthen the Independent Payment Advisory Board (IPAB) to reduce long-term drivers of Medicare cost growth ...	......	......	......	......	......	......	......	......	−250	−370	−3,480	......	−4,100
Total, Medicare structural reforms ...	......	−350	−500	−540	−3,720	−3,910	−5,300	−8,610	−11,500	−14,000	−19,360	−9,020	−67,790
Interactions	......	......	......	20	30	50	1,770	2,500	2,950	1,860	5,290	100	14,470

S–9. Mandatory and Receipt Proposals—Continued

(Deficit increases (+) or decreases (−) in millions of dollars)

	2013	2014	2015	2016	2017	2018	2019	2020	2021	2022	2023	Totals 2014–2018	Totals 2014–2023
Medicaid and other:													
Medicaid:													
Limit Medicaid reimbursement of durable medical equipment based on Medicare rates	......	−250	−290	−374	−402	−434	−469	−503	−543	−586	−632	−1,750	−4,483
Rebase future Medicaid Disproportionate Share Hospital (DSH) allotments	......	......	......	......	......	......	......	......	......	......	−3,630	......	−3,630
Begin Affordable Care Act Medicaid Disproportionate Share Hospital (DSH) reductions in FY 2015	......	360	......	−216	−144	......	......	......	......	......	......	......	......
Reduce fraud, waste and abuse in Medicaid	......	−156	−252	−338	−358	−374	−394	−420	−441	−466	−492	−1,478	−3,691
Improve Medicaid drug rebate and payment policies	......	−411	−761	−811	−851	−882	−922	−972	−1,017	−1,057	−1,117	−3,716	−8,801
Expand State flexibility to provide benchmark benefit packages	......	......	......	......	......	......	......	......	......	......	......	......	......
Extend the Qualified Individuals (QI) program through CY 2014	......	405	185	......	......	......	......	......	......	......	......	590	590
Extend the Transitional Medical Assistance (TMA) program through CY 2014	......	480	560	15	......	......	......	......	......	......	......	1,055	1,055
Total, Medicaid	......	428	−558	−1,724	−1,755	−1,690	−1,785	−1,895	−2,001	−2,109	−5,871	−5,299	−18,960
Pharmaceutical savings:													
Prohibit brand and generic drug companies from delaying the availability of new generic drugs and biologics	......	−750	−820	−900	−960	−1,020	−1,110	−1,210	−1,310	−1,410	−1,510	−4,450	−11,000
Modify length of exclusivity to facilitate faster development of generic biologics	......	10	−50	−100	−190	−310	−420	−480	−530	−580	−630	−640	−3,280
Total, pharmaceutical savings	......	−740	−870	−1,000	−1,150	−1,330	−1,530	−1,690	−1,840	−1,990	−2,140	−5,090	−14,280
Medicare-Medicaid enrollees:													
Ensure retroactive Part D coverage of newly-eligible low-income beneficiaries	......	......	......	......	......	......	......	......	......	......	......	......	......
Integrate appeals process for Medicare-Medicaid enrollees	......	......	......	......	......	......	......	......	......	......	......	......	......
Total, Medicare-Medicaid Enrollees	......	......	......	......	......	......	......	......	......	......	......	......	......
Accelerate the issuance of State innovation waivers	......	......	......	......	......	......	......	......	......	......	......	......	......
Enact survey and certification revisit fees	......	......	......	......	......	......	......	......	......	......	......	......	......

S–9. Mandatory and Receipt Proposals—Continued

(Deficit increases (+) or decreases (−) in millions of dollars)

	2013	2014	2015	2016	2017	2018	2019	2020	2021	2022	2023	Totals 2014–2018	Totals 2014–2023
Extend Centers for Medicare and Medicaid Services (CMS) quality measurement		10	30	30	30	......						100	100
Total, Medicaid and other	......	–302	–1,398	–2,694	–2,875	–3,020	–3,315	–3,585	–3,841	–4,099	–8,011	–10,289	–33,140
Provide administrative resources for implementation		100	250	50	......	......						400	400
Total, HHS health proposals	......	–6,182	–15,128	–20,744	–28,595	–33,740	–38,715	–47,625	–56,211	–66,339	–79,411	–104,389	–392,690
Office of Personnel Management:													
Modernize the Federal Employees Health Benefits Program (FEHBP):													
Streamline FEHBP pharmacy benefit contracting	......	......	–74	–140	–157	–167	–180	–195	–211	–227	–247	–538	–1,598
Offer an FEHBP Self+One option and domestic partner benefits	......	......	–345	–504	–519	–548	–581	–617	–653	–684	–721	–1,916	–5,172
Expand FEHBP plan types	......	......	–4	–11	–15	–18	–24	–31	–41	–51	–69	–48	–264
Adjust FEHBP premiums for wellness	......	......	3	–11	–34	–60	–101	–154	–230	–316	–430	–102	–1,333
Total, modernize FEHBP	......	......	–420	–666	–725	–793	–886	–997	–1,135	–1,278	–1,467	–2,604	–8,367
Total, health savings	......	–6,182	–15,548	–21,410	–29,320	–34,533	–39,601	–48,622	–57,346	–67,617	–80,878	–106,993	–401,057
Other Mandatory Savings:													
Agriculture:													
Streamline conservation programs	......	–37	127	–10	–50	–193	–238	–273	–298	–358	–383	–163	–1,713
Reduce subsidies for crop insurance companies and farmer premiums	......	–513	–1,005	–1,238	–1,244	–1,256	–1,274	–1,280	–1,294	–1,302	–1,310	–5,256	–11,716
Eliminate direct payments	......	......	–3,300	–3,300	–3,300	–3,300	–3,300	–3,300	–3,300	–3,300	–3,300	–13,200	–29,700
Provide assistance for dairy and livestock producers	......	400	400	400	400	400	400	400	400	400	400	2,000	4,000
Provide assistance for specialty crops, bioenergy and beginning farmers	......	235	235	235	235	235	20	20	20	20	20	1,175	1,275
Total, Agriculture	......	85	–3,543	–3,913	–3,959	–4,114	–4,392	–4,433	–4,472	–4,540	–4,573	–15,444	–37,854
Health and Human Services:													
Provide dedicated, mandatory funding for Health Care Fraud and Abuse Control Program (HCFAC) program integrity:													
Administrative costs	303	329	672	706	725	745	765	786	807	829	852	3,177	7,216
Benefit savings	–450	–496	–546	–599	–628	–659	–690	–722	–755	–789	–824	–2,928	–6,708
Subtotal, provide dedicated, mandatory funding for HCFAC program integrity	–147	–167	126	107	97	86	75	64	52	40	28	249	508
Annual reduction to discretionary spending limits (non-add)	–147	......	–311	–311	–311	–311	–311	–311	–311	–311	–311	–1,244	–2,799

S–9. Mandatory and Receipt Proposals—Continued

(Deficit increases (+) or decreases (–) in millions of dollars)

	2013	2014	2015	2016	2017	2018	2019	2020	2021	2022	2023	Totals 2014–2018	Totals 2014–2023
Homeland Security:													
Reform the aviation passenger security user fee to more accurately reflect the costs of aviation security	....	–200	–1,139	–1,410	–1,675	–1,950	–2,235	–2,279	–2,324	–2,370	–2,418	–6,374	–18,000
Interior:													
Enact Federal oil and gas management reforms	....	–50	–120	–125	–150	–170	–185	–200	–215	–225	–240	–615	–1,680
Authorize U.S.-Mexico Transboundary Agreement on Gulf of Mexico Leasing	....	–50	....	....	....	....	....	....	....	....	....	–50	–50
Terminate Abandoned Mine Lands (AML) payments to certified States	....	–32	–33	–27	–31	–40	–47	–39	–36	–32	–10	–163	–327
Make permanent net receipts sharing for energy minerals	....	....	–44	–44	–43	–44	–45	–47	–49	–52	–53	–175	–421
Total, Interior	....	–132	–197	–196	–224	–254	–277	–286	–300	–309	–303	–1,003	–2,478
Labor:													
Improve Pension Benefit Guaranty Corporation (PBGC) solvency	....	....	–2,778	–2,778	–2,778	–2,778	–2,778	–2,778	–2,778	–2,778	–2,778	–11,112	–25,002
Improve unemployment insurance (UI) program integrity [1,2]	....	–10	–40	–42	–40	–31	–25	413	2	–62	–10	–163	155
Implement cap adjustments for UI program integrity [1,2]	....	–33	–77	–96	–113	–116	582	–25	–140	–1,493	–296	–435	–1,807
Outlays from discretionary cap adjustment (non-add)	....	20	25	30	35	36	37	38	39	40	41	146	341
Total, Labor	....	–43	–2,895	–2,916	–2,931	–2,925	–2,221	–2,390	–2,916	–4,333	–3,084	–11,710	–26,654
Treasury:													
Implement tax enforcement program integrity cap adjustment [1,3]	....	–458	–1,252	–2,503	–3,766	–5,052	–5,955	–6,525	–6,816	–7,017	–7,158	–13,031	–46,502
Outlays from discretionary cap adjustment (non-add)	....	387	718	1,012	1,322	1,643	1,640	1,649	1,708	1,769	1,832	5,082	13,680
Other Defense—Civil Programs:													
Increase TRICARE pharmacy copayments	....	–4	–81	–141	–220	–405	–525	–637	–781	–917	–1,051	–851	–4,762
Increase annual premiums for TRICARE-For-Life (TFL) enrollment	....	....	–4	–21	–53	–80	–109	–138	–169	–201	–234	–158	–1,009
Total, Other Defense - Civil Programs	....	–4	–85	–162	–273	–485	–634	–775	–950	–1,118	–1,285	–1,009	–5,771
Office of Personnel Management:													
Increase Civil Service Retirement System (CSRS) and Federal Employees Retirement System (FERS) contributions [1]	....	–800	–1,569	–2,325	–2,300	–2,273	–2,237	–2,197	–2,153	–2,104	–2,050	–9,267	–20,008

S–9. Mandatory and Receipt Proposals—Continued

(Deficit increases (+) or decreases (−) in millions of dollars)

	2013	2014	2015	2016	2017	2018	2019	2020	2021	2022	2023	Totals 2014–2018	Totals 2014–2023
Social Security Administration (SSA):													
Prevent improper use of the Death Master File [1]	....	−65	−131	−132	−135	−138	−137	−137	−140	−143	−145	−601	−1,303
Provide dedicated, mandatory funding for program integrity:													
Administrative costs	266	1,227	1,750	1,800	1,710	1,625	1,543	1,543	1,543	1,543	1,620	8,112	15,904
Benefit savings	−76	−559	−2,437	−3,809	−4,417	−4,824	−5,760	−6,466	−7,040	−7,890	−8,124	−16,046	−51,326
Subtotal, provide dedicated, mandatory funding for program integrity	190	668	−687	−2,009	−2,707	−3,199	−4,217	−4,923	−5,497	−6,347	−6,504	−7,934	−35,422
Annual reduction to discretionary spending limits (non-add)	....	....	−273	−273	−273	−273	−273	−273	−273	−273	−273	−1,092	−2,457
Offset DI benefits for period of concurrent UI receipt	....	−100	−100	−100	−100	−100	−100	−100	−100	−100	−100	−500	−1,000
Improve collection of pension information from States and localities	....	18	28	24	−232	−500	−650	−685	−619	−577	−524	−662	−3,717
Total, SSA	190	521	−890	−2,217	−3,174	−3,937	−5,104	−5,845	−6,356	−7,167	−7,273	−9,697	−41,442
Other Independent Agencies:													
Civilian Property Realignment Board:													
Dispose of unneeded real property	....	−87	−203	−376	−990	−130	−100	−120	−120	−120	−120	−1,786	−2,366
Total, Other Mandatory Savings	43	−1,285	−11,647	−15,911	−19,195	−21,034	−23,080	−24,786	−26,355	−29,038	−28,236	−69,072	−200,567
Chained CPI:													
Adjust indexing and protect vulnerable populations [1]	....	....	−3,000	−8,000	−14,000	−19,000	−24,000	−31,000	−37,000	−44,000	−50,000	−44,000	−230,000
Revenues:													
Reduce the value of certain tax expenditures	....	−24,568	−39,800	−43,014	−46,800	−51,100	−55,639	−60,271	−64,995	−69,214	−73,860	−205,282	−529,261
Implement the Buffett Rule [4]	....	−5,327	−1,726	−3,486	−5,542	−6,177	−5,967	−5,968	−6,146	−6,393	−6,655	−22,258	−53,387
Total, revenues	....	−29,895	−41,526	−46,500	−52,342	−57,277	−61,606	−66,239	−71,141	−75,607	−80,515	−205,282	−582,648
Upfront Investments:													
Invest in immediate surface transportation priorities	....	5,600	17,850	12,170	5,770	3,870	1,530	1,560	870	480	240	45,260	49,940
Total, savings consistent with the December Compromise Deficit Reduction Package	43	−31,762	−53,871	−79,651	−109,087	−127,974	−146,757	−169,087	−190,972	−215,782	−239,389	−402,345	−1,364,332
Accrual effects:													
Increase TRICARE pharmacy copayments	....	528	850	900	951	1,006	1,063	1,125	1,190	1,258	1,330	4,235	10,201
Increase annual premiums for TFL enrollment	....	66	93	98	103	109	115	123	130	137	144	469	1,118
Total accrual effects	....	594	943	998	1,054	1,115	1,178	1,248	1,320	1,395	1,474	4,704	11,319

S–9. Mandatory and Receipt Proposals—Continued

(Deficit increases (+) or decreases (−) in millions of dollars)

	2013	2014	2015	2016	2017	2018	2019	2020	2021	2022	2023	Totals 2014–2018	Totals 2014–2023
Additional Mandatory and Receipt Proposals:													
Early Childhood Investments:													
Support preschool for all	......	130	1,235	3,110	5,456	7,360	8,773	9,787	10,560	10,275	9,356	17,291	66,042
Extend and expand home visiting	......	......	150	250	625	900	1,150	1,450	1,900	2,075	2,225	1,925	10,725
Total, early childhood investments	......	130	1,385	3,360	6,081	8,260	9,923	11,237	12,460	12,350	11,581	19,216	76,767
Increase tobacco taxes and index for inflation [2]	......	−7,725	−9,844	−9,264	−8,718	−8,205	−7,723	−7,268	−6,842	−6,440	−6,062	−43,756	−78,091
Infrastructure and Jobs Investments:													
Invest in rail transportation through reauthorization	......	333	1,419	1,759	2,678	3,409	3,032	2,977	2,565	1,804	790	9,598	20,766
Reserve additional resources for surface transportation reauthorization	......	......	399	2,879	6,855	10,865	15,045	19,343	15,795	7,679	4,112	20,998	82,972
Create infrastructure bank	......	22	116	350	630	919	1,218	1,403	1,465	1,441	1,271	2,037	8,835
Provide funding for Project Rebuild	......	50	4,650	7,100	3,200	......	......					15,000	15,000
Create a Pathways Back to Work fund	625	10,750	1,125	......								11,875	11,875
Recognize Educational Success, Professional Excellence, and Collaborative Teaching (RESPECT)	100	2,650	1,750	500								4,900	4,900
Provide for teacher stabilization	625	11,875										11,875	11,875
Establish Veterans Job Corps	......	50	237	237	238	238	......	......	......	......	......	1,000	1,000
Enact Reemployment NOW	200	3,000	800									3,800	3,800
Support first responders	......	2,450	2,200	350								5,000	5,000
Total, infrastructure and jobs investments	1,550	31,180	12,696	13,175	13,601	15,431	19,295	23,723	19,825	10,924	6,173	86,083	166,023
Savings in OCO reserved for infrastructure and jobs investments (non-add)	−968	−4,027	−38,088	−59,134	−65,606	−69,395	−41,232	......	......	......	......	−236,250	−277,482
Other Mandatory Initiatives and Savings:													
Agriculture:													
Enact biobased labeling fee	......	−1	......	......	......	......	......	......	......	......	......	−1	−1
Reauthorize Secure Rural Schools	......	214	242	154	94	58	12	......	......	......	......	762	774
Enact Animal Plant and Health Inspection Service (APHIS) fee	......	−20	−27	−27	−28	−29	−30	−31	−32	−33	−34	−131	−291
Enact Natural Resources Conservation Service (NRCS) fee	......	−22	−22	−22	−22	−22	−22	−22	−22	−22	−22	−110	−220
Enact Grain Inspection, Packers, and Stockyards Administration (GIPSA) fee	......	−27	−27	−28	−28	−28	−29	−29	−29	−30	−30	−138	−285
Enact Food Safety and Inspection Service (FSIS) fee	......	−4	−4	−4	−5	−5	−5	−5	−5	−5	−5	−22	−47
Restore temporary Supplemental Nutrition Assistance Program (SNAP) benefit increase	2,223	41	......	......								2,264	2,264
Reauthorize stewardship contracting permanently	......	−12	......	1	1	1	1	2	2	2	1	−9	−1

S–9. Mandatory and Receipt Proposals—Continued

(Deficit increases (+) or decreases (−) in millions of dollars)

	2013	2014	2015	2016	2017	2018	2019	2020	2021	2022	2023	Totals 2014-2018	Totals 2014-2023
Outyear mandatory effects of discretionary changes to the Conservation Stewardship Program	......	......	−10	−13	−13	−13	−13	−13	−13	−13	−13	−49	−114
Total, Agriculture	......	2,351	193	61	−1	−38	−86	−98	−99	−101	−103	2,566	2,079
Commerce:													
Develop a national network of manufacturing innovation institutes	......	38	112	180	186	156	122	102	74	30	......	672	1,000
Education:													
Reform student loan interest rates	8,489	11,954	8,772	4,686	1,394	−1,387	−4,118	−6,678	−8,683	−9,912	−10,915	25,419	−14,887
Expand Pay-As-You-Earn to all borrowers	463	3,460	400	381	332	350	239	221	238	163	191	4,923	5,975
Reform and expand Perkins loan program	......	−673	−2,012	−1,863	−1,693	−1,540	−1,453	−1,402	−1,324	−1,195	−1,124	−7,781	−14,279
Adjust guaranty agency loan rehabilitation compensation	......	−3,657	......	......	......	......	......	......	......	......	......	−3,657	−3,657
Provide mandatory appropriation to sustain recent Pell Grant increases	......	......	866	3,589	4,035	2,948	2,494	869	905	1,113	1,116	11,438	17,935
Overhaul TEACH Grants and replace with Presidential Teaching Fellows	......	5	126	176	181	176	164	28	−28	−43	−46	664	739
Establish the Community College to Career Fund	......	......	134	533	933	1,134	800	400	67	......	......	2,733	4,000
Total, Education	8,952	11,089	8,286	7,502	5,182	1,681	−1,874	−6,562	−8,825	−9,874	−10,778	33,739	−4,174
Energy:													
Repeal ultra-deepwater oil and gas research and development program	......	−20	−20	−10	......	......	......	......	......	......	......	−50	−50
Reauthorize special assessment from domestic nuclear utilities [1]	......	−200	−204	−209	−213	−218	−223	−228	−233	−238	−243	−1,044	−2,209
Establish Energy Security Trust Fund	......	60	140	180	200	200	200	200	200	200	200	780	1,780
Enact nuclear waste management program	......	......	......	......	90	170	390	520	720	−1,334	740	260	1,296
Provide HomeStar rebates for energy efficient home retrofits	......	300	1,800	2,100	1,020	600	180	......	......	......	......	5,820	6,000
Total, Energy	......	140	1,716	2,061	1,097	752	547	492	687	−1,372	697	5,766	6,817
Health and Human Services:													
Reauthorize Family Connection Grants	......	......	11	14	14	4	1	1	......	......	......	43	45
Expand child care access	......	406	683	735	745	749	750	750	750	750	750	3,318	7,068
Make TANF supplemental grant funding permanent and reduce the annual amount available in the TANF contingency fund	......	......	......	......	......	......	......	......	......	......	......	......	......

S–9. Mandatory and Receipt Proposals—Continued

(Deficit increases (+) or decreases (−) in millions of dollars)

	2013	2014	2015	2016	2017	2018	2019	2020	2021	2022	2023	Totals 2014–2018	Totals 2014–2023
Modernize child support	....	8	53	158	177	247	280	320	312	302	159	643	2,016
Supplemental Security Income (SSI) effects		....	....	–3	–3	–6	–7	–9	–9	–8	–8	–12	–53
SNAP effects	....			–33	–34	–58	–74	–90	–87	–85	–82	–125	–543
Total, Health and Human Services		414	747	871	899	936	950	972	966	959	819	3,867	8,533
Housing and Urban Development:													
Provide funding for the Affordable Housing Trust Fund		10	140	290	230	190	100	20	20	....	....	860	1,000
Interior:													
Extend funding for Payments in Lieu of Taxes (PILT)		410	....	....	....	....	....	....	....	....	....	410	410
Increase coal AML fee to pre–2006 levels [1]		–53	–37	–28	–16	–8	....	–2	–2	54	39	–142	–53
Reauthorize and reform DOI's helium program		–152	–110	–94	–64	–33	–21	–6	....	....	....	–453	–480
Permanently reauthorize the Federal Lands Recreation Enhancement Act (FLREA)		....	....	....	....	....	....	....	....	....	....	....	....
Reallocate State share of NPR-A revenues to fund priority Alaska programs		–2	....	....	....	–15	–3	1	1	1	16	–17	–1
Establish an AML hardrock reclamation fund [1]		....	–200	–150	–100	–50	....	....	....	....	....	–500	–500
Reform hardrock mining on public lands		....	–2	–4	–5	–5	–6	–6	–11	–17	–24	–16	–80
Repeal geothermal payments to counties		–4	–4	–5	–5	–5	–5	–5	–5	–5	–5	–23	–48
Extend the Palau Compact of Free Association		66	28	22	15	13	12	11	10	9	6	144	192
Reauthorize the Federal Land Transaction Facilitation Act of 2000 (FLTFA)		–3	–5	–8	–9	–3	....	....	....	....	....	–28	–28
Increase duck stamp fees [1]		–4	....	....	....	–4	....	....	....	....	....	–4	–4
Establish dedicated funding for Land and Water Conservation Fund (LWCF) programs		70	421	755	927	908	900	900	900	900	900	3,081	7,581
Total, Interior	....	328	91	488	743	802	877	893	893	942	932	2,452	6,989
Labor:													
Reform the Federal Employees' Compensation Act (FECA)		–9	–10	–19	–29	–39	–49	–60	–71	–82	–94	–106	–462
Reform the Defense Base Act by establishing a Government-wide self-insurance program		....	–214	....	....	....	....	....	....	....	....	–214	–214
Strengthen UI system solvency [1,2]	606	2,922	2,746	–6,910	–9,324	–7,227	–6,847	–5,495	–4,924	–8,036	–7,929	–17,793	–51,024
Establish a Universal Displaced Worker program [5]		4,014	3,547	3,116	2,763	2,559	2,389	2,257	2,111	1,963	1,814	15,999	26,533

S–9. Mandatory and Receipt Proposals—Continued

(Deficit increases (+) or decreases (–) in millions of dollars)

	2013	2014	2015	2016	2017	2018	2019	2020	2021	2022	2023	Totals 2014–2018	Totals 2014–2023
Establish the Community College to Career Fund	......	......	134	533	933	1,134	800	400	67	......	......	2,733	4,000
Total, Labor	606	6,927	6,203	–3,280	–5,657	–3,574	–3,707	–2,898	–2,817	–6,155	–6,209	619	–21,167
Transportation:													
Establish a mandatory surcharge for air traffic services [1]	......	–605	–632	–660	–690	–719	–745	–766	–790	–812	–836	–3,306	–7,255
Establish a co-insurance program for aviation war risk insurance	......	–110	–107	–51	15	91	203	175	125	80	48	–162	469
Reduction in interagency ocean freight differential reimbursement as a result of food aid reform	......	–50	–50	–50	–50	–50	–50	–50	–50	–50	–50	–250	–500
Total, Transportation	......	–765	–789	–761	–725	–678	–592	–641	–715	–782	–838	–3,718	–7,286
Treasury:													
Increase levy authority for payments to Medicare providers with delinquent tax debt [1]	......	–46	–67	–70	–71	–72	–74	–76	–76	–77	–78	–326	–707
Authorize Treasury to locate and recover assets of the United States and to retain a portion of amounts collected to pay for the costs of recovery	......	–3	–3	–3	–3	–3	–3	–3	–3	–3	–3	–15	–30
Allow offset of Federal income tax refunds to collect delinquent State income taxes for out-of-state residents	......											......	......
Establish a Pay for Success Incentive Fund	......	1	1	10	24	40	56	49	42	24	15	76	262
Provide authority to contact delinquent debtors via their cell phones	......	–12	–12	–12	–12	–12	–12	–12	–12	–12	–12	–60	–120
Total, Treasury	......	–60	–81	–75	–62	–47	–33	–42	–49	–68	–78	–325	–595
Veterans Affairs:													
Extend round-down of cost of living adjustments (compensation)	......	–42	–91	–148	–193	–239	–264	–286	–311	–336	–347	–713	–2,257
Extend round-down of cost of living adjustments (education)	......	–1	–1	–2	–2	–3	–2	–2	–3	–3	–3	–9	–22
Exclude Temporary Residence Adaptation grants from Specially Adapted Housing (SAH) grant limit [6]	......											......	......
Restore eligibility for housing grant adaptation	......	5	5	5	6	6	6	6	7	7	7	27	60
Replace housing grant limits with limits to grant type [7]	......					......	1	1	1	1	1	......	5
Provide SAH grants to veterans living with family	......	6	7	7	7	7	8	8	9	9	9	34	77

S-9. Mandatory and Receipt Proposals—Continued

(Deficit increases (+) or decreases (–) in millions of dollars)

	2013	2014	2015	2016	2017	2018	2019	2020	2021	2022	2023	Totals 2014–2018	Totals 2014–2023
Extend supplemental service disabled veterans insurance coverage [8]	....	....	....	....	....	....	....	....	....	....	....	....	....
Expand eligibility for veterans medallion for headstones [9]	....	....	....	....	....	....	....	....	....	....	....	....	....
Allow for Government furnished headstones [10]	....	....	....	....	....	....	....	....	....	....	....	....	....
Increase cap on vocational rehabilitation contract counseling	....	1	1	1	1	1	1	1	1	1	1	5	10
Make permanent the pilot for certain work-study activities	....	1	1	1	1	1	1	1	1	1	1	5	10
Provide refunds for the Montgomery GI Bill Buy-Up program [11]	....	....	....	....	....	....	....	....	....	....	....	....	....
Increase annual limitation on new Independent Living cases [12]	....	....	....	....	....	....	4	4	4	4	4	....	20
Expand authority to provide headstones and markers at tribal veterans cemeteries [13]	....	....	....	....	....	....	....	....	....	....	....	....	....
Cover burial expenses for remains of unclaimed veterans [14]	....	....	....	....	....	....	....	....	....	....	....	....	....
Provide burial receptacles for certain new casketed gravesites	....	3	4	3	1	6	....	....	3	3	4	17	27
Total, Veterans Affairs	....	–27	–74	–133	–179	–221	–245	–267	–288	–313	–323	–634	–2,070
Corps of Engineers:													
Reform inland waterways funding [1]	....	–82	–113	–113	–113	–113	–113	–113	–113	–113	–114	–534	–1,100
International Assistance Programs:													
Implement 2010 IMF agreement:													
PAYGO effects	–1,994	....	....	....	....	....	....	....	....	....	....	....	....
Non-scorable effects	....	....	....	....	....	....	....	....	....	....	....	....	....
Total, implement 2010 IMF agreement	–1,994	....	....	....	....	....	....	....	....	....	....	....	....
Office of Personnel Management:													
Eliminate the FERS Supplement for new employees (accrual effects)	....	17	31	46	61	78	96	114	133	153	174	233	903
Social Security Administration (SSA):													
Terminate step-child benefits in the same month as step-parent [15]	....	....	....	....	....	....	....	....	....	....	....	....	....
Lower electronic wage reporting threshold to 50 employees [16]	....	....	....	....	....	....	....	....	....	....	....	....	....
Move from annual to quarterly wage reporting	....	20	30	90	....	....	....	....	....	....	....	140	140
Establish Workers Compensation Information Reporting	....	5	5	....	....	....	....	....	....	....	....	10	10

S–9. Mandatory and Receipt Proposals—Continued

(Deficit increases (+) or decreases (−) in millions of dollars)

	2013	2014	2015	2016	2017	2018	2019	2020	2021	2022	2023	Totals 2014–2018	Totals 2014–2023
Extend SSI time limits for qualified refugees	......	46	53	......	......	......	......	......	......	......	......	99	99
Medicaid effects	......	11	13	......	......	......	......	......	......	......	......	24	24
SNAP effects	......	−8	−9	......	......	......	......	......	......	......	......	−17	−17
Conform treatment of State and local government earned income tax credit (EITC) and child tax credit (CTC) for SSI [17]													
Total, Social Security Administration (SSA)	......	74	92	90	......	......	......	......	......	......	......	256	256
Other Independent Agencies:													
Postal Service:													
Enact Postal Service financial relief and reform:													
PAYGO effects	582	2,894	−903	−3,057	−3,185	−3,185	−3,185	−3,185	−3,185	−3,185	−3,185	−7,436	−23,361
Non-scoreable effects	972	1,822	5,117	8,675	2,835	2,835	2,835	2,835	2,835	2,835	2,835	21,284	35,459
Railroad Retirement Board (RRB):													
Allow the electronic certification of certain RRB benefits													
Total, other independent agencies	1,554	4,716	4,214	5,618	−350	−350	−350	−350	−350	−350	−350	13,848	12,098
Multi-Agency:													
Provide the Secretary of the Treasury authority to access and disclose prisoner data to prevent and identify improper payments:													
Labor effects	......	−5	−10	−10	−10	−10	−10	−10	−11	−11	−12	−45	−99
Treasury effects [1]	......	−24	−35	−36	−37	−38	−39	−40	−41	−42	−43	−170	−375
SSA effects	......	15	......	......	......	......	......	......	......	......	......	15	15
Total, Provide the Secretary of the Treasury authority to access and disclose prisoner data to prevent and identify improper payments	......	−14	−45	−46	−47	−48	−49	−50	−52	−53	−55	−200	−459
Increase TRICARE Prime enrollment fee, impose Standard/Extra annual enrollment fee, and deductible/catastrophic cap adjustments (mandatory effects in Coast Guard, Public Health Service and National Oceanic and Atmospheric Administration)	......	−5	−13	−19	−25	−30	−32	−35	−37	−40	−43	−92	−279
Enact Spectrum License User Fee and allow the FCC to auction predominantly domestic satellite services	−50	−225	−325	−425	−550	−550	−550	−550	−550	−550	−550	−2,075	−4,825

S–9. Mandatory and Receipt Proposals—Continued

(Deficit increases (+) or decreases (–) in millions of dollars)

	2013	2014	2015	2016	2017	2018	2019	2020	2021	2022	2023	Totals 2014–2018	Totals 2014–2023
Auction or assign via fee 1675–1680 megahertz [18]	......	......	......	......	–80	–150	......	......	......	......	......	–230	–230
Establish hold harmless for Federal poverty guidelines	......	......	......	......	......	......	......	......	......	......	......	......	......
Total, multi-agency	–50	–244	–383	–490	–702	–778	–631	–635	–639	–643	–648	–2,597	–5,793
Total, other mandatory initiatives and savings ...	**9,068**	**24,926**	**20,384**	**12,355**	**609**	**–1,204**	**–4,939**	**–9,013**	**–11,122**	**–17,687**	**–16,819**	**57,070**	**–2,510**
Other Revenue Proposals:													
Tax relief to create jobs and jumpstart growth:													
Provide small businesses a temporary 10-percent tax credit for new jobs and wage increases [19]		10,356	9,446	2,752	1,648	932	444	179	40	......	......	25,134	25,797
Provide additional tax credits for investment in qualified property used in a qualified advanced energy manufacturing project		85	390	640	614	261	–6	–64	–54	–29	–10	1,990	1,827
Designate Promise Zones [19]		......	107	316	522	697	769	757	744	734	730	1,642	5,376
Total, tax relief to create jobs and jumpstart growth		10,441	9,943	3,708	2,784	1,890	1,207	872	730	705	720	28,766	33,000
Incentives for investment in infrastructure:													
Provide America Fast Forward Bonds [19]		–1	–1	......	1	......	......	......	......	......	......	–1	–1
Allow eligible uses of America Fast Forward Bonds to include financing all qualified private activity bond categories [19]		2	4	8	15	20	25	30	37	44	49	49	234
Increase the Federal subsidy rate for America Fast Forward Bonds for school construction [19]		251	794	1,117	1,147	1,147	1,147	1,147	1,147	1,147	1,147	4,456	10,191
Allow current refundings of State and local governmental bonds [20]		......	......	......	......	......	......	......	......	......	......	......	......
Repeal the $150 million nonhospital bond limitation on all qualified 501(c)(3) bonds ...		1	3	5	7	9	11	13	16	17	18	25	100
Increase national limitation amount for qualified highway or surface freight transfer facility bonds		......	......	3	16	34	52	72	92	113	133	53	515
Eliminate the volume cap for private activity bonds for water infrastructure ...		3	5	9	14	20	27	33	41	49	57	51	258
Increase the 25-percent limit on land acquisition restriction on private activity bonds		2	4	8	11	15	19	23	27	32	35	40	176
Allow more flexible research arrangements for purposes of private business use limits		......	......	1	1	1	1	3	3	3	3	3	16

S–9. Mandatory and Receipt Proposals—Continued

(Deficit increases (+) or decreases (−) in millions of dollars)

	2013	2014	2015	2016	2017	2018	2019	2020	2021	2022	2023	Totals 2014–2018	Totals 2014–2023
Repeal the government ownership requirement for certain types of exempt facility bonds	16	71	152	238	330	410	459	488	518	549	549	1,201	3,764
Exempt certain foreign pension funds from the application of FIRPTA	......	109	187	196	206	216	227	238	250	263	276	914	2,168
Total, incentives for investment in infrastructure	16	438	1,148	1,585	1,748	1,872	1,968	2,047	2,131	2,217	2,267	6,791	17,421
Tax cuts for families and individuals:													
Provide for automatic enrollment in IRAs, including a small employer tax credit, and double the tax credit for small employer plan start-up costs [19]	......	......	1,086	1,303	1,434	1,584	1,809	2,098	2,383	2,734	3,195	5,407	17,626
Expand child and dependent care tax credit [19]	......	251	953	954	946	957	955	949	947	937	926	4,061	8,775
Extend exclusion from income for cancellation of certain home mortgage debt [19]	......	1,058	1,252	300	......	......	......	......	......	......	......	2,610	2,610
Provide exclusion from income for student loan forgiveness for students in certain income-based or income-contingent repayment programs who have completed payment obligations											2	......	2
Provide exclusion from income for student loan forgiveness and for certain scholarship amounts for participants in the IHS Health Professions Programs	......	5	13	14	14	15	16	18	19	20	21	61	155
Total, tax cuts for families and individuals	......	1,314	3,304	2,571	2,394	2,556	2,780	3,065	3,349	3,691	4,144	12,139	29,168
Modify estate and gift tax provisions:													
Restore the estate, gift and GST tax parameters in effect in 2009						......	−12,235	−13,284	−14,343	−15,356	−16,475	......	−71,693
Require consistency in value for transfer and income tax purposes		......	−158	−171	−183	−197	−210	−223	−237	−251	−266	−709	−1,896
Require a minimum term for GRATs		......	−131	−194	−261	−335	−412	−494	−581	−683	−803	−921	−3,894
Limit duration of GST tax exemption		......	......	......	......	......	......	......	......	......	......	......	......
Coordinate certain income and transfer tax rules applicable to grantor trusts		......	−36	−47	−62	−79	−102	−129	−164	−207	−261	−224	−1,087
Extend the lien on estate tax deferrals provided under section 6166		......	−12	−15	−16	−17	−18	−19	−20	−21	−22	−60	−160
Clarify GST tax treatment of HEETs [19]	......	−47	30	29	27	26	24	23	21	20	18	65	171
Total, modify estate and gift tax provisions	......	−47	−307	−398	−495	−602	−12,953	−14,126	−15,324	−16,498	−17,809	−1,849	−78,559

S–9.   Mandatory and Receipt Proposals—Continued

(Deficit increases (+) or decreases (−) in millions of dollars)

	2013	2014	2015	2016	2017	2018	2019	2020	2021	2022	2023	Totals 2014–2018	Totals 2014–2023
Reform treatment of financial and insurance industry and products:													
Impose a financial crisis responsibility fee	....	....	−2,991	−6,066	−6,321	−6,581	−6,839	−7,159	−7,470	−7,794	−8,128	−21,959	−59,349
Require current inclusion in income of accrued market discount and limit the accrual amount for distressed debt	....	−6	−21	−42	−67	−95	−126	−160	−197	−236	−276	−231	−1,226
Require that the cost basis of stock that is a covered security must be determined using an average cost basis method	91	75	−61	−126	−200	−248	−266	−284	−301	−319	−339	−560	−2,069
Total, reform treatment of financial and insurance industry and products	91	69	−3,073	−6,234	−6,588	−6,924	−7,231	−7,603	−7,968	−8,349	−8,743	−22,750	−62,644
Other revenue changes and loophole closers:													
Increase Oil Spill Liability Trust Fund financing rate by one cent and update the law to include other sources of crudes [2]	....	−64	−88	−92	−102	−106	−109	−116	−121	−127	−133	−452	−1,058
Reinstate Superfund taxes [2]	....	−1,369	−1,818	−1,899	−1,970	−2,053	−2,123	−2,152	−2,206	−2,257	−2,358	−9,109	−20,205
Make UI surtax permanent [2]	....	−1,044	−1,459	−1,489	−1,520	−1,551	−1,576	−1,597	−1,618	−1,641	−1,660	−7,063	−15,155
Tax carried (profits) interests as ordinary income	....	−3,407	−3,096	−2,389	−1,718	−1,247	−1,105	−1,065	−864	−612	−406	−11,857	−15,909
Eliminate the deduction for contributions of conservation easements on golf courses	....	−37	−53	−55	−59	−61	−64	−68	−71	−74	−77	−265	−619
Restrict deductions and harmonize the rules for contributions of conservation easements for historic preservation	....	−8	−11	−16	−22	−26	−27	−28	−31	−32	−33	−83	−234
Require non-spouse beneficiaries of IRA owners and retirement plan participants to take inherited distributions over no more than five years	....	−86	−224	−369	−517	−668	−699	−660	−612	−563	−513	−1,864	−4,911
Limit the total accrual of tax-favored retirement benefits	....	−802	−831	−839	−876	−964	−1,010	−1,054	−923	−1,082	−961	−4,312	−9,342
Total, other revenue changes and loophole closers	....	−6,817	−7,580	−7,148	−6,784	−6,676	−6,713	−6,740	−6,446	−6,388	−6,141	−35,005	−67,433
Reduce the tax gap and make reforms:													
Expand information reporting:													
Require information reporting for private separate accounts of life insurance companies	....	....	....	....	−1	−1	−1	−1	−1	−1	−1	−2	−7
Require a certified TIN from contractors and allow certain withholding	....	−25	−58	−99	−135	−141	−147	−154	−161	−168	−176	−458	−1,264

S–9. Mandatory and Receipt Proposals—Continued

(Deficit increases (+) or decreases (−) in millions of dollars)

	2013	2014	2015	2016	2017	2018	2019	2020	2021	2022	2023	Totals 2014–2018	Totals 2014–2023
Modify reporting of tuition expenses and scholarships on Form 1098-T[19]	......	−8	−105	−111	−114	−117	−120	−124	−128	−132	−136	−455	−1,095
Provide for reciprocal reporting of information in connection with the implementation of FATCA	......	......										......	......
Subtotal, expand information reporting	......	−33	−163	−210	−250	−259	−268	−279	−290	−301	−313	−915	−2,366
Improve compliance by businesses:													
Require greater electronic filing of returns		......										......	......
Make e-filing mandatory for exempt organizations		......										......	......
Authorize the Department of the Treasury to require additional information to be included in electronically filed Form 5500 Annual Reports and electronic filing of certain other employee benefit plan reports		......										......	......
Implement standards clarifying when employee leasing companies can be held liable for their clients' Federal employment taxes		−5	−6	−6	−6	−7	−7	−8	−8	−8	−8	−30	−69
Increase certainty with respect to worker classification	−4	−73	−361	−706	−857	−945	−1,035	−1,129	−1,226	−1,328	−1,437	−2,942	−9,097
Repeal special estimated tax payment provision for certain insurance companies													
Subtotal, improve compliance by businesses	−4	−78	−367	−712	−863	−952	−1,042	−1,137	−1,234	−1,336	−1,445	−2,972	−9,166
Strengthen tax administration:													
Impose liability on shareholders participating in "Intermediary Transaction Tax Shelters" to collect unpaid corporate income taxes		−304	−421	−444	−469	−493	−517	−540	−562	−586	−611	−2,131	−4,947
Streamline audit and adjustment procedures for large partnerships		−78	−114	−138	−174	−208	−227	−232	−233	−234	−235	−712	−1,873
Revise offer-in-compromise application rules		−1	−1	−1	−1	−1	−1	−1	−1	−1	−1	−5	−10
Expand IRS access to information in the National Directory of New Hires for tax administration purposes		......										......	......
Make repeated willful failure to file a tax return a felony					−1	−1	−1	−1	−2	−2	−2	−2	−10
Facilitate tax compliance with local jurisdictions	−1	−1	−1	−1	−1	−1	−2	−2	−2	−2	−2	−5	−15

S–9. Mandatory and Receipt Proposals—Continued

(Deficit increases (+) or decreases (–) in millions of dollars)

	2013	2014	2015	2016	2017	2018	2019	2020	2021	2022	2023	Totals 2014–2018	Totals 2014–2023
Extend statute of limitations where State adjustment affects Federal tax liability	......	......	......	–1	–4	–4	–4	–4	–4	–4	–4	–9	–29
Improve investigative disclosure statute	......	......	......	......	–1	–1	–1	–1	–2	–2	–2	–2	–10
Require taxpayers who prepare their returns electronically but file their returns on paper to print their returns with a 2-D bar code	......	......	......	......	......	......	......	......	......	......	......	......	......
Allow the IRS to absorb credit and debit card processing fees for certain tax payments	......	–1	–2	–2	–2	–2	–2	–2	–2	–2	–2	–9	–19
Extend IRS math error authority in certain circumstances [19]	......	–16	–17	–16	–17	–18	–19	–19	–21	–21	–21	–84	–185
Impose a penalty on failure to comply with electronic filing requirements	......	......	......	......	–1	–1	–1	–1	–2	–2	–2	–2	–10
Provide whistleblowers with protection from retaliation	......	......	......	......	......	......	......	......	......	......	......	......	......
Provide stronger protection from improper disclosure of taxpayer information in whistleblower actions	......	......	......	......	......	......	......	......	......	......	......	......	......
Index all penalties to inflation	......	–349	–544	–699	–844	–995	–1,147	–1,303	–1,462	–1,625	–1,791	–3,431	–10,759
Extend paid preparer EITC due diligence requirements to the CTC	......	......	......	......	......	......	......	......	......	......	......	......	......
Extend IRS authority to require truncated SSNs on Form W–2	......	......	......	......	......	......	......	......	......	......	......	......	......
Add tax crimes to the Aggravated Identity Theft Statute	......	......	......	......	......	......	......	......	......	......	......	......	......
Impose a civil penalty on tax identity theft crimes	......	......	......	......	......	......	......	......	......	......	......	......	......
Subtotal, strengthen tax administration	......	–750	–1,100	–1,302	–1,515	–1,725	–1,922	–2,106	–2,293	–2,481	–2,673	–6,392	–17,867
Total, reduce the tax gap and make reforms	–4	–861	–1,630	–2,224	–2,628	–2,936	–3,232	–3,522	–3,817	–4,118	–4,431	–10,279	–29,399
Simplify the tax system:													
Simplify the rules for claiming the EITC for workers without qualifying children [19]	......	42	562	576	589	599	578	590	604	617	632	2,368	5,389
Modify adoption credit to allow tribal determination of special needs	......	......	......	......	......	......	1	1	1	1	1	......	5
Eliminate MRD requirements for IRA/plan balances of $75,000 or less	......	4	7	9	14	17	23	29	35	39	45	51	222
Allow all inherited plan and IRA accounts to be rolled over within 60 days	......	......	......	......	......	......	......	......	......	......	......	......	......
Repeal non-qualified preferred stock designation	......	–29	–49	–48	–45	–42	–37	–33	–29	–26	–23	–213	–361

S–9. Mandatory and Receipt Proposals—Continued

(Deficit increases (+) or decreases (−) in millions of dollars)

	2013	2014	2015	2016	2017	2018	2019	2020	2021	2022	2023	Totals	
												2014–2018	2014–2023
Repeal preferential dividend rule for publicly offered REITs	......	......	......	......	......	......	......	......	......	......	......	......	......
Reform excise tax based on investment income of private foundations	......	4	4	5	5	5	5	6	6	7	7	23	54
Remove bonding requirements for certain taxpayers subject to Federal excise taxes on distilled spirits, wine, and beer	......	......	......	......	......	......	......	......	......	......	......	......	......
Simplify arbitrage investment restrictions	2	9	18	26	37	46	57	66	76	86	97	136	518
Simplify single-family housing mortgage bond targeting requirements	......	......	......	......	1	1	1	3	3	3	3	2	15
Streamline private business limits on governmental bonds	1	3	5	7	9	11	13	15	17	19	20	35	119
Exclude self-constructed assets of small taxpayers from the UNICAP rules	......	46	48	51	69	80	92	97	101	105	110	294	799
Repeal technical terminations of partnerships	......	−7	−14	−17	−18	−19	−20	−21	−22	−22	−23	−75	−183
Repeal anti-churning rules of section 197	......	23	95	187	250	281	295	298	298	298	298	836	2,323
Total, simplify the tax system	3	95	676	796	911	979	1,008	1,051	1,090	1,127	1,167	3,457	8,900
Trade initiative:													
Extend GSP [2]	......	394	613	......	......	......	......	......	......	......	......	1,007	1,007
Other initiatives:													
Authorize the limited sharing of business tax return information to improve the accuracy of important measures of the economy	......	......	......	......	......	......	......	......	......	......	......	......	......
Eliminate certain reviews conducted by the U.S. TIGTA	......	......	......	......	......	......	......	......	......	......	......	......	......
Modify indexing to prevent deflationary adjustments	......	......	......	......	......	......	......	......	......	......	......	......	......
Total, other initiatives	......	......	......	......	......	......	......	......	......	......	......	......	......
Total, other revenue proposals [21]	106	5,026	3,094	−7,344	−8,658	−9,841	−23,166	−24,956	−26,255	−27,613	−28,826	−17,723	−148,539
Total, December offer and additional mandatory and receipt proposals	10,767	22,369	−25,213	−66,371	−105,118	−122,418	−152,189	−174,116	−201,586	−242,853	−271,868	−296,751	−1,339,363
Addendum, Business Tax Policies Reserved for Revenue-Neutral Reform:													
Incentives for manufacturing, research, clean energy, and insourcing and creating jobs:													
Provide tax incentives for locating jobs and business activity in the United States and remove tax deductions for shipping jobs overseas	......	5	10	10	10	12	12	12	13	14	14	47	112

S–9. Mandatory and Receipt Proposals—Continued

(Deficit increases (+) or decreases (–) in millions of dollars)

	2013	2014	2015	2016	2017	2018	2019	2020	2021	2022	2023	Totals 2014–2018	Totals 2014–2023
Provide new Manufacturing Communities tax credit	......	19	103	240	392	516	618	701	729	641	452	1,270	4,411
Enhance and make permanent the R&E tax credit	......	3,893	7,282	8,121	8,975	9,832	10,669	11,439	12,225	13,052	13,890	38,103	99,378
Extend certain employment tax credits, including incentives for hiring veterans	......	359	817	1,006	1,060	1,049	1,009	968	943	936	939	4,291	9,086
Provide a tax credit for the production of advanced technology vehicles	......	50	283	461	784	1,079	1,175	933	144	–352	–345	2,657	4,212
Provide a tax credit for medium- and heavy-duty alternative-fuel commercial vehicles	......	71	362	411	488	471	247	217	–108	–66	–37	1,803	2,056
Modify and permanently extend renewable electricity production tax credit [19]	......	43	177	664	1,160	1,543	1,915	2,320	2,778	3,192	3,651	3,587	17,443
Modify and permanently extend the deduction for energy-efficient commercial building property	......	83	217	350	489	575	624	701	736	729	718	1,714	5,222
Total, incentives for manufacturing, research, clean energy, and insourcing and creating jobs	......	4,523	9,251	11,263	13,358	15,077	16,269	17,291	17,460	18,146	19,282	53,472	141,920
Tax relief for small business:													
Extend increased expensing for small business	......	6,839	9,626	7,732	6,974	6,543	6,344	6,182	6,064	6,130	6,227	37,714	68,661
Eliminate capital gains taxation on investments in small business stock	......	......	......	......	......	......	262	730	1,163	1,615	2,040	......	5,810
Double the amount of expensed start-up expenditures	223	251	311	310	308	304	300	297	296	294	292	1,484	2,963
Expand and simplify the tax credit provided to qualified small employers for non-elective contributions to employee health insurance [19]	......	720	1,386	1,453	1,299	1,167	1,044	972	857	796	802	6,025	10,496
Total, tax relief for small business	223	7,810	11,323	9,495	8,581	8,014	7,950	8,181	8,380	8,835	9,361	45,223	87,930
Incentives to promote regional growth:													
Extend and modify the NMTC	20	47	109	231	393	588	809	1,023	1,240	1,416	1,507	1,368	7,363
Restructure assistance to New York City, provide tax incentives for transportation infrastructure	......	200	200	200	200	200	200	200	200	200	200	1,000	2,000
Modify tax-exempt bonds for Indian tribal governments	4	12	12	12	12	12	12	12	12	12	12	60	120
Reform and expand the LIHTC	......	12	38	67	96	127	157	188	208	238	256	340	1,387
Total, incentives to promote regional growth	24	271	359	510	701	927	1,178	1,423	1,660	1,866	1,975	2,768	10,870
Reform U.S. international tax system:													
Defer deduction of interest expense related to deferred income of foreign subsidiaries	......	–2,612	–4,466	–4,653	–4,840	–5,025	–5,196	–5,361	–2,662	–836	–869	–21,596	–36,520
Determine the foreign tax credit on a pooling basis	......	–3,478	–5,948	–6,197	–6,447	–6,693	–6,920	–7,140	–7,373	–7,630	–7,926	–28,763	–65,752

S-9. Mandatory and Receipt Proposals—Continued

(Deficit increases (+) or decreases (−) in millions of dollars)

	2013	2014	2015	2016	2017	2018	2019	2020	2021	2022	2023	Totals 2014–2018	Totals 2014–2023
Tax currently excess returns associated with transfers of intangibles offshore	....	−1,552	−2,612	−2,659	−2,667	−2,605	−2,512	−2,433	−2,358	−2,315	−2,292	−12,095	−24,005
Limit shifting of income through intangible property transfers	....	−47	−96	−126	−157	−189	−222	−257	−295	−336	−383	−615	−2,108
Disallow the deduction for non-taxed reinsurance premiums paid to foreign affiliates	....	−312	−532	−556	−591	−630	−650	−681	−717	−752	−788	−2,621	−6,209
Limit earnings stripping by expatriated entities	....	−234	−401	−421	−442	−464	−488	−512	−538	−565	−593	−1,962	−4,658
Modify tax rules for dual capacity taxpayers	....	−552	−946	−998	−1,054	−1,109	−1,162	−1,214	−1,268	−1,302	−1,359	−4,659	−10,964
Tax gain from the sale of a partnership interest on look-through basis	....	−133	−229	−240	−252	−265	−278	−292	−307	−322	−338	−1,119	−2,656
Prevent use of leveraged distributions from related foreign corporations to avoid dividend treatment	....	−172	−293	−306	−318	−330	−341	−352	−364	−376	−391	−1,419	−3,243
Extend section 338(h)(16) to certain asset acquisitions	....	−60	−100	−100	−100	−100	−100	−100	−100	−100	−100	−460	−960
Remove foreign taxes from a section 902 corporation's foreign tax pool when earnings are eliminated	....	−10	−20	−27	−36	−46	−50	−50	−50	−50	−50	−139	−389
Total, reform U.S. international tax system	....	−9,162	−15,643	−16,283	−16,904	−17,456	−17,919	−18,392	−16,032	−14,584	−15,089	−75,448	−157,464
Reform treatment of financial and insurance industry institutions and products:													
Require that derivative contracts be marked to market with resulting gain or loss treated as ordinary	....	−2,419	−4,576	−4,148	−2,614	−1,682	−1,148	−705	−510	−532	−555	−15,439	−18,889
Modify rules that apply to sales of life insurance contracts	....	−17	−54	−58	−62	−66	−70	−73	−77	−80	−84	−257	−641
Modify proration rules for life insurance company general and separate accounts	....	−294	−515	−532	−552	−566	−549	−526	−500	−465	−602	−2,459	−5,101
Extend pro rata interest expense disallowance for corporate-owned life insurance	....	−26	−60	−131	−278	−478	−651	−817	−986	−1,158	−1,334	−973	−5,919
Total, reform treatment of financial and insurance industy institutions and products	....	−2,756	−5,205	−4,869	−3,506	−2,792	−2,418	−2,121	−2,073	−2,235	−2,575	−19,128	−30,550
Eliminate fossil fuel preferences:													
Eliminate oil and gas preferences:													
Repeal enhanced oil recovery credit [20]	....	....	....	....	....	....	....	....	....	....	....	....	....
Repeal credit for oil and gas produced from marginal wells [20]	....	....	....	....	....	....	....	....	....	....	....	....	....
Repeal expensing of intangible drilling costs	....	−1,663	−2,460	−2,125	−1,639	−1,099	−748	−514	−366	−289	−90	−8,986	−10,993
Repeal deduction for tertiary injectants	....	−8	−12	−12	−11	−11	−11	−11	−11	−10	−10	−54	−107
Repeal exception to passive loss limitations for working interests in oil and natural gas properties	....	−7	−10	−9	−8	−8	−7	−7	−6	−6	−6	−42	−74

S–9. Mandatory and Receipt Proposals—Continued

(Deficit increases (+) or decreases (–) in millions of dollars)

	2013	2014	2015	2016	2017	2018	2019	2020	2021	2022	2023	Totals 2014–2018	Totals 2014–2023
Repeal percentage depletion for oil and natural gas wells	....	–1,039	–1,044	–1,042	–1,041	–1,045	–1,052	–1,067	–1,091	–1,121	–1,181	–5,211	–10,723
Repeal domestic manufacturing deduction for oil and natural gas production	....	–1,119	–1,926	–1,951	–1,944	–1,884	–1,783	–1,717	–1,703	–1,705	–1,715	–8,824	–17,447
Increase geological and geophysical amortization period for independent producers to seven years	....	–60	–220	–333	–304	–221	–141	–64	–11	–2	–7	–1,138	–1,363
Subtotal, eliminate oil and gas preferences	....	–3,896	–5,672	–5,472	–4,947	–4,268	–3,742	–3,380	–3,188	–3,133	–3,009	–24,255	–40,707
Eliminate coal preferences:													
Repeal expensing of exploration and development costs	....	–25	–43	–45	–47	–49	–48	–47	–44	–44	–40	–209	–432
Repeal percentage depletion for hard mineral fuels	....	–113	–193	–196	–198	–201	–206	–209	–216	–222	–228	–901	–1,982
Repeal capital gains treatment for royalties	....	–14	–31	–37	–42	–45	–48	–50	–53	–55	–57	–169	–432
Repeal domestic manufacturing deduction for the production of coal and other hard mineral fuels	....	–33	–34	–36	–39	–40	–41	–44	–45	–48	–49	–182	–409
Subtotal, eliminate coal preferences	....	–185	–301	–314	–326	–335	–343	–350	–358	–369	–374	–1,461	–3,255
Total, eliminate fossil fuel tax preferences	....	–4,081	–5,973	–5,786	–5,273	–4,603	–4,085	–3,730	–3,546	–3,502	–3,383	–25,716	–43,962
Other revenue changes and loophole closers:													
Repeal the excise tax credit for distilled spirits with flavor and wine additives [2]	....	–85	–112	–112	–112	–112	–112	–112	–112	–112	–112	–533	–1,093
Repeal LIFO method of accounting for inventories	....	–3,493	–7,595	–8,538	–8,287	–8,290	–8,732	–8,739	–8,402	–9,045	–9,701	–36,203	–80,822
Repeal lower-of-cost-or-market inventory accounting method	....	–617	–1,344	–1,460	–1,470	–864	–259	–270	–283	–296	–309	–5,755	–7,172
Modify depreciation rules for purchases of general aviation passenger aircraft	....	–65	–201	–299	–334	–404	–437	–341	–231	–197	–193	–1,303	–2,702
Repeal gain limitation for dividends received in reorganization exchanges	....	–146	–252	–259	–267	–275	–283	–292	–300	–309	–319	–1,199	–2,702
Expand the definition of built-in loss for purposes of partnership loss transfers	....	–5	–6	–7	–7	–7	–7	–8	–8	–8	–10	–32	–73
Extend partnership basis limitation rules to nondeductible expenditures	....	–56	–77	–85	–91	–95	–98	–102	–107	–114	–123	–404	–948
Limit the importation of losses under related party loss limitation rules	....	–53	–71	–79	–84	–88	–92	–95	–99	–105	–113	–375	–879

S–9. Mandatory and Receipt Proposals—Continued

(Deficit increases (+) or decreases (−) in millions of dollars)

	2013	2014	2015	2016	2017	2018	2019	2020	2021	2022	2023	Totals 2014–2018	Totals 2014–2023
Deny deduction for punitive damages	.....	–25	–35	–36	–36	–38	–39	–39	–41	–41	–42	–170	–372
Eliminate section 404(k) ESOP dividend deduction for large C corporations	.....	–407	–614	–665	–674	–682	–691	–699	–707	–716	–722	–3,042	–6,577
Total, other revenue changes and loophole closers	.....	–4,952	–10,307	–11,540	–11,362	–10,855	–10,750	–10,697	–10,290	–10,943	–11,644	–49,016	–103,340
Reserve for revenue-neutral business tax reform	.....	.....	.....	.....	.....	.....	.....	.....	.....	.....	.....	.....	.....

Note: For receipt effects, positive figures indicate lower receipts. For outlay effects, positive figures indicate higher outlays. For net costs, positive figures indicate higher deficits.

[1] The estimates for this proposal include effects on receipts. The receipt effects included in the totals above are as follows:

	2013	2014	2015	2016	2017	2018	2019	2020	2021	2022	2023	Totals 2014–2018	Totals 2014–2023
Implement unemployment insurance integrity	.....	.....	.....	1	4	9	12	448	35	–29	21	14	501
Implement cap adjustments for UI program integrity	.....	.....	.....	4	10	21	725	123	14	–1,332	–132	35	–567
Implement tax enforcement program integrity cap adjustment	.....	–458	–1,252	–2,503	–3,766	–5,052	–5,955	–6,525	–6,816	–7,017	–7,158	–13,031	–46,502
Increase Civil Service Retirement System (CSRS) and Federal Employees Retirement System (FERS) contributions	.....	–800	–1,569	–2,325	–2,300	–2,273	–2,237	–2,197	–2,153	–2,104	–2,050	–9,267	–20,008
Prevent improper use of the Death Master File	.....	–65	–87	–89	–91	–93	–91	–92	–94	–96	–97	–425	–895
Adjust indexing and protect vulnerable populations	.....	.....	–1,000	–3,000	–6,000	–8,000	–10,000	–13,000	–16,000	–20,000	–23,000	–18,000	–100,000
Reauthorize special assessment from domestic nuclear utilities	.....	–200	–204	–209	–213	–218	–223	–228	–233	–238	–243	–1,044	–2,209
Increase coal AML fee to pre–2006 levels	.....	–53	–52	–53	–53	–53	–53	–55	–55			–264	–427
Establish an AML hardrock reclamation fund	.....		–200	–200	–200	–200	–200	–200	–200	–200	–200	–800	–1,800
Increase duck stamp fees	.....	–14	–14	–14	–14	–14	–14	–14	–14	–14	–14	–70	–140
Strengthen unemployment insurance system solvency	.....	2,467	2,746	–6,910	–9,324	–7,227	–6,847	–5,495	–4,924	–8,036	–7,929	–18,248	–51,479
Establish a mandatory surcharge for air traffic services	.....	–605	–632	–660	–690	–719	–745	–766	–790	–812	–836	–3,306	–7,255

S–9. Mandatory and Receipt Proposals—Continued

(Deficit increases (+) or decreases (−) in millions of dollars)

	2013	2014	2015	2016	2017	2018	2019	2020	2021	2022	2023	Totals 2014–2018	Totals 2014–2023
Increase levy authority for payments to Medicare providers with delinquent tax debt	....	−46	−67	−70	−71	−72	−74	−76	−76	−77	−78	−326	−707
Reform inland waterways funding	....	−82	−113	−113	−113	−113	−113	−113	−113	−113	−114	−534	−1,100
Disclose prisoner data for improper payments	....	−24	−35	−36	−37	−38	−39	−40	−41	−42	−43	−170	−375
Total receipt effects of mandatory proposals [2]	....	120	−2,479	−16,177	−22,858	−24,042	−25,854	−28,230	−31,460	−40,110	−41,873	−65,436	−232,963

[2] Net of income offsets.

[3] Savings in 2022 and 2023 include sustainment of enforcement initiatives beyond the sunset of the discretionary spending caps contained in the Budget Control Act of 2011.

	2013	2014	2015	2016	2017	2018	2019	2020	2021	2022	2023	Totals 2014–2018	Totals 2014–2023
Increased revenues associated with implementing the Buffett Rule prior to estimating the effects of the proposal to reduce the value of certain tax expenditures [4]	....	−7,710	−5,525	−7,824	−10,148	−10,887	−10,760	−10,929	−11,333	−11,814	−12,273	−42,094	−99,203

[5] This proposal would also result in discretionary savings of $7.2 billion over 10 years.

[6] This proposal has outlays of less than $500,000 per year. The total cost is $1 million from 2014–2018 and $2 million from 2014–2023.

[7] This proposal has outlays of less than $500,000 per year. The total cost is $2 million in 2014–2018.

[8] This proposal has outlays of less than $500,000 per year. The total cost is $1 million from 2014–2018 and $3 million from 2014–2023.

[9] This proposal has outlays of less than $500,000 per year. The total cost over 2014–2023 is $1 million.

[10] This proposal has outlays of less than $500,000 per year. The total cost over 2014–2023 is $1 million.

[11] This proposal has outlays of less than $500,000 per year. The total cost over 2014–2023 is also less than $500,000.

[12] This proposal has outlays of less than $500,000 per year in years 2014–2018. The total cost is $1 million from 2014–2018.

[13] This proposal has outlays of less than $500,000 per year. The total cost over 2014–2023 is also less than $500,000.

[14] This proposal has outlays of less than $500,000 per year. The total cost over 2014–2023 is also less than $500,000.

[15] This proposal has outlays of less than $500,000 per year. The total savings are $1 million over 2014–2018 and $4 million over 2014–2023.

[16] This proposal has no estimated costs.

[17] This proposal has outlays of less than $500,000 per year. The total cost over 2014–2023 is also less than $500,000.

[18] Overall, the proposal generates $300 million in additional proceeds. Total savings are net of Federal agency relocation costs.

[19] The estimates for this proposal include effects on outlays. The outlay effects included in the totals above are as follows:

	2013	2014	2015	2016	2017	2018	2019	2020	2021	2022	2023	Totals 2014–2018	Totals 2014–2023
Provide small businesses a temporary 10-percent tax credit for new jobs and wage increases	....	133	417	....	....	....	....	....	....	....	....	550	550
Designate Promise Zones [5]	....	....	13	28	30	30	33	35	37	40	41	101	287
Provide America Fast Forward Bonds [6]	....	230	1,022	2,117	3,202	4,372	5,656	7,029	8,476	9,977	11,511	10,943	53,592
Allow eligible uses of America Fast Forward Bonds to include financing all qualified private activity bond categories	....	47	213	460	723	999	1,288	1,589	1,902	2,224	2,552	2,442	11,997
Increase the Federal subsidy rate for America Fast Forward Bonds for school construction	....	409	1,522	2,512	2,799	2,799	2,799	2,799	2,799	2,799	2,799	10,041	24,036

S–9. Mandatory and Receipt Proposals—Continued

(Deficit increases (+) or decreases (−) in millions of dollars)

	2013	2014	2015	2016	2017	2018	2019	2020	2021	2022	2023	Totals 2014–2018	Totals 2014–2023
Provide for automatic enrollment in IRAs, including a small employer tax credit, and double the tax credit for small employer plan start-up costs	....	....	203	209	212	216	222	228	231	234	239	840	1,994
Expand child and dependent care tax credit	....	....	331	344	357	371	383	393	407	415	421	1,403	3,422
Modify reporting of tuition expenses and scholarships on Form 1098-T	....	....	−29	−33	−34	−35	−36	−37	−38	−39	−40	−131	−321
Extend IRS math error authority in certain circumstances	....	−7	−7	−7	−7	−8	−8	−8	−9	−9	−9	−36	−79
Simplify the rules for claiming the EITC for workers without qualifying children	....	25	494	506	518	528	510	521	533	544	558	2,071	4,737
Total, outlay effects of receipt proposals	....	837	4,179	6,136	7,800	9,272	10,847	12,549	14,338	16,185	18,072	28,224	100,215
Addendum, business tax policies reserved for revenue-neutral reform:													
Modify and permanently extend renewable electricity production tax credit		21	88	332	580	771	957	1,159	1,388	1,595	1,825	1,792	8,716
Expand and simplify the tax credit provided to qualified small employers for non-elective contributions to employee health insurance		92	177	186	166	149	134	124	109	102	103	770	1,342

[20] The provision is estimated to have zero receipt effect under the Administration's current economic projections.

[21] These additional revenue savings could be used to pay for continuing tax benefits provided under the American Taxpayer Relief Act, if the Congress decided those costs should be offset.

Table S–10. Funding Levels for Appropriated ("Discretionary") Programs by Category

(Budget authority in billions of dollars)

	Actuals			Requests		Outyears									Totals	
	2010	2011	2012	2013	2014	2015	2016	2017	2018	2019	2020	2021	2022	2023	2014-2018	2014-2023
Discretionary Current Law Caps by Category:[1]																
Security category	684	688	684	684	n/a	n/a	n/a	n/a	n/a	n/a	n/a	n/a	n/a	n/a	n/a	n/a
Nonsecurity category	407	374	377	359	n/a	n/a	n/a	n/a	n/a	n/a	n/a	n/a	n/a	n/a	n/a	n/a
Defense category	n/a	n/a	n/a	n/a	552	566	577	590	603	616	630	644	660	677	2,888	6,115
Non-Defense category	n/a	n/a	n/a	n/a	506	520	530	541	553	566	578	590	605	620	2,650	5,609
Total, Base Discretionary Funding	1,092	1,062	1,060	1,043	1,058	1,086	1,107	1,131	1,156	1,182	1,208	1,234	1,265	1,297	5,538	11,724
Proposed Changes to Base Discretionary Caps:[2]																
Reclassify Transportation Rail Programs	-2	-1	-1	-1	-1	-1	-2	-2	-2	-2	-2	-2	-2	-2	-8	-16
Proposed cap reductions:																
Defense cap reductions	......	......	......	......	......	......	......	-4	-8	-12	-16	-20	-26	-33	-12	-119
Non-defense cap reductions	......	......	......	......	......	......	......	-4	-8	-12	-16	-20	-27	-33	-12	-120
Non-defense reductions of base program integrity funding for shift to mandatory	......	......	......	......	......	-1	-1	-1	-1	-1	-1	-1	-1	-1	-2	-5
Total, Proposed Changes to Base Caps	-2	-1	-1	-1	-1	-2	-2	-10	-18	-26	-34	-42	-55	-68	-34	-260
Total, Base Discretionary with changes	1,090	1,061	1,059	1,042	1,057	1,084	1,105	1,121	1,138	1,156	1,174	1,192	1,210	1,229	5,504	11,464
Discretionary Cap Adjustments and Other Funding (not included above):[3]																
Overseas Contingency Operations[4,5]	163	159	127	97	92	37	37	37	37	37	37	37	......	......	241	353
Disaster relief	......	......	10	11	6										6	6
Program integrity	*	*	*	*	*	1	1	1	2	2	2	2	2	2	5	14
Other emergency/supplemental funding[6]	10	-1	*	41												
Total, Cap Adjustments and Other	173	159	137	149	99	38	38	39	39	39	39	39	2	2	253	373
Grand Total, Discretionary Budget Authority	1,263	1,219	1,196	1,190	1,155	1,122	1,143	1,160	1,177	1,195	1,213	1,231	1,212	1,231	5,757	11,837
Grand Total, Discretionary Budget Authority Adjusted for Inflation and Population	*1,431*	*1,338*	*1,272*	*1,228*	*1,155*	*1,087*	*1,074*	*1,056*	*1,038*	*1,022*	*1,005*	*989*	*944*	*929*	*5,410*	*10,298*

Table S–10. Funding Levels for Appropriated ("Discretionary") Programs by Category—Continued

(Budget authority in billions of dollars)

* $500 million or less.

[1] The Budget Control Act of 2011 (BCA) amended the Balanced Budget and Emergency Deficit Control Act of 1985 (BBEDCA) by establishing statutory discretionary caps for 2012 through 2021 with separate categories in 2012 and 2013 for "Security" and "Nonsecurity". These categories were revised on January 15, 2012 to equal all accounts in budget function 050 for the "Defense" category with all other amounts in the "Non-defense" category. The American Taxpayer Relief Act of 2012 reinstated the Security and Nonsecurity caps for 2013.

[2] The 2014 Budget proposes changes to the current law caps in the BBEDCA, as amended, for the reclassification of certain Transportation programs and further reductions as part of the Administration's policy to achieve additional deficit reduction.

[3] Where applicable, amounts in 2012 through 2023 are existing or proposed cap adjustments designated pursuant to Section 251(b)(2) of the BBEDCA, as amended. Amounts in 2010 and 2011 are not so designated but are shown for comparability purposes.

[4] Because final decisions about the pace of the drawdown in Afghanistan have not yet been made, the Budget includes a placeholder for the Department of Defense's 2014 OCO funding, equivalent to the amount provided in the 2013 Budget. The Administration will submit a Budget amendment to Congress updating the DOD OCO request after a determination has been made on required force levels in Afghanistan.

[5] The Budget includes placeholder amounts of $37.3 billion per year for Government-wide OCO funding from 2015 to 2021. These amounts reflect the Administration's proposal to cap total OCO budget authority from 2013 to 2021 at $450 billion but do not reflect any specific decisions or assumptions about OCO funding in any particular year.

[6] Amounts in 2010–2012 are not designated as emergency funding pursuant to Section 251(b)(2)(A) of the BBEDCA, as amended, as they include congressionally-designated emergencies, rescissions of funding provided in the American Recovery and Reinvestment Act of 2009 (P.L. 111–5), and other supplemental funding.

Table S–11. Funding Levels for Appropriated ("Discretionary") Programs by Agency

(Budget authority in billions of dollars)

	Actuals			Requests					Outyears						Totals	
	2010	2011	2012	2013	2014	2015	2016	2017	2018	2019	2020	2021	2022	2023	2014– 2018	2014– 2023
Base Discretionary Funding by Agency:[1][2]																
Agriculture	27.0	23.2	23.7	23.0	21.5	23.1	23.6	24.1	24.6	25.2	25.8	26.3	27.0	27.7	117.0	248.9
Commerce	13.9	5.6	7.7	8.0	8.6	9.1	9.4	9.9	10.9	12.0	18.2	10.4	10.2	10.4	47.8	109.1
Census Bureau	*7.2*	*–0.7*	*0.9*	*0.9*	*1.0*	*1.3*	*1.5*	*1.7*	*2.5*	*3.5*	*9.5*	*1.5*	*1.1*	*1.1*	*8.0*	*24.6*
Defense[3]	530.1	528.3	530.4	525.4	526.6	540.8	551.4	560.0	568.6	577.1	586.7	596.3	605.9	615.5	2,747.4	5,728.9
Education	64.3	68.3	67.4	69.8	71.2	71.9	72.8	73.9	75.1	76.3	77.4	78.6	80.0	81.5	365.0	758.7
Energy	26.5	25.7	26.4	27.2	28.4	28.3	28.9	29.5	30.1	30.8	31.5	32.2	33.0	33.8	145.2	306.5
National Nuclear Security Administration[3]	*9.9*	*10.5*	*11.0*	*11.5*	*11.7*	*11.0*	*11.2*	*11.4*	*11.7*	*11.9*	*12.2*	*12.4*	*12.8*	*13.1*	*56.9*	*119.3*
Health & Human Services (HHS)[4]	84.4	78.5	78.3	71.7	78.3	83.9	85.5	87.4	89.3	91.3	93.3	95.3	97.7	100.2	424.3	902.2
Homeland Security	39.8	41.9	39.9	39.5	39.0	39.7	40.4	41.2	42.0	42.8	43.8	44.7	45.8	47.0	202.3	426.4
Housing and Urban Development	42.8	37.1	36.3	34.5	33.1	33.9	34.4	35.0	35.8	36.5	37.2	37.9	38.8	39.6	172.2	362.2
Interior	12.1	11.7	11.3	11.4	11.7	12.1	12.4	12.6	12.9	13.2	13.5	13.8	14.2	14.5	61.8	131.0
Justice	27.6	26.9	26.9	17.9	16.3	28.8	29.3	29.9	30.6	31.3	32.0	32.7	33.5	34.4	135.0	298.8
Labor	13.5	12.5	13.2	12.0	12.1	12.3	11.6	11.9	12.1	12.3	12.6	12.8	13.1	13.4	60.0	124.3
State and Other International Programs	49.0	48.5	41.6	46.5	48.1	49.4	50.3	51.4	52.6	53.7	54.9	56.0	57.5	58.9	251.8	532.8
Transportation	20.2	15.4	16.4	16.5	16.3	17.2	17.5	17.9	18.3	18.7	19.1	19.5	20.0	20.5	87.2	185.1
Treasury	13.4	13.4	13.1	12.5	12.9	14.2	14.7	15.3	15.8	16.4	17.0	17.5	18.1	18.7	72.9	160.5
Veterans Affairs	53.1	56.4	58.7	61.0	63.5	64.9	66.1	67.5	69.0	70.5	72.1	73.6	75.5	77.5	330.9	700.1
Corps of Engineers	5.5	4.9	5.1	4.7	4.7	5.0	5.0	5.2	5.3	5.4	5.5	5.6	5.8	5.9	25.2	53.4
Environmental Protection Agency	10.3	8.7	8.5	8.3	8.2	8.2	8.2	8.2	7.7	7.9	8.0	8.2	8.4	8.5	40.4	81.4
General Services Administration	0.4	–1.0	–0.8	–0.8	0.2	0.3	0.3	0.3	0.3	0.3	0.3	0.3	0.3	0.3	1.3	2.8
National Aeronautics & Space Administration	18.7	18.4	17.8	17.7	17.7	18.2	18.5	18.9	19.4	19.8	20.2	20.7	21.2	21.7	92.7	196.3
National Science Foundation	6.9	6.8	7.0	7.4	7.6	7.8	8.0	8.2	8.3	8.5	8.7	8.9	9.1	9.4	39.9	84.5
Small Business Administration	0.8	0.7	0.9	0.9	0.8	0.8	0.8	0.9	0.9	0.9	0.9	0.9	1.0	1.0	4.2	8.9
Social Security Administration (SSA)[4]	8.9	8.6	9.0	9.0	9.1	9.0	9.2	9.4	9.6	9.8	10.0	10.3	10.5	10.8	46.4	97.8
Corporation for National & Community Service	1.2	1.1	1.0	1.1	1.1	1.1	1.1	1.1	1.2	1.2	1.2	1.2	1.3	1.3	5.6	11.8
Other Agencies	19.5	18.8	18.8	18.9	19.4	19.5	19.9	20.3	20.8	21.2	21.7	22.2	22.7	23.3	100.0	211.1
Required savings[5]	....	....	....	–2.6	....	–15.6	–14.6	–19.0	–23.2	–27.4	–37.9	–34.1	–40.7	–47.0	–72.4	–259.5
Subtotal, Base Discretionary Funding	1,090.0	1,060.6	1,058.8	1,041.6	1,056.5	1,083.9	1,104.9	1,120.9	1,137.8	1,155.8	1,173.8	1,191.8	1,209.7	1,228.7	5,504.1	11,463.9

Table S–11. Funding Levels for Appropriated ("Discretionary") Programs by Agency—Continued

(Budget authority in billions of dollars)

	Actuals		Requests			Outyears									Totals	
	2010	2011	2012	2013	2014	2015	2016	2017	2018	2019	2020	2021	2022	2023	2014–2018	2014–2023
Discretionary Cap Adjustments and Other Funding (not included above):[6]																
Overseas Contingency Operations	**162.6**	**159.4**	**126.5**	**96.7**	**92.3**	**37.3**	**37.3**	**37.3**	**37.3**	**37.3**	**37.3**	**37.3**	....	....	**241.4**	**353.3**
Defense[7]	162.3	158.8	115.1	88.5	88.5	....	....	....	....	....	....	....	....	....	88.5	88.5
Homeland Security	0.2	0.3	0.3	....	....	....	....	....	....	....	....	....	....	....	....	....
Justice	0.1	0.1	....	....	....	....	....	....	....	....	....	....	....	....	....	....
State and Other International Programs	....	0.3	11.2	8.2	3.8	....	....	....	....	....	....	....	....	....	3.8	3.8
Overseas Contingency Operations Outyears[8]	....	....	....	....	....	37.3	37.3	37.3	37.3	37.3	37.3	37.3	....	....	149.1	261.0
Disaster Relief	....	....	**10.5**	**11.0**	**5.8**	....	....	....	....	....	....	....	....	....	**5.8**	**5.8**
Homeland Security	....	....	6.4	10.9	5.6	....	....	....	....	....	....	....	....	....	5.6	5.6
Transportation	....	....	1.7	....	....	....	....	....	....	....	....	....	....	....	....	....
Corps of Engineers	....	....	1.7	....	....	....	....	....	....	....	....	....	....	....	....	....
Small Business Administration	....	....	....	0.2	0.2	....	....	....	....	....	....	....	....	....	0.2	0.2
Other Agencies	....	....	0.7	....	....	....	....	....	....	....	....	....	....	....	....	....
Program Integrity	....	**0.5**	**0.5**	**0.5**	**0.4**	**0.8**	**1.1**	**1.4**	**1.7**	**1.7**	**1.7**	**1.8**	**1.8**	**1.9**	**5.3**	**14.1**
Treasury	....	0.5	0.5	0.5	0.4	0.7	1.0	1.3	1.7	1.6	1.7	1.7	1.8	1.8	5.2	13.8
HHS, Labor, and SSA	....	0.5	0.5	0.5	*	*	*	*	*	*	*	*	*	*	*	*
Other Emergency/Supplemental Funding[9]	**9.6**	**-1.3**	*	**40.6**	....	....	....	....	....	....	....	....	....	....	....	....
Agriculture	0.6	....	....	0.2	....	....	....	....	....	....	....	....	....	....	....	....
Commerce	-0.5	....	....	0.3	....	....	....	....	....	....	....	....	....	....	....	....
Defense	-1.9	....	....	*	....	....	....	....	....	....	....	....	....	....	....	....
Energy	-1.5	....	....	-0.5	....	....	....	....	....	....	....	....	....	....	....	....
Health and Human Services	0.2	-1.3	....	0.3	....	....	....	....	....	....	....	....	....	....	....	....
Homeland Security	5.5	....	*	6.7	....	....	....	....	....	....	....	....	....	....	....	....
Housing and Urban Development	0.1	....	....	16.0	....	....	....	....	....	....	....	....	....	....	....	....
Interior	*	....	....	0.8	....	....	....	....	....	....	....	....	....	....	....	....
State and Other International Programs	6.1	....	....	....	....	....	....	....	....	....	....	....	....	....	....	....
Transportation	....	*	....	13.1	....	....	....	....	....	....	....	....	....	....	....	....
Corps of Engineers	0.2	....	....	1.9	....	....	....	....	....	....	....	....	....	....	....	....

Table S–11. Funding Levels for Appropriated ("Discretionary") Programs by Agency—Continued

(Budget authority in billions of dollars)

	Actuals			Requests		Outyears									Totals	
	2010	2011	2012	2013	2014	2015	2016	2017	2018	2019	2020	2021	2022	2023	2014–2018	2014–2023
Environmental Protection Agency	*	....	....	0.6	....	....	....	....	....	....	....	....	....	....	....	....
Small Business Administration		1.0	....	0.8	....	....	....	....	....	....	....	....	....	....	....	....
Other Agencies	–0.1	....	....	0.3	....	....	....	....	....	....	....	....	....	....	....	....
Grand Total, Discretionary Funding	1,262.7	1,219.2	1,196.2	1,190.4	1,155.0	1,122.0	1,143.2	1,159.5	1,176.8	1,194.8	1,212.8	1,230.8	1,211.5	1,230.6	5,756.6	11,837.1

Memorandum:

2014 Base Defense Category Request by agency:

	2014
Defense	526.6
Energy (including NNSA)	17.8
Justice (FBI)	4.9
Homeland Security	1.6
Other	1.0
Total, Base Defense Category	552.0

* $50 million or less.

[1] Amounts in the actuals years of 2010 through 2012 exclude changes in mandatory programs enacted in appropriations bills since those amounts have been rebased as mandatory, whereas amounts in 2013 and 2014 are net of these proposals.

[2] The 2014 Budget proposes changes to the current law caps in the BBEDCA, as amended, for the reclassification of certain Transportation programs and further reductions as part of the Administration's policy to achieve additional deficit reduction.

[3] The Department of Defense (DOD) levels in 2015–2023 include funding that will be allocated, in annual increments, to the National Nuclear Security Administration (NNSA). Current estimates by which DOD's budget authority will decrease and NNSA's will increase are, in millions of dollars: 2015: $1,196; 2016: $1,444; 2017: $1,602; 2018: $1,665; 2019: $1,702; 2014–2023: $14,816. DOD and NNSA continue to review aspects of NNSA's outyear requirements and this will affect outyear allocations made by DOD to NNSA.

[4] Funding from the Hospital Insurance and Supplementary Medical Insurance trust funds for administrative expenses incurred by the Social Security Administration that support the Medicare program are included in the Health and Human Services total and not in the Social Security Administration total.

[5] The 2014 Budget includes allowances, similar to the Function 920 allowances used in Budget Resolutions, to represent amounts to be allocated among the respective agencies to reach the proposed defense and non-defense caps for 2015 and beyond. These levels are determined for illustrative purposes but do not reflect specific policy decisions. 2013 also includes an allowance amount to bridge from the 2013 request level to 2013 caps, as enacted in ATRA.

[6] Where applicable, amounts in 2012 through 2023 are existing or proposed cap adjustments designated pursuant to Section 251(b)(2) of the BBEDCA, as amended. Amounts in 2010 and 2011 are not so designated but are shown for comparability purposes.

[7] Because final decisions about the pace of the drawdown in Afghanistan have not yet been made, the Budget includes a placeholder for DOD's 2014 Overseas Contingency Operations (OCO) funding, equivalent to the amount provided in the 2013 Budget. The Administration will submit a Budget amendment to Congress updating the DOD OCO request after a determination has been made on required force levels in Afghanistan.

[8] The Budget includes placeholder amounts of $37.3 billion per year for Government-wide OCO funding from 2015 to 2021. These amounts reflect the Administration's proposal to cap total OCO budget authority from 2013 to 2021 at $450 billion but do not reflect any specific decisions or assumptions about OCO funding in any particular year.

[9] Amounts in 2010–2012 are not designated as Emergency funding pursuant to Section 251(b)(2)(A) of the BBEDCA, as amended, as they include congressionally-designated emergencies, rescissions of funding provided in the American Recovery and Reinvestment Act of 2009 (P.L. 111–5), and other supplemental funding.

Table S–12. Economic Assumptions[1]

(Calendar years)

	2011 Actual	2012	2013	2014	2015	2016	2017	2018	2019	2020	2021	2022	2023
							Projections						
Gross Domestic Product (GDP):													
Nominal level, billions of dollars	15,076	15,705	16,384	17,235	18,181	19,192	20,247	21,275	22,247	23,219	24,216	25,252	26,331
Percent change, nominal GDP, year/year	4.0	4.2	4.3	5.2	5.5	5.6	5.5	5.1	4.6	4.4	4.3	4.3	4.3
Real GDP, percent change, year/year	1.8	2.3	2.3	3.2	3.5	3.6	3.5	3.1	2.6	2.4	2.4	2.3	2.3
Real GDP, percent change, Q4/Q4	2.0	2.0	2.6	3.4	3.6	3.6	3.5	2.9	2.4	2.4	2.3	2.3	2.3
GDP chained price index, percent change, year/year	2.1	1.9	2.0	1.9	1.9	1.9	1.9	1.9	1.9	1.9	1.9	1.9	1.9
Consumer Price Index, [2] **percent change, year/year**	3.1	2.1	2.1	2.2	2.2	2.2	2.2	2.2	2.2	2.2	2.2	2.2	2.2
Interest rates, percent: [3]													
91-day Treasury bills [4]	0.1	0.1	0.1	0.2	0.4	1.2	2.3	3.2	3.6	3.7	3.7	3.7	3.7
10-year Treasury notes	2.8	1.8	2.0	2.6	3.1	3.7	4.1	4.4	4.6	4.8	5.0	5.0	5.0
Unemployment rate, civilian, percent [3]	8.9	8.1	7.7	7.2	6.7	6.2	5.7	5.5	5.4	5.4	5.4	5.4	5.4

Note: A more detailed table of economic assumptions is in Chapter 2, "Economic Assumptions and Interactions with the Budget," in the *Analytical Perspectives* volume of the Budget, Table 2–1.

[1] Based on information available as of mid-November 2012.
[2] Seasonally adjusted CPI for all urban consumers.
[3] Annual average.
[4] Average rate, secondary market (bank discount basis).

Table S–13. Federal Government Financing and Debt

(Dollar amounts in billions)

	Actual 2012	Estimate										
		2013	2014	2015	2016	2017	2018	2019	2020	2021	2022	2023
Financing:												
Unified budget deficit:												
Primary deficit (+)/surplus (−)	867	750	521	323	228	113	14	−45	−106	−162	−197	−323
Net interest	220	223	223	254	300	373	461	543	609	663	715	763
Unified budget deficit	1,087	973	744	576	528	487	475	498	503	501	519	439
As a percent of GDP	7.0%	6.0%	4.4%	3.2%	2.8%	2.4%	2.3%	2.3%	2.2%	2.1%	2.1%	1.7%
Other transactions affecting borrowing from the public:												
Changes in financial assets and liabilities:[1]												
Change in Treasury operating cash balance	27	−5	....	....	....	....	....	....	....	....	....	....
Net disbursements of credit financing accounts:												
Direct loan accounts	86	144	138	153	144	133	124	119	118	120	119	120
Guaranteed loan accounts	12	15	17	12	12	11	13	13	9	5	*	−2
Troubled Asset Relief Program (TARP) equity purchase accounts	−61	−3	−5	−4	*	*	*	*	*	*	−*	*
Net purchases of non-Federal securities by the National Railroad Retirement Investment Trust (NRRIT)	1	−1	−1	−1	−2	−1	−1	−1	−1	−1	−1	−*
Net change in other financial assets and liabilities[2]	1	....	....	....	....	....	....	....	....	....	....	....
Subtotal, changes in financial assets and liabilities	66	150	148	160	154	143	135	131	126	123	118	118
Seigniorage on coins	....	−*	−*	−*	−*	−*	−*	−*	−*	−*	−*	−*
Total, other transactions affecting borrowing from the public	66	150	148	160	154	142	135	131	126	123	118	118
Total, requirement to borrow from the public (equals change in debt held by the public)	1,153	1,122	892	736	682	629	611	629	629	624	637	557
Changes in Debt Subject to Statutory Limitation:												
Change in debt held by the public	1,153	1,122	892	736	682	629	611	629	629	624	637	557
Change in debt held by Government accounts	134	76	105	165	197	221	209	140	130	124	94	94
Change in other factors	−6	1	*	*	1	*	−*	−*	−1	−1	−1	*
Total, change in debt subject to statutory limitation	1,280	1,200	998	901	879	850	820	768	757	747	730	651
Debt Subject to Statutory Limitation, End of Year:												
Debt issued by Treasury	16,024	17,221	18,218	19,118	19,996	20,846	21,665	22,432	23,190	23,937	24,667	25,318
Adjustment for discount, premium, and coverage[3]	3	5	7	8	9	10	10	11	11	11	11	11
Total, debt subject to statutory limitation[4]	16,027	17,227	18,225	19,126	20,005	20,855	21,675	22,443	23,200	23,948	24,677	25,329

Table S–13. Federal Government Financing and Debt—Continued

(Dollar amounts in billions)

	Actual 2012	Estimate 2013	2014	2015	2016	2017	2018	2019	2020	2021	2022	2023
Debt Outstanding, End of Year:												
Gross Federal debt:[5]												
Debt issued by Treasury	16,024	17,221	18,218	19,118	19,996	20,846	21,665	22,432	23,190	23,937	24,667	25,318
Debt issued by other agencies	27	28	29	30	30	31	31	33	34	35	36	35
Total, gross Federal debt	16,051	17,249	18,247	19,148	20,027	20,876	21,696	22,465	23,224	23,972	24,702	25,353
Held by:												
Debt held by Government accounts	4,770	4,846	4,951	5,116	5,312	5,533	5,742	5,882	6,011	6,136	6,229	6,324
Debt held by the public [6]	11,281	12,404	13,296	14,032	14,714	15,344	15,954	16,583	17,212	17,836	18,473	19,030
As a percent of GDP	72.6%	76.6%	78.2%	78.2%	77.7%	76.8%	75.9%	75.3%	74.9%	74.4%	73.9%	73.0%
Debt Held by the Public Net of Financial Assets:												
Debt held by the public	11,281	12,404	13,296	14,032	14,714	15,344	15,954	16,583	17,212	17,836	18,473	19,030
Less financial assets net of liabilities:												
Treasury operating cash balance	85	80	80	80	80	80	80	80	80	80	80	80
Credit financing account balances:												
Direct loan accounts	803	947	1,086	1,239	1,383	1,515	1,639	1,758	1,877	1,996	2,115	2,235
Guaranteed loan accounts	–10	5	22	34	46	57	70	83	92	97	97	96
TARP equity purchase accounts	14	10	5	1	1	1	1	*	*	*	*	*
Government-sponsored enterprise preferred stock	109	109	109	109	109	109	109	109	109	109	109	109
Non-Federal securities held by NRRIT	23	22	20	19	18	16	15	14	13	12	10	10
Other assets net of liabilities	–25	–25	–25	–25	–25	–25	–25	–25	–25	–25	–25	–25
Total, financial assets net of liabilities	999	1,149	1,297	1,457	1,611	1,753	1,889	2,020	2,146	2,269	2,387	2,505
Debt held by the public net of financial assets	10,282	11,255	11,999	12,575	13,103	13,590	14,065	14,563	15,066	15,567	16,085	16,524
As a percent of GDP	66.1%	69.5%	70.5%	70.1%	69.2%	68.0%	66.9%	66.2%	65.6%	65.0%	64.4%	63.4%

* $500 million or less.

[1] A decrease in the Treasury operating cash balance (which is an asset) is a means of financing a deficit and therefore has a negative sign. An increase in checks outstanding (which is a liability) is also a means of financing a deficit and therefore also has a negative sign.

[2] Includes checks outstanding, accrued interest payable on Treasury debt, uninvested deposit fund balances, allocations of special drawing rights, and other liability accounts; and, as an offset, cash and monetary assets (other than the Treasury operating cash balance), other asset accounts, and profit on sale of gold.

[3] Consists mainly of debt issued by the Federal Financing Bank (which is not subject to limit), debt held by the Federal Financing Bank, the unamortized discount (less premium) on public issues of Treasury notes and bonds (other than zero-coupon bonds), and the unrealized discount on Government account series securities.

[4] Legislation enacted February 4, 2013, (P.L. 113–3) temporarily suspended the debt limit through May 18, 2013.

[5] Treasury securities held by the public and zero-coupon bonds held by Government accounts are almost all measured at sales price plus amortized discount or less amortized premium. Agency debt securities are almost all measured at face value. Treasury securities in the Government account series are otherwise measured at face value less unrealized discount (if any).

[6] At the end of 2012, the Federal Reserve Banks held $1,645.3 billion of Federal securities and the rest of the public held $9,635.8 billion. Debt held by the Federal Reserve Banks is not estimated for future years.

OMB CONTRIBUTORS TO THE 2014 BUDGET

The following personnel contributed to the preparation of this publication. Hundreds, perhaps thousands, of others throughout the Government also deserve credit for their valuable contributions.

A

Andrew Abrams
Chandana Achanta
Brenda Aguilar
Shagufta I. Ahmed
Steven D. Aitken
Jameela R. Akbari
David Alekson
Clydea M. Allaire
Julie Allen
Victoria L. Allred
Lois E. Altoft
Aaron Ampaw
Scott J. Anchin
Lauren Antelo
Anna R. Arroyo
Emily E. Askew
Ari Isaacman Astles
Lisa L. August
Renee Austin

B

Peter M. Babb
Susan Badgett
Jessie W. Bailey
Paul W. Baker
Carol Bales
Bethanne Barnes
Patti Barnett
Jody Barringer
Avital Bar-Shalom
Mary C. Barth
Sarah Bashadi
Alison Beason
Margot Beausey
Jennifer Wagner Bell

Steven Bennett
Joseph Berger
Sam K. Berger
Lindsey R. Berman
Scott A. Bernard
Elizabeth Bernhard
Boris Bershteyn
Mathew C. Blum
James Boden
Melissa B. Bomberger
Dan Bonesteel
Cole Borders
Bill Boyd
Chantel M. Boyens
Brianna Bradford-
   Benesh
Paul B. Bradley
Betty I. Bradshaw
Nicole A. Bradstreet
Joshua J. Brammer
Michael Branson
Shannon Bregman
Andrea Brian
Candice M. Bronack
Jonathan M. Brooks
Christopher Broome
Calla R. Brown
Dustin S. Brown
Elizabeth M. Brown
Eric Brown
Jamal T. O. Brown
James A. Brown
Jontia Brown
Kelly D. Brown
Michael Brunetto
Paul Bugg
Tom D. Bullers
Robert Bullock

Erin Boeke Burke
Benjamin Burnett
Ryan M. Burnette
John D. Burnim
John C. Burton
Nathaniel Buss
Mark Bussow

C

Kathleen Cahill
Steven Cahill
William H. Campbell
Mark F. Cancian
Malissa Candland
Eric D. Cardoza
J. Kevin Carroll
Mario J. Carroll
William S. Carroll
Scott Carson
Adam Case
Mary I. Cassell
David Cassidy
Benjamin Chan
Daniel E. Chandler
James Chase
Anita Chellaraj
Michael C. Clark
Ashley Cleaves
Braye Gregory Cloud
Rosye B. Cloud
Daniel Cohen
Victoria Collin
Debra M. Collins
Kelly T. Colyar
Nicole E. Comisky
David C. Connolly
Martha B. Coven

Catherine Crato
Joseph Crilley
Rosemarie C. Crow
Michael F. Crowley
Craig Crutchfield
C. Tyler Curtis
William P. Curtis

D

Rowena Dagang
Veronica Daigle
Neil B. Danberg
Kristy L. Daphnis
Michael P. Darling
Alexander J. Daumit
Joanne Davenport
John Davis
Ken Davis
Margaret B. Davis-
   Christian
Brian Dewhurst
John H. Dick, Jr.
China Dickerson
Frank DiGiammarino
Jason Dixson
Angela M. Donatelli
Norman Dong
Paul Donohue
Bridget C. E. Dooling
Shamera Dorsey
Lisa Driskill
Francis DuFrayne
Laura Duke

E

Jacqueline A. Easley

Mabel E. Echols
Jeanette Edwards
Emily M. Eelman
C. J. Elliot
Lisa Ellman
Noah Engelberg
Michelle A. Enger
Sally Ericsson
Andrew H. Erwin
Mark Erwin
Victoria Espinel
Edward V. Etzkorn
Rowe Ewell

F

Chris Fairhall
Robert S. Fairweather
Edna T. Falk Curtin
Michael C. Falkenheim
Kara Farley-Cahill
Christine Farquharson
Kira R. Fatherree
Andrew R. Feldman
Nicole A. Fernandes
Patricia A. Ferrell
Lesley A. Field
Mary Fischietto
E. Holly Fitter
Mary E. Fitzpatrick
Darlene B. Fleming
Tera Fong
Keith Fontenot
James Ford-Fleming
Nicholas A. Fraser
Marc Freiman
Farrah B. Freis
Virginia French
Nathan J. Frey
Patrick J. Fuchs

G

Arti Garg
Marc Garufi
Thomas Gates
Benjamin P.O. Geare
Elaine Geiser

Jeremy J. Gelb
Brian Gillis
Dori Glanz
David Glaudemans
Joshua Glazer
Kimberly G. Glenn
Gary Glickman
Ja'Cia D. Goins
Ariel Gold
Jeffrey Goldstein
Oscar Gonzalez
Robert M. Gordon
Tom Grannemann
Kathleen Gravelle
Richard E. Green
Aron Greenberg
Hester Grippando
Rebecca Grusky

H

Michael B. Hagan
Susan J. Haggerty
Christopher C. Hall
Erika S. Hamalainen
Kathleen D. Hamm
Christina Hansen
Eric V. Hansen
Linda W. Hardin
Dionne M. Hardy
David Harmon
Patsy W. (Pat) Harris
Brian Harris-Kojetin
Nicholas R. Hart
Paul Harvey
Ryan Harvey
Aisha Hasan
Tomer Hasson
Adam Hatton
David J. Haun
Laurel Havas
Mark H. Hazelgren
John Henson
Kevin W. Herms
Alex Hettinger
Gretchen T. Hickey
Michael Hickey
Beth N. Higa

Heather A.
   Higginbottom
Cortney J. Higgins
Mary Lou Hildreth
Andrew Hire
Thomas E. Hitter
Jennifer Hoef
Michael C. Hoehn
Joanne Cianci Hoff
Adam Hoffberg
Stuart Hoffman
Troy Holland
Jim Holm
Peter M. Holm
Daniel Hornung
Lynette Hornung-
   Kobes
Laura E. House
Grace Hu
Kathy M. Hudgins
Jeremy D. Hulick
James Hundt
Alexander T. Hunt
Lorraine D. Hunt
James C. Hurban
Jaki Mayer Hurwitz
Kristen D. Hyatt
Dana J. Hyde

I

Robert Ikoku
Tae H. Im
Janet Irwin
Paul Iwugo

J

Laurence R. Jacobson
Carol D. Jenkins
Aaron D. Joachim
Barbara A. Johnson
Carol Johnson
Kim I. Johnson
Michael D. Johnson
Bryant A. Jones
Danielle Y. Jones
Denise Bray Jones

Lisa M. Jones
Scott W. Jones
Joseph G. Jordan
Hee K. Jun

K

Paul Kagan
Richard Kane
Jamie Kanselbaum
Jacob H. Kaplan
Irene B. Kariampuzha
Jenifer Karwoski
Molly M. Kawahata
Nathaniel Kayhoe
Regina Kearney
Ed Kearns
Dan Keenaghan
Matthew J. Keeneth
Hunter Kellett
John W. Kelly
Ann H. Kendrall
Nancy Kenly
Amanda R. Kepko
Paul E. Kilbride
Cristina Killingsworth
Barry D. King
Kelly Kinneen
Carole E. Kitti
Ben Klay
Sarah Klein
Emily Kornegay
Steven M. Kosiak
John Kraemer
Lori A. Krauss
Shannon Kroll
Alison C. Kukla
Joydip Kundu

L

Chris LaBaw
Katherine T. LaBeau
Leonard L. Lainhart
James A. Laity
Chad A. Lallemand
Lawrence L. Lambert
Daniel LaPlaca

Phil Larson
Janisa LaSalle
Eric P. Lauer
Jessie LaVine
David Lee
Jessica Lee
Karen F. Lee
Sarah S. Lee
Susan Leetmaa
Maximillian Lehman
Bryan León
Jeremy León
Andrea Leung
Stuart Levenbach
Anthony Lewandowsky
George Lewis
Sheila D. Lewis
Wendy Liberante
Richard A.
    Lichtenberger
Sara Rose Lichtenstein
Kristina E. Lilac
Jennifer M. Lipiew
Lin C. Liu
Patrick G. Locke
Brandi M. Lofton
Aaron M. Lopata
Alexander W. Louie
Adrienne C. Erbach
    Lucas
Kimberley Luczynski
Thomas S. Lue
Gideon F. Lukens
Sarah Lyberg
Laura E. Lynch
Randolph M. Lyon

M

Chi T. Mac
Debbie Macaulay
Ryan J. MacMaster
John S. MacNeil
Natalia Mahmud
Claire A. Mahoney
Mikko Mäkäräinen
Kathryn (Katie)
    Malague
Margaret A. Malanoski

Thomas J. Mancinelli
Dominic J. Mancini
Robert Mann
Sharon Mar
Celinda A. Marsh
Brendan A. Martin
Kathryn Martin
Rochelle Wilkie
    Martinez
Meg Massey
Daniel P. Matheny
Surujpat J. Adrian
    Mathura
Shelly McAllister
George McArdle
Alexander J.
    McClelland
Jeremy McCrary
Brenda McCullough
Anthony W. McDonald
Christine McDonald
Katrina A. McDonald
Renford McDonald
Mark McDonnell
Luther McGinty
Christopher McLaren
Robin J. McLaughry
Andrew McMahon
William J. McQuaid
William J. Mea
Inna L. Melamed
Flavio Menasce
Jessica Nielsen Menter
P. Thaddeus
    Messenger
Shelley Metzenbaum
William L. Metzger
Joanna M. Mikulski
Julie L. Miller
Kimberly Miller
Asma Mirza
Amanda Mitchum
Joe Montoni
Cindy Moon
Jamesa C. Moone
Roxana Moussavian
Whitney Moyer
Moira Mack Muntz
Edward A. Murphy, Jr.

Jennifer Winkler
    Murray
Chris Music

N

Jennifer Nading
Jeptha E. Nafziger
Larry Nagl
Barry Napear
Ashley Michelle
    Nathanson
Allie Neill
Adam Neufeld
Melissa K. Neuman
Betsy Newcomer
Joan F. Newhart
John Newman
Kimberly A. Newman
Kevin F. Neyland
Teresa Nguyen
Eric C. Ngwa
Alex Niejelow
Abigail P. Norris
Tim H. Nusraty

O

Erin L. O'Brien
Devin O'Connor
Matthew J. O'Kane
Matthew Olsen
Dennis P. O'Neil
Steve Onley
Jared Ostermiller
Tyler J. Overstreet
Brooke Owens

P

Ben Page
Jennifer Park
Sangkyun Park
Joel R. Parriott
John Pasquantino
Terri B. Payne
Jacqueline M. Peay
Falisa L. Peoples-Tittle
Kathleen Peroff

Andrew B. Perraut
Mike Perz
Andrea M. Petro
Stacey Que-Chi Pham
Carolyn R. Phelps
Karen A. Pica
Joseph G. Pipan
Verite Pitts
Alisa M. Ple-Plakon
Rachel C. Pollock
Ruxandra I. Pond
Steven C. Posner
Jonathan B. Porat
Lindsey Powell
Celestine M. Pressley
Jamie Price Pressly
Larrimer Prestosa
Marguerite Pridgen
Robert B. Purdy

Q

John P. Quinlan

R

Jonathan E. Rackoff
Lucas R. Radzinschi
Latonda Glass Raft
Jose Angelo Ramilo
Jamil Ramsey
Maria Raphael
Jeffrey Reczek
McGavock D. Reed
Tiffany Reeser
Rudy Regner
Paul B. Rehmus
Jake Reilly
Sean Reilly
Thomas M. Reilly
Scott Renda
Richard J. Renomeron
Kent Reynolds
Keri A. Rice
M. David Rice
Gavette A. Richardson
Shannon Richter
Justin Riordan
Emma K. Roach

Benjamin Roberts
Donovan O. Robinson
Marshall Rodgers
Alexandra Rogers
Meredith B. Romley
Dan T. Rosenbaum
Adam J. Ross
David Rowe
Mario D. Roy
Trevor H. Rudolph
Chris Rupar
Ryan Rusnak
Latisha Russell
Kristin Rzeczkowski

S

Fouad P. Saad
Aparna Saha
John Asa Saldivar
Dominic K. Sale
Mark S. Sandy
Jessica R. Santillo
Kristen J. Sarri
Aschley Schiller
Lisa A. Schlosser
Tricia Schmitt
Andrew M. Schoenbach
Daniel Schory
Margo Schwab
Nancy Schwartz
Jasmeet K. Seehra
Will Sellheim
Emily L. Sharp
Dianne Shaughnessy
Paul Shawcross
Sophie M. Shulman
Gary Shortencarrier
Sophie M. Shulman
Mary Jo Siclari
Sara R. Sills
Samantha Silverberg
Angela M. Simms
Rhonda M. Sinkfield

Benjamin Skidmore
Jack A. Smalligan
Curtina O. Smith
Jan Smith
Nikolis R. Smith
Joanne E. Snow
Carolyn Snyder
Sarah Snyder
Silvana Solano
Kathryn B. Stack
Scott Stambaugh
Melanie A. Stansbury
Andrea M. Staron
Nora Stein
Gary Stofko
Carla B. Stone
Shayna Strom
Shannon Stuart
Tom Suarez
Brett J. Sullivan
Kevin J. Sullivan
Jessica Sun
Indraneel Sur
Harry K. Swann
Jennifer Swartz
Benjamin R. Sweezy
Christina Swoope

T

Teresa A. Tancre
Naomi Stern Taransky
Benjamin K. Taylor
Myra Taylor
Raina Thiele
Amanda I. Thomas
Judith F. Thomas
LaTina Thomas
Paul E. Thomas
Will Thomas
Shelley Thompson
Courtney B.
   Timberlake
Thomas Tobasko

Toinita Tolson
Richard Toner
Taryn H. Toyama
Gilbert Tran
Minh-Hai Tran-Lam
Susan M. Truslow
Donald L. Tuck
Benjamin J. Turpen

U

Nick Uchalik
Darrell J. Upshaw

V

Matthew J. Vaeth
Kathleen M. Valentine
Ofelia M. Valeriano
Amanda L. Valerio
Cynthia A. Vallina
Sarita Vanka
Steven L. VanRoekel
David W. Varvel
Areletha L. Venson
Alexandra Ventura
Patricia A. Vinkenes
Dean Vonk
Kathy Voorhees
David Vorhaus
Ann M. Vrabel

W

James A. Wade
James (Rusty) Walker
Martha A. Wallace
Katherine K. Wallman
Heather V. Walsh
Timothy Wang
Sharon A. Warner
Gary Waxman
Mark A. Weatherly
Bessie M. Weaver

Jeffrey A. Weinberg
Philip R. Wenger
Daniel Werfel
Mike Wetklow
Arnette C. White
Catherine White
Kamela G. White
Kim S. White
Sherron R. White
Chad S. Whiteman
Robert T. Whitley
Sarah Widor
Mary Ellen Wiggins
Shimika Wilder
Chavon Renee
   Wilkerson
Debra L. (Debbie)
   Williams
Monique C. Williams
Ross D. Williams
Julia B. Wise
Julie A. Wise
Elizabeth Wolkomir
Gary Wong
Hermine Wong
Raymond Wong
Lauren Wright
Sophia Wright
Steven Wynands

Y

Abra Yeh
Melany N. Yeung
Theany Yin

Z

Diane Zayas-Veles
Jeff Zients
Gail S. Zimmerman
Rachel Zinn
Rita Zota
Lindsay Zwiener

www.ingramcontent.com/pod-product-compliance
Lightning Source LLC
Chambersburg PA
CBHW080531220326
41599CB00032B/6272